ROUTLEDGE LIBRARY EDITIONS:
CHINA UNDER MAO

Volume 8

THE CULTURAL REVOLUTION
IN CHINA

THE CULTURAL REVOLUTION IN CHINA

An Annotated Bibliography

JAMES C.F. WANG

Routledge
Taylor & Francis Group

LONDON AND NEW YORK

First published in 1976 by Garland Publishing, Inc.

This edition first published in 2019
by Routledge
2 Park Square, Milton Park, Abingdon, Oxon OX14 4RN

and by Routledge
711 Third Avenue, New York, NY 10017

Routledge is an imprint of the Taylor & Francis Group, an informa business

British Library Cataloguing in Publication Data
A catalogue record for this book is available from the British Library

ISBN: 978-1-138-32344-5 (Set)
ISBN: 978-0-429-43659-8 (Set) (ebk)
ISBN: 978-1-138-34772-4 (Volume 8) (hbk)
ISBN: 978-1-138-34780-9 (Volume 8) (pbk)
ISBN: 978-0-429-43687-1 (Volume 8) (ebk)

Publisher's Note
The publisher has gone to great lengths to ensure the quality of this reprint but points out that some imperfections in the original copies may be apparent.

Disclaimer
The publisher has made every effort to trace copyright holders and would welcome correspondence from those they have been unable to trace.

The Cultural Revolution in China:
An Annotated Bibliography

James C.F. Wang

Garland Publishing, Inc., New York & London

1976

Copyright © 1976

by James C.F. Wang

All Rights Reserved

Library of Congress Cataloging in Publication Data

Wang, James C   F
    The cultural revolution in China.

    (Garland reference library of social science ;
v. 16)
    Includes indexes.
    1. China--Politics and government--1949-
--Bibliography. 2. Chung-kuo kung ch'an tang--
Purges--Bibliography. I. Title.
Z3108.A5W35   [DS777.55]   016.95105   75-24099
ISBN 0-8240-9973-7

To my wife, Sally, for her infinite patience and invaluable assistance

Contents

Abbreviations

CCP	Chinese Communist Party
PLA	People's Liberation Army

Introduction to the Annotated Bibliography

.The Cultural Revolution in China has generated a cascade of commentaries and interpretations on the development and meaning of the upheaval. Many students and researchers of contemporary China, especially those interested in the period of the Cultural Revolution, have often found it inconvenient, if not difficult at times, to locate and identify literature on the period. This annotated bibliography is an effort to correct this situation. The bibliography includes all books, monographs, and journal articles in English on the Cultural Revolution which are commonly available to students and researchers. Each entry is annotated to show its relevance to the study of the Cultural Revolution. The bibliography is designed as a reference tool for use by both the university community and the general public in locating published works and ascertaining the coverage and major themes in each.

The bibliography covers a wide range of topics related to the Cultural Revolution and its impact on China. For the readers' convenience, the material is arranged by general topics in nine chapters. An introduction to each chapter outlines the main themes and major points of discussion to orient the user. Chapter I includes works which provide broad interpretations and explanations on the origin and meaning of the Cultural Revolution. Chapter II covers material on the Chinese Communist

9

INTRODUCTION

Party (CCP) and includes the question of the ideological purity of the cadres, the reshuffling of the Central Committee and the Politburo, the routinization of the party apparatus, purges of top leaders, and the rehabilitation of veteran cadres. The Red Guards and the effects of the Cultural Revolution on China's youth are dealt with in Chapter III. Chapter IV includes works on the complex role that the People's Liberation Army (PLA) played during the Cultural Revolution. Closely related to the military's role in the upheaval is the establishment of Temporary Revolutionary Committees at all levels of the decision-making process, covered in Chapter V. These committees, in most cases dominated by the military, were formed in the midst of the Cultural Revolution to replace the dismantled party structure. Entries for Chapter V cover the major controversies emanating from the formation or the inability to form Revolutionary Committees at the regional and local levels and include questions such as the extent of the party control over the regional and local jurisdictions, the rivalry among the feuding revolutionary mass groups, and participation in the decision-making process.

The impact of the Cultural Revolution on economic policy and the functioning of the economy is covered in Chapter VI. Chapter VII deals with the Cultural Revolution's relationship to disruption and reform in education, policies for science and technology and their implications for China's modernization process, developments in literature, drama and opera, and, finally, changes in the social milieu in China. Chapter VIII on China's foreign policy and foreign policy-making during the Cultural Revolution includes works which provide interpretations and analysis on questions such as: was there any foreign policy for the period; who actually made foreign policy during the period; and how was the foreign policy apparatus affected by the Cultural Revolution. Finally, Chapter IX covers works which assess the Cultural Revolution from the perspective of the aftermath period. Included are the relationship of the Cultural Revolution to the demise of Lin Piao, the leadership succession question, the reorganization of the party's Central Committee, the reestablishment of the party structure, profound changes in education, and the party-army relationship.

A few words must be said about the items in this bibliography. No items originating from the Chinese source, either in English or in translation, are included. The reason for this omission is two-fold. First, there are several reference tools now available which provide a comprehensive collection of official documentation on the Cultural Revolution. Four are included in this bibliography: the Asian Research Centre's *The Great Cultural Revolution in China* and *The Great Power Struggle in China,* Union Research Institute's *CCP Documents of the Great Proletarian Cultural Revolution: 1966-1967,* and Dr. Chi's *Readings in the Chinese Communist Cultural Revolution.* Second, the main purpose of this bibliography is to assemble and annotate works in English which provide interpretations and analyses of the Cultural Revolution by China scholars and commentators from the West. Books and articles from American and British publications are cited as well as a few from Indian and the Soviet Union sources. Most, however, are American. No unpublished papers are included for the simple reason that these are not generally available to college and public libraries not specializing in research on contemporary China.

The indexing system for this bibliography is designed

INTRODUCTION

for the convenience of students, researchers and librarians. The system consists of two separate indices: an author index and a subject index. The alphabetical author index lists the full citation for each of the author's works annotated in the bibliography. The subject index list covers main topics or themes, arranged in alphabetical order. The arabic numerals, assigned to each entry in the sequence of its placement in the bibliography, are given in both indices to facilitate location of the items.

Articles annotated in this bibliography come from the following journal sources commonly available to any college and public library not specializing in contemporary Chinese affairs:

1. *American Political Science Review*
2. *American Sociological Review*
3. *Asian Studies in Hawaii*
4. *Asian Survey: A Monthly Review of Contemporary Asian Affairs*
5. *Bulletin of the Atomic Scientists*
6. *China News Analysis*
7. *China Report*
8. *Columbia Journal of World Business*
9. *Current History: A World Affairs Monthly*
10. *Current Scene: Development in People's Republic of China*
11. *Far Eastern Economic Review*
12. *Foreign Affairs: An American Quarterly Review*
13. *Issues and Studies: A Monthly Journal of Communist Problems and World Affairs*
14. *Journal of Asian and African Studies*
15. *Journal of Contemporary China*
16. *Journal of International Affairs* (Catham House)
17. *Journal of International Affairs* (Columbia University)

INTRODUCTION

18. *Monthly Review: An Independent Socialist Magazine*
19. *New Scientists*
20. *Orbis: A Quarterly Journal of World Affairs*
21. *Pacific Affairs*
22. *Phi Delta Kappan*
23. *Physics Today*
24. *Problems of Communism*
25. *Saturday Review World*
26. *Studies in Comparative Communism: An International Interdisciplinary Journal*
27. *The Center Magazine* (Center for Study of Democratic Institutions)
28. *The China Quarterly: An International Journal for the Study of China*
29. *The New Republic*
30. *The Political Quarterly*
31. *The World Today*
32. *World Politics: A Quarterly Journal of International Relations*
33. *Reprint from the Soviet Press*

It is hoped that this annotated bibliography will render needed assistance to its users appropriate to their needs and will contribute in some small measure to stimulating interest for research on this momentous event and its far-reaching consequences for the People's Republic of China.

CHAPTER I

ORIGIN AND MEANING OF THE CULTURAL REVOLUTION

The items listed in this chapter represent a myriad of interpretations and explanations about the origin and meaning of the Chinese Cultural Revolution, which lasted from 1966 to 1969. Several major themes seem to run through these annotated entries. These major themes tend to fall into three groups: (1) struggle for political power, (2) conflict over the means for achieving China's goals, and (3) basic disagreement over the goals, and thus also the means, for communism in China. Many observers see elements of two or three major themes in the Cultural Revolution, and there is a wide variation of points of view and interpretations within each of the categories.

Many proponents of the power struggle thesis advance the proposition that a basic cleavage existed within the top leadership of the Chinese Communist Party over the policies to be pursued and that at some stage this policy cleavage became intertwined with a power struggle to such an extent that the power struggle obscured the importance of the policy conflict. This thesis frequently traces the origin of the Cultural Revolution back to the 1959 Lushan Conference, when Chairman Mao's leadership and authority were seriously challenged. A few scholars have related this challenge to signs of the growing power of an entrenched bureaucracy in the party and government.

14

Others have stressed the concern over succession of leadership both on the part of Mao and on the part of those vying for increased power in the regime's top echelon. Some observers believe that the Cultural Revolution represented the inevitable disruption of a regime as it reached the end of its dynasty.

The Cultural Revolution was, as interpreted by some, the manifestation of the top leadership's frustration and its inability to answer the fundamental question: what was the correct approach and strategy to promote sustained development toward the regime's ultimate goals. These observers tend to focus on the failure of the Great Leap Forward, which led to the challenge of Mao's leadership at Lushan in 1959, on the controversy between "red" versus "expert" and between a radical revolutionary style versus a pragmatic bureaucratic approach.

Finally, a number of observers see the concern of the Cultural Revolution as something more basic than merely policy differences among the top leaders. Those who embrace this view maintain that the Cultural Revolution was an attempt to resolve the central question of the nature of the Chinese communist society by the Maoists, who have faith in voluntarism, which among many other things stresses the human will and the transformation of values. The Cultural Revolution seen in this perspective was a struggle over a choice of priorities, a choice between development with a heavy reliance upon technology and economic production versus the Maoist vision of a good society. Thus the Cultural Revolution has been interpreted as an "ideological crusade" against the orthodox Soviet revisionistic model

15

of development.

The desire on the part of Chairman Mao and others to prevent the resurgence of elitism or special classes in the advancement toward an egalitarian society, the need to develop the politics of activism to "restart the engine of mobilization," the appropriate role of the culture and of the intellectuals in a revolutionary society, and, finally, the necessity for China to develop a mass mobilization and participation model for community action and responsiveness are but examples of many other themes interwoven in the items annotated in this chapter. A few entries present the psychological aspects of the revolution in terms of an authority crisis and a conflict in the Chinese political culture.

1 ADIE, W. A. C.
"China's 'Second Liberation' in Perspective," China After the
Cultural Revolution, A Selection from Bulletin of the Atomic
Scientists, Vol. XXV, No. 2, February 1969, Vintage Books,
New York, 1970, pp. 27-56.
Adie attempts to provide an answer to the question: was the
Cultural Revolution an ideological crusade or a struggle for
power and succession? After giving an analytical account of
China's major political developments from 1949-1966, Adie
concludes that the Cultural Revolution was a combination of
these forces: "an enigmatic multiple power struggle, wrapped
in a crusade, and superimposed on a scattering of more or less
spontaneous, more or less politicized student riots, strikes,
peasant uprisings, mutinies and palace coups." The background
for the Cultural Revolution was made up of conflicts between
Mao's thought and practical politics in modernizing China. The
ideological split between a revolutionary set of goals and
techniques and the pragmatic professional approach was the
vortex of these conflicts.

2 AHN, Byung-joon.
"The Cultural Revolution and China's Search for Political
Order," The China Quarterly, No. 58, April-June 1974,
pp. 249-285.
Ahn views the Cultural Revolution as a major shift in the
pattern of China's political order, which was proceeded by
intra-party conflict. Questions about the purge of top party
leaders and the dismantling of party structure can only be
understood in the context of China's search for political
order--in the leadership style and the policy-making processes.
This article summarizes current literature in the social
sciences which analyze political orders in changing societies,
particularly as these relate to Chinese politics. The pattern
of Chinese political order for the Cultural Revolution, 1966-67,
was categorized as the "movement regime" under a supreme leader.
The political order that existed during the early stages of the
Cultural Revolution was, therefore, characterized by a low level
of institutionalization but a high level of mass participation--
the elite were linked directly with the masses. Mao, as the
supreme leader, was the source of all wisdom and proper policies.
Mass movement became the mode of life for everyone. In order to
build the mass polity, the supreme leader had to employ instruments such as the military and Red Guards to destroy the
institutionalized structure and to remove party leaders. The
Cultural Revolution represented a confrontation between one-man
leadership and the party as well as a conflict between mass
participation and institutionalization. When mass participation
became excessive, the movement brought internal civil war, which
could only be averted by the intervention of the military to
restore order.

3 AN, Tai Sung.
Mao Tse-tung's Cultural Revolution, Pegasus, a Division of The

Bobs-Merrill Company, Inc., Indianapolis, Ind., 1972, 211p.
An presents the thesis that the Cultural Revolution was
basically an ideological remolding campaign with the specific
purpose of making China over in Mao's own image. It represented Mao's last attempt to re-revolutionize China. In
launching an upheaval of this magnitude, Mao really was attempting to avoid the mistakes made by Stalin. Mao believes that
class struggle, a key tenent of Marxism-Leninism, does not
cease when a socialist base is constructed. The Cultural
Revolution was launched to perpetuate a "permanent revolution"
and to prevent the revival of bourgeois tendencies in China.
Viewed in this perspective, the only major policy dispute among
the top leaders was "revolutionary radicalism" versus "pragmatic
realism." The roots of this struggle go back to the failure of
the Great Leap in 1958, which created doubt among the leaders
on the validity of Mao's strategy for developing China. Coupled
with the economic disorder were China's setbacks in her foreign
relations with Southeast Asian countries and the Soviet Union
in the mid-1960's. Liu Shao-chi became the chief target for the
Cultural Revolution because he repudiated Mao's radical policies
at home and abroad. The book contains a summary of the development of the Cultural Revolution. Three appendixes give the
membership of the Ninth Central Committee and lists the
leaders of the provincial revolutionary committees and the party
committees.

4 ARMBRUSTER, Frank E.; LEWIS, John W., MOZINGO, David, and
TANG TSOU.
China Briefing, University of Chicago, Center for Policy Study,
The University of Chicago Press, Chicago, 1968, 72p.
Five articles were selected for this book from those presented
at a briefing session held at the University of Chicago for
"in-depth analysis and instructional give-and-take probing
between China experts and journalists." Separate annotation of
articles from this book are found under author entry in various
sections of this bibliography.

5 ASIAN RESEARCH CENTRE.
The Great Cultural Revolution in China, Charles E. Tuttle
Company, Rutland, Vt., and Tokyo, 1968, 507p.
This is a collection of official documents, some in full text
but most in excerpt form, which traces the origin and development of the Cultural Revolution. Part one of the book contains
background material about the cultural aspects of the revolution: Mao's 1942 talks at the Yenan arts forum, excerpts from
the National Conference of Writers and Artists in 1963, debate
over the philosophical concepts of "one divides into two" and
"two combine into one," reform of the Peking opera, and the
Socialist Education Campaign. Part two contains documents from
official sources on the Cultural Revolution in the early stages:
policy pronouncements on the Cultural Revolution, the army's
role in the upheaval, key party decisions on launching the
revolution, and material on the birth of the Red Guards. Two

appendixes need to be mentioned as reference aids: (1) a
glossary of the special terms and slogans used in the Cultural
Revolution, both in the original Chinese and in English translation, (2) a chronology of events from November 1965 to
November 1966.

6 . ASIAN RESEARCH CENTRE.
The Great Power Struggle in China, Hong Kong, 1969, 303p.
This is a sequel to the book The Great Cultural Revolution in
China, published in 1968 by the Asian Research Centre in Hong
Kong. It is a collection of official documents, radio broadcasts, and speeches by party leaders concerning events occurring
between the fall of 1967 and the fall of 1968. Part one deals
with the Red Guard movement and the spread of the revolution
both to the countryside and to the production sectors of the
economy. Part two covers the January 1967 revolution, the
"February adverse current," and the impact of the purge. Part
three deals with the role of the military and the problems it
encountered.

7 BARNETT, Doak A.
China After Mao, Princeton University Press, Princeton, N. J.,
1967, 287p.
This book is a collection of three lectures given by Barnett at
Princeton University when the Cultural Revolution was in full
progress. The central theme of these lectures is that the
process of modernization in China will produce changing conditions which might raise questions about the lasting validity of
Mao's revolutionary ideals and values, which were formulated
during the days of guerrilla warfare. These lectures, particularly the first chapter of the book, point out China's dilemma:
how to enable the younger generation to develop a commitment to
revolutionary values in view of the attractiveness of the
material benefits that have resulted from the Soviet Union's
revisionism. The analysis of Mao's attack on the Soviet Union's
brand of "phoney communism" reveals Mao's obsession with the
possible gradual erosion of revolutionary elan in China. Mao's
prescription for future generations, the successors to his
revolution, would be continuous revolution and adoption of his
revolutionary values, such as self-sacrifice, austerity, ideological reform, and egalitarianism. Mao believes that mass
participation and mobilization techniques must be continuously
applied in social and economic construction. Mao, according to
these lectures, represents a hero of the bygone years, who was
essentially a romantic revolutionary and who wanted desperately
to adhere to values and concepts which are inappropriate for a
modernizing state. Appended to the book are four key documents.
One is the ninth letter addressed to the Soviet Union on
Khrushchev's "phoney communism," which revealed a great deal of
Mao's thinking about the erosion of revolutionary elan and his
formula for preventing revisionism. The others are Lin Piao's
article on the people's war and the two documents by the Central
Committee on the launching of the Cultural Revolution. These

are good sources for an understanding of the causes for the
Cultural Revolution.

8   BAUM, Richard D.
"Ideology Redivivus," Problem of Communism, May-June 1967,
Vol. XVI, No. 3, pp. 1-11. Also in Richard Baum with Louise B.
Bennett, eds., China in Ferment: Perspectives on the Cultural
Revolution, Prentice-Hall, Inc., Englewood Cliffs, N. J., 1971,
pp. 67-77.
This article is written by a young American Scholar specializing
in contemporary Chinese studies. As a political scientist, he
places China's Cultural Revolution in the theoretical framework
of a "modernizing Marxist-Leninist society" undergoing ideological revivalism. The author begins with a sweeping sketch of
his analysis of the chain of events from the rise of a new class
of bureaucrats and technicians in China after the Great Leap to
China's concern over the revisionistic programs launched by
Khrushchev in the Soviet Union. Baum argues in the article that
China, on the eve of the Cultural Revolutions, was experiencing
instrumentalism, defined as "the substitution of a largely
apolitical production and managerial ethic for the consummatory
ethic of the 'command economy.'" This article argues further
that the post-Leap economic moderation policies brought about
an alarming trend in the domestic scene--increasing bureaucratization which led to "routinization" of the revolutionary
functions of the party and, thus, the attack on Khrushchev's
revisionism by the Chinese coincident with their own apprehen-
sion of instrumentalism and bureaucratization within their party
and government. The author then proceeds with a detailed
description of China's efforts in ideological revivalism as a
means by which solutions to these problems of modernization
could be found. The Socialist Education Campaign of 1963-64
was launched to prevent "ideological degeneration" of the
cadres. The hsia-fang movement in 1964 and the mass emulation
campaign of the army heroes were intended as ideological reeducation for the cadres and masses alike. The Cultural
Revolution was merely a gigantic purge from the party ranks of
those "anti-socialistic" elements who had embarrassed the
bourgeois and revisionist ideology.

9   BAUM, Richard D.
"'Red and Expert': The Politico-Ideological Foundations of
China's Great Leap Forward," Asian Survey, Vol. IV, No. 9,
September 1964, pp. 1048-1057.
In this article written prior to the Cultural Revolution, Baum
analyzes underlying factors involved in the dialects of "red"
and "expert" in China's development strategy. He sees the
Great Leap as a "convergence of two inveterate strands of
communist development strategy." One was the Stalinist
"revolution from above," and the other, the Maoist "mind over
matter." The campaign for both "red" and "expert" was launched
in 1957 to overcome the difficulties of insufficient enthusiasm
on the part of the intellectuals and the inadequacies of

20

material resources. Very soon, however, the concept of "red"
was emphasized more than that of "expert." The results of the
Great Leap showed that ideology and politics did not really
produce coal, steel and grain. A shift in emphasis from "red"
to "expert" became imperative by 1959. The new stress on
technology, skills and expertise was Liu Shao-chi's answer for
restoring the economy wrought by the mass mobilization techniques of the Great Leap. Baum's conclusion in this article is
that the pendulum might swing back and forth so long as the
contradictions between "red" and "expert" remain. The contradictions could be eliminated in two ways: a maturing of the
economy or the mellowing of revolutionary elan.

10 BAUM, Richard, with BENNETT, Louise B., eds.
China in Ferment: Perspectives on the Cultural Revolution,
Prentice-Hall, Inc., Englewood Cliffs, N. J., 1971, 246p.
This book is a collection of articles on the background, origins,
meaning, development and trends of the Cultural Revolution.
Since all of the articles included in the reader have been
annotated in this bibliography, the entry will deal exclusively
with the introduction and conclusion of the book. The introduction, written by Baum, answers a number of questions raised by
the general reader about the nature and consequences of the
Cultural Revolution: was China in a state of anarchy; what was
the extent of damage to the political system caused by the
revolution; who were the Red Guards, and what happened to them;
who were the victims of the purge; and what was involved in the
army take-over. By clearing up the queries at the beginning,
it becomes easier for the reader to understand the substantive
sections of the analytical articles on various aspects of the
Cultural Revolution. The conclusion, written by Bennett, is an
examination of the assumptions commonly shared by scholars
investigating the Cultural Revolution. We might label these
shared assumptions as main themes of the revolution as interpreted by scholars and observers of Chinese political development. Six major themes are briefly examined: (1) Maoism versus
modernization, (2) individualism versus socialistic collectivism,
(3) revolution versus evolution, or mass mobilization goals
versus modernization goals, (4) masses versus elites, (5) mass
emotional outbursts, (6) the decentralization goals.

11 BRIDGHAM, Philip.
"Mao's 'Cultural Revolution': Origin and Development," The
China Quarterly, No. 29, January-March 1967, pp. 1-35.
The Cultural Revolution, according to Bridgham, originated in
the Chinese political situation. Mao felt betrayed following
the attack by his long-time comrade, Defense Minister Peng
Teh-huai, at the party's enlarged Central Committee meetings at
Lushan in 1959. Although Peng was purged at Lushan, many
continued in his defense. Mao's crisis of confidence reached
its peak during the three years of 1959-61 when serious food
shortages and near economic collapse proved that his policies
for mass mobilization during the Great Leap had failed. Mao's

own explanation for this failure was that the cadres had not understood the necessity for revolutionary elan in carrying out the party's policies. He, therefore, concluded that socialist education, or "cultural revolution," was necessary to "educate man anew" and to reorganize the "revolutionary ranks." The Socialist Education Movement was launched in mid-1964 to combat "revisionism" among party cadres, to cultivate revolutionary successors among the youth, to eliminate corruption among rural cadres, and to have all emulate the work-style of the PLA. The article goes on to describe Mao's dissatisfaction, by 1960, with the results of the Socialist Education Campaign, which he attributed to disloyalty of his top lieutenants in the party. Thus, a new rectification-purge campaign aimed at members at the top of the party apparatus was launched under the direction of Lin Piao and the PLA. The analysis of these key political developments was based on original Chinese sources, mainly editorials of the People's Daily and the Hung Chi (Red Flag).

12   BULLETIN OF THE ATOMIC SCIENTISTS.
China After the Cultural Revolution, A Selection from Bulletin of the Atomic Scientists, Vol. XXV, No. 2, February 1969, Vintage Books, New York, 1970, 247p.
Separate annotation of articles selected from the Bulletin of the Atomic Scientists for this book are listed under author entry in various sections of this bibliography.

13   CHANG, Chun-shu; CRUMP, James; and MURPHEY, Rhoads, eds.
The Cultural Revolution: 1967 in Review, Michigan Papers in Chinese Studies No. 2, Center for Chinese Studies, University of Michigan, Ann Arbor, 1968, 125p.
This collection of four essays covers occupational groups in the Chinese society, the Chinese economy, China's foreign policy, and structural changes in China during 1967. Separate annotation of these essays can be found under author entry in various parts of this bibliography.

14   CHANG, Parris H.
"Mao's Great Purge: A Political Balance Sheet," Problems of Communism, Vol. XVIII, No. 2, March-April 1969, pp. 1-10.
This article summarizes and evaluates the events of the Cultural Revolution from 1966 to 1969. Chang sees the turbulent develop- ment in China, not as a well directed revolution from above, but as "drastic twists and turns" by a "shifting balance of opposing forces." He analyzes the successive shifts from the "Left in command" in 1966-67 through the sharp swing to the right after the military intervened in the fall of 1967 and the "upsurge of the Left" in 1968 to a period of stabilization in 1969. The article gives a detailed account of the purges in the Politburo, in the party Secretariat, in the Central Committee, and in regional and provincial offices. Chang also shows the differ- ences between purges under Stalin and those during the Cultural Revolution. According to Chang, the Cultural Revolution ful- filled some of the classical function of purges, for example,

promotion of upward political mobility at the expense of
institutional stability and orderly economic and educational
progress.

15 CHEN, Theodore Hsi-en.
"A Nation in Agony," Problems of Communism, Vol. XV, No. 6,
November-December 1966, pp. 14-20.
This article investigates the reasons for the Chinese leaders'
willingness to risk the gains made since 1949 in the Cultural
Revolution, which brought chaos and destruction to China's
development. In Chen's opinion, the Cultural Revolution was
"in essence a redoubled effort to change the minds and hearts
of China's millions." The upheaval was not a "sudden development" but a "new and more violent phase of the continuing battle
the communists are waging for the minds and hearts of China's
millions." Chen argues that it was easier for the regime to
design new economic institutions than to revive "the elan and
the patriotic zeal that characterized the early 1950's."
Revisionism in China meant "not only the Khrushchev brand of
communism but any ideas at variance with the orthodox Chinese
Communist Party line." The major sources of revisionism in
China are also analyzed in this article.

16 CHENG, Chu-yuan.
"The Power Struggle in Red China," Asian Survey, Vol. VI,
No. 9, September 1966, pp. 469-483.
Cheng, a research economist for the Center for Chinese Studies
at the University of Michigan, presents the thesis that the
Cultural Revolution was, in essence, a power rivalry among
potential successors to Mao. He traces the power struggle from
the Kao Kang-Jao Shu-shih affair during 1954-1956 through the
emergence of Lin Piao as heir apparent. The purge of Kao and
Jao paved the way for Liu Shao-chi to gain control over the
party machine. Liu's rival was Premier Chou En-lai, who had
the support of the intellectuals and government cadres. The
power struggle among Mao's lieutenants became more complicated
when Lin Piao rose to power as the result of the 1959 Lushan
Conference and with the purge of Mao's critic, Defense Minister
Peng Teh-huai. Lin pledged personal loyalty to Mao and molded
the PLA into a model instrument for the support of Mao. Lin
Piao's rise to power coincided with widespread discontent among
party and non-party intellectuals due to the failure of the
Great Leap. As literary criticism of Mao's policies appeared,
Lin Piao, with the PLA under his firm control and in alliance
with Chou En-lai, launched an attack on those top party leaders
who were actually behind the literary criticism. These attacks
led finally to the purge of Peng Chen, chief ally of Liu
Shao-chi, and to the reshuffling of the party's entire literary
and propaganda machinery. The article concludes with a picture
of the emergence of the radical line in China's political
development: intensification of class struggle in the countryside, dramatic educational reform, and the reshaping of the
party organization by Lin Piao.

17 CHENG, Peter.
"Liu Shao-chi and the Cultural Revolution," _Asian Survey_,
Vol. XI, No. 10, October 1971, pp. 943-957.
Cheng argues that the Cultural Revolution had its origin in the
leadership styles of the two top Chinese leaders: Mao and
Liu Shao-chi. By using editorials of the party's theoretical
journal, _Hung-chi_ (Red Flag), Cheng analyzes the allegations
against Liu and the circumstances under which these allegations
were made. For instance, Liu was accused of attempting to
circumvent Mao's policies in 1958-59, of repudiating the class
struggle, and of opposing Mao's collectivization of agriculture.
Some of the sources for this article were unsubstantiated Red
Guard materials. The article concludes that Mao's feud with
Liu was over the basic question of strategy for development:
rapid implementation of revolutionary programs or consolidation
of revolutionary gains.

18 CHENG, Peter.
"The Root of China's Cultural Revolution: The Feud between
Mao Tse-tung and Liu Shao-chi," _Orbis_, Vol. XI, No. 4,
Winter 1968, pp. 1160-1178.
The major theme of this article is that the feud between
Chairman Mao and President Liu Shao-chi made the Cultural
Revolution inevitable. The key to the feud was Liu's shift
from a position promoting the personality cult of Mao to one
opposing it. Liu's efforts since 1956 to de-emphasize the
"Thought of Mao" are attributed to two developments: the
influence of de-Stalinization in the Soviet Union and discontent
with Mao's radical policies. After establishing the argument
that the personality cult was the core of the feud, Cheng points
out that the feud was also the manifestation of basic differences on domestic policies: (1) the duration of the class
struggle, (2) economic development strategy, including priorities for industrialization and agricultural collectivization,
the use of material incentives and profit realization, and
reliance on experts, (3) attitudes toward intellectuals. Cheng
concludes that the conflict will result in "a weakened party
machine and an erosion of discipline" and that the moderate
line advocated by Liu will persist in party councils.

19 CHI, Wen-shun, compiler and ed.
Readings in the Chinese Communist Cultural Revolution, A Manual
for Students of the Chinese Language, University of California
Press, Berkeley, Los Angeles, and London, 1971, 530p.
This collection of twenty-one key documents of the Cultural
Revolution in both Chinese and English, with English commentary
and Chinese glossary, has two purposes: a textbook for Chinese
language students and a basic text for social science students.
The collection begins with Yao Wen-yuan's criticism of Wu Han's
play, "Hai Jui Dismissed from Office," which launched the
Cultural Revolution, and ends with the enlarged 12th Plenum of
the 8th Central Committee communique of October 1968, which
finally denounced Liu Shao-chi by name. In addition to being a

useful tool for Chinese scholars who wish to use the original
Chinese text, the selection of key documents gives a complete
picture of the vicissitudes of the Cultural Revolution.

20   COMMITTEE OF CONCERNED ASIAN SCHOLARS.
China! Inside the People's Republic, Bantam Books, Inc.,
New York, 1972, 433p.
The bulk of this book contains the impressions and insights
gained by members of the Committee of Concerned Asian Scholars
who were invited by the Chinese government to visit China in the
summer of 1971. Chapter 3 deals exclusively with the Cultural
Revolution. The cause of the Cultural Revolution is attributed
to the leadership's feeling of "loss of the revolutionary goals
in the material success of modernization and death of the Yenan
spirit in the birth of a new class hierarchy." The Cultural
Revolution, in the view of this group, was a struggle between
two elites, each adhering to a different approach, or model, for
the construction of socialism in China. The events that led to
the launching of the Cultural Revolution are traced in Chapter 3.
Then, based on conversations with the group's hosts, the arrival
of the Cultural Revolution in Shanghai and the organization of
the revolutionary committee are examined. The chapter ends with
a brief discussion of the goals of the Cultural Revolution.

21   DAUBIER, Jean.
A History of the Cultural Revolution, Vintage Books, A Division
of Random House, New York, 1974, 336p.
This book on the Cultural Revolution and its origins was written
by a westerner who participated in the upheaval. From 1966-68,
Daubier was a French translator for the Chinese government.
The book was originally written in French and subsequently
translated into English. The book traces the vicissitudes of
the upheaval in terms of Marxist-Leninist ideology as applied
by Mao. The basic objective of the Cultural Revolution, as
seen by this participant and observer, was the re-making of the
human spirit for a collectivist social system under which there
was to be no room for individualism. View from this perspective, Daubier argues, the Cultural Revolution was a perfectly
logical endeavor of Marxist-Leninism. The book is introduced
by an analysis on the origin of the Cultural Revolution focusing
on the theme that Marxist theory and Mao's thought call for
the elimination of all inequalities, which requires constant
struggle against deeply rooted individualistic traditions. The
eradication of these human inequalities demands, not only
complete disruption of customs and ways of thinking, but the
recasting of "the entire body of administrative, cultural, and
pedagogical superstructures." The remainder of the book is
devoted to a detailed account of the developments during the
Cultural Revolution, based essentially on Chinese source material and the author's own firsthand knowledge of these events as
a participant. The appendix of key documents on the events is
a very useful tool for further understanding about the upheaval.
In short, the author tries rather successfully to enable his

readers to understand this momentous event in Chinese contemporary history as the Chinese see it.

22 DESHINGKAR, G. D.
"The Causes of the Cultural Revolution," China Report, Vol. 3, No. 1, December 1966-January 1967, pp. 9-12 and 17.
Deshingkar takes the position that the Cultural Revolution was "an inevitable feature of the Chinese revolution as charted by Mao Tse-tung." He reviews events from 1962 to 1965, when Mao confronted his opponents. The confrontation was over the issues of the concept of class struggle and the manner the struggle was to be handled; the need to remove differences between workers and peasants; and the bureaucratic contradictions within the party. The reasons for the party's loss of revolutionary elan are also explored. Mao's fear of revisionism and the lack of revolutionary successors were contributing factors in the planning of the revolution. According to Deshingkar, the Cultural Revolution was "intended to destroy old attitudes in the society, eliminate the so-called revisionist group from the party, and arrest the process of bureaucratization."

23 DORRILL, William F.
"Leadership and Succession in Communist China," Current History, Vol. 49, No. 289, September 1965, pp. 129-135 and 179-180.
An underlying cause for the Cultural Revolution is discussed in this article on the Chinese leadership's overriding concern with finding a successor to Mao and the related problem of recruiting and training a new generation of leaders. Dorrill sees the rectification and the socialist education campaigns in the early 1960's as expressions of the party's concern over tightening control in cadres discipline and combating various "revisionist" tendencies. He views the campaign of "learn from the PLA," not as a device to enable Lin Piao to gain control over the army and the party, but as a sincere attempt to make the PLA into a model for political and ideological emulation. The point is made that although the top leaders are old, "they are also remarkable for their continuity in power over the years and their maintenance of an almost unbroken united front despite the vicissitudes of the internal and external situation." However, Mao's eventual departure would introduce tensions in terms of disagreements and dissent on policies and programs leading to factionalism. To prevent instability, efforts have been made to prepare the party for the succession to Mao, including the creation of the honorary chairmanship of the party's central committee for Mao and the resignation of Mao from the presidency of the republic.

24 DUTT, Gardi and DUTT, Vidya P.
China's Cultural Revolution, Asia Publishing House, Bombay and Calcutta, 1970, 260p.
This book presents the views on the Cultural Revolution of two China scholars from India. It was written during the early summer of 1967 and, therefore, contains some premature

26

evaluations of the events. The book is an attempt to give a
full picture of the upheaval, mainly using primary source
material from the Chinese press. The Cultural Revolution,
according to the Dutts, was the culmination of many factors:
power struggle, fear of restoration of capitalism, Mao's
obsession for the future, and the rift between the bureaucrats
and ideologues. These conditions made the upheaval inevitable.
The seeds for the revolution were sown during the failure of
the Great Leap Program in 1958 and 1959 and in the party
professionals' disenchantment with Mao's radical policies.
Thus, ideology versus professional competence became one of the
major issues. Mao's personality cult was also an important
issue because the professionals could not accept the infalli-
bility of Mao and, thus, were the targets of his wrath. A
related issue was the problem of subjecting the intellectuals
to ideological conformity. The upheaval brought to light
China's divided leadership and revealed the thinking of a
revolutionary Mao.

25 ELEGANT, Robert S.
Mao's Great Revolution, The World Publishing Company, New York
and Cleveland, 1971, 478p.
This is a monumental attempt to put the background and events of
the Cultural Revolution into a highly readable narrative form,
similar to a novel. Although the author does not cite any of
the sources, many of the materials used for this narrative are
official documents and Red Guard publications from the period of
the Cultural Revolution. Part I begins with the 1959 Lushan
Conference of the Central Committee of the CCP, when the infal-
libility of Chairman Mao was discarded and his programs were
subject to severe criticism by some of his close associates.
The line for struggle was then drawn between a visionary Mao
and his pragmatic lieutenants. When the moderates in power
launched a literary attack on Mao's ideas in the form of satire,
Mao began to map out his counterattack and selected the military,
headed by his disciple Lin Piao, as his instrument. Part II
describes in detail (1) how Mao selected his targets for attack,
from Peng Chen, Mayor of Peking, to Wang Kwang-mei, Liu
Shao-chi's wife, (2) how the criticism campaign was launched at
two leading universities, and (3) how the student revolt
expanded into a rampaging rebellion and a power seizure.

26 ESMEIN, Jean.
The Chinese Cultural Revolution, Anchor Books, New York, 1973,
346p.
This book contains a lucid analysis of the Cultural Revolution
as seen by the press attache of the French Embassy in Peking.
It is a very detailed account of the development of the Cultural
Revolution, based upon a variety of well documented sources,
most from the Chinese. The chapter on the roots of the Cultural
Revolution is most instructive. It outlines the framework of
Mao's thought and its essential ingredients: criticism and
self-criticism, mass line, and the will to accomplish the

27

impossible. In her development, China encountered the inevitable: the superstructures, in terms of art and literature,
education, social consciousness, and political awareness, became
bourgeois and capitalistic. One reason for the Cultural Revolution, therefore, was to make a revolution in the superstructures
in order to transform them. Put in ideological terms, it was an
attempt by Mao to denounce and reject "mechanistic materialism."
Another reason for the revolution was to fulfill the need to
wage continuous class struggle in order to preserve the ideal
world in Mao's vision. There is no room in the construction of
a visionary socialistic state for the conventional development
strategies of professional economists and technocrats. Disorder,
collectivization, and decentralization must be part of the
developmental experience. The Cultural Revolution was, in the
final analysis, a campaign to gain control of the party through
mass line and to awaken political awareness and enthusiasm among
the people and cadres.

27 FAN, Kuang-huan.
The Chinese Cultural Revolution: Selected Documents, Grove
Press, Inc., New York, 1968, 320p.
This book is a collection of selected documents which shows the
Cultural Revolution, not only in its historical perspective, but
also in its development during 1966-67. All the documents
selected for this collection come from controlled press publications, such as the People's Daily, Kuangmin Daily, Red Flag, and
Liberation Army Daily. English translations of these documents
are taken from the Peking Review. The documents are arranged in
pertinent groupings, designated by chapter captions. Mao's
essays on contradiction and practice, literature and art, and
theory of knowledge are grouped under ideological roots of the
Cultural Revolution. Documents which indicate the progression
of the Cultural Revolution are arranged according to military,
political, educational, and economic aspects of the development.
Key documents on the mobilization of the Red Guards, the intervention of the military, and attacks against Liu Shao-chi are
grouped under the high tide of the Cultural Revolution. The
last two chapters of the book contain a set of documents which
the compiler believes to be the world significance of the
Cultural Revolution.

28 FITZGERALD, Stephen.
"China Visited: A View of the Cultural Revolution," China and
Ourselves: Explorations and Revisions by a New Generation,
Bruce Douglass and Ross Terrill, eds., Beacon Press, Boston,
1970, pp. 1-29.
The Cultural Revolution was a struggle within the leadership
over "fundamental questions of doctrine and socialist construction in China." It was a struggle fought essentially on
ideological grounds. Fitzgerald argues that the revolution
should not be viewed as a "typical communist power struggle"
and offers the following to support this conclusion: Mao's open
encouragement to those outside of the party to attack the party

structure and the suspension of controls for mobilizing attacks
on the party elite. Nor did the Cultural Revolution resemble
Stalin's purge; there were no secret trials nor physical exter-
mination of opponents. Fitzgerald presents his impressions
about the Cultural Revolution in the various places he visited
while on a tour of China in 1968. By relating events encountered and entanglements with feuding factions of Red Guard
groups, Fitzgerald illustrates how the conflict and much of the
violence occurred. He also discusses the reasons why there was
no "civil war" in China under these conditions. Other topics,
such as the role of cultural, the arts and literature, and
education, are discussed to show that these were major issues
in the ideological struggle.

29 FRIEDMAN, Edward.
"Cultural Limits of the Cultural Revolution," Asian Survey,
Vol. IX, No. 3, March 1969, pp. 188-201.
The Cultural Revolution, as seen by Friedman, was not the
creation of a few leaders like Mao but was an integral part of
the modernization process with many universal aspects. As a
nation modernizes, tensions, problems and even contradictions
produce unexpected responses. The article examines the social
and political origins of the Cultural Revolution from 1955 to
1969 with particular reference to the modernizing process.
Mao's strategy was to collectivise agriculture by mass mobilization, disregarding the level of technical progress in the
countryside. In his desire to impose his own will on the party,
Mao acted arbitrarily, undermining the collective decision-
making process. The Great Leap had made the peasants conservative. Rural cadres were demoralized by mass criticism and,
therefore, became entrenched. Anxiety and tension were the norm
among the youth, especially the middle school graduates who had
to gain admission to the university or go down to the farms. As
the party's authority was weakened, self-interest groups organized on regional, institutional and occupational lines and began
to exert pressure and to make demands on the political system.
Friedman concludes that developments in China will be limited by
the "cultural givens of modernization and that the egalitarian
and developmental ideas proclaimed by China's leaders cannot be
achieved or even approached for generations."

30 FUNNELL, Victor C.
"Social Stratification," Problems of Communism, Vol. XVII,
No. 2, March-April 1968, pp. 14-20.
Funnell sees Mao's dislike of the disparities in income and
social standing, produced by China's economic and educational
systems, as the underlying reason for the Cultural Revolution.
Viewed in this light, the Cultural Revolution was an attempt by
Mao to break down economic and social distinctions, neo-
capitalism, that existed in China during 1965-66. Funnell
analyzes China's industrial wage system, the criteria for
differential salary systems among the state bureaucracy, and
the material incentives for agricultural production to show how

widespread the disparity in personal income and social standing was in China before the Cultural Revolution.

31 GELMAN, Harry.
"Mao and the Permanent Purge," Problems of Communism, Vol. XV, No. 6, November-December 1966, pp. 2-14.
The events of 1965-66 in China are viewed as attempts by Mao to obtain absolute loyalty from his subordinates and long-time colleagues. The purpose of the Cultural Revolution, Gelman argues, "was not merely to purge, but actually to terrorize, the party's central, regional and provincial apparatus in a manner that would leave a permanent imprint and secure an atmosphere in which footdragging or hidden opposition to Mao's will would no longer be conceivable." The article discusses the disagreement between Mao and Marshal Peng at Lushan in 1959, the criticisms of Wu Han's play, and the 10th Plenum of the 8th Central Committee in 1962 as orchestrated moves by Mao to launch his counteroffensive against the opposition within the party. Thus, the purge of the Peking party committee in 1966 was a culmination of the struggle between loyal military components and the long-established party cultural apparatus. According to Gelman, the real sin committed by the purged leaders in the initial stage of the upheaval "lay simply in daring to oppose Mao's will and question his policies."

32 GITTINGS, John.
"The Prospects of the Cultural Revolution," China After the Cultural Revolution, A Selection from Bulletin of the Atomic Scientists, Vol. XXV, No. 2, February 1969, Vintage Books, New York, 1970, pp. 57-72.
The Chinese Cultural Revolution revealed the conflicts in the society, with groupings and factions formed along lines of economic and political interests. The "leftists" were the unemployed students and unskilled workers, the have-nots; and the "rightists" were those with good jobs and secure status. Gittings points out that for a time in the winter of 1967 China seemed to have returned to normal as the party was reorganized, cadres were rehabilitated, and students were about to return to school. However, this period was followed in 1968 by an upsurge from the left and a counter reaction from the right with the army swinging to the right on the side of the status quo.
Viewed in light of the shifting events in 1968, Gittings points out the continuing role of Mao's ideology and his charisma in influencing the events unfolding in China.

33 GITTINGS, John.
"What Was It All About," Far Eastern Economic Review, Vol. LXVI, No. 40, October 20, 1969, pp. 36-37.
In this short essay, Gittings has succinctly stated his view of the meaning of the Cultural Revolution: it was an attempt made by the leaders, Mao in particular, to change people's "world outlook," or "social conscience," and to clarify the "strategy" by which the Chinese people could develop the kind of society

they desired. Programs of the Great Leap failed, this article asserts in agreement with Mao's conclusion, not because the programs were inappropriate for China in 1958 but simply because the people were ideologically unprepared for it. Thus, this essay argues, the Cultural Revolution was not merely about politics but was an attempt to inculcate a new set of socialist values to govern people's behavior. Moral values of self-sacrifice, service-to-the-people, and the collective good must be substituted for material incentives. The Cultural Revolution, from this point of view, was a struggle between two value systems: the proletarian and the bourgeois. Gittings does not dismiss the relevance of disagreements on economic and foreign policy issues; instead he raises what he considers the real question for China: how has the Cultural Revolution affected the Chinese people's view on the nature of their society and their role in it?

34 GOLDMAN, Merle.
Literary Dissent in Communist China, Harvard University Press, Cambridge, Mass., 1967, 343p.
If we accept the assumption that ideological dissent and devia-tion among the intellectuals in China on programs designed by the regime to develop an industrial society is a major under-lying cause for the Cultural Revolution, then this book, which focuses on the inner conflicts and struggles of the intellec-tuals in the 1950's, may serve as a good starting point for an understanding of the unprecedented upheaval. Basically, there was a constant conflict between the writers and the party functionaries over the writers insistence on voicing their criticism and dissatisfaction and over the functionaries control of this. Although many of the writers were party members and all embraced the humanitarian aspects of Marxism, each defined communism in his own way. Factionalism along ideological lines formed among the writers, upon whose services the regime depended for transmitting messages to the masses. As a group, the alienated intellectuals criticized and indicted the party for its arbitrariness and bureaucratic tendencies. As a group, they resisted the party's demand for control over their artistic and intellectual activities. The history of China's literary dissent seems to suggest that the party had failed at various times prior to the Cultural Revolution to incorporate the intellectual community into the regime's overall design. The nagging question on the eve of the Cultural Revolu-tion was what freedom for dissent could be permitted in China. For dissent, masked frequently by allegories, poems and satires, could erode ideological orthodoxy. This, to a large extent, may be what the Cultural Revolution was all about.

35 GRAY, Jack, and CAVENDISH, Patrick.
Chinese Communism in Crisis: Maoism and the Cultural Revolution, Frederick A. Praeger, New York, 1968, 279p.
This is a book written by two historians, whose purpose is to present the background and issues of the 1966 crisis in China.

In the first two chapters the main phases of Mao's revolution
and the regime's problems and policies from 1949 to 1965 are
described. Throughout this period strategies for development
had vacillated with much discussion and debate among the top
leaders on the application of the alternating strategies. The
debate in 1961 and most of 1962, according to Gray and Cavendish,
departed from the norm in that any reference to class struggle
was conspicuously absent. It was not until the 10th Plenum of
the 8th Central Committee in the fall of 1962 that the concept
of class struggle was inserted in the party's papers at Mao's
insistence. Class struggle is a crucial ingredient in the
application of the mass line, a key issue contended by the top
leaders on the eve of the Cultural Revolution. The Cultural
Revolution was an attack on the whole cultural "superstructure"
of the Chinese society: from art and literature to science and
technology. Viewed in this light, the attack was an assault on
the intellectuals, who by then were responsible for the development of the primary and secondary social institutions. It was
through the Cultural Revolution that the question of the proper
role of the cultural superstructure must be resolved: education,
technical and professional skills, and bureaucratic apparatus
and services. The Cultural Revolution of 1966 was preceded by
the abortive Socialist Education Campaign of 1963, which was a
mass campaign for political and ideological indoctrination in
the countryside. The 1966 campaign should be called the
cultural rectification campaign, personally initiated by Mao.
It became a political crisis when the campaign met resistance
from the central party authorities who wanted to exercise
control over the movement and over the surge of mass action by
the Red Guards. The Red Guards wanted no party control at all.
From here on the struggle became multi-leveled and the targets
escalated into a purge within the party.

36 HARDING, Harry, Jr.
"China: Toward Revolutionary Pragmatism," Asian Survey,
Vol. XI, No. 1, January 1971, pp. 51-67.
The theme of this article is that the Cultural Revolution was
essentially a visionary program to provide more equity in the
economic system and to prevent further rigidification of the
bureaucracy. It was the continuous pursuit for the realization
of revolutionary goals in political, economic, military, educational, and foreign policy. Harding reconstructs the meaning
of the Cultural Revolution using post-1970 events in China.
Politically the Cultural Revolution was an attempt to make the
party organization more responsive to the masses. The Central
Committee's discussion in 1970 of a revised constitution
centered on the incorporation of revolutionary principles of
organization, which were implemented during the Cultural
Revolution: simplified bureaucratic structure, institutionalization of mass criticism, mass participation in decision-
making at all levels. The army had been employed as a political
instrument for domestic control during the Cultural Revolution;
efforts were made in the 1970's to de-emphasize that aspect of

the army's work and to place the army under party control.
Rational planning and decentralization in decision-making in
the economic sector, educational reforms aimed at "working
class leadership," and preparation for war against the Soviet
Union, along with a less militant attitude elsewhere, all
indicate the return to "revolutionary pragmatism." Harding
argues that Mao was basically a pragmatic revolutionary, who
only permitted excesses during the Cultural Revolution in order
to shake-up, or "unfreeze," the Chinese society to halt its
trend toward revisionism.

37 HINTON, Harold.
An Introduction to Chinese Politics, Praeger Publishers,
New York, 1973, 323p.
Basically this is an introductory textbook on Chinese politics
for undergraduates. The various chapters cover topics on
political history up to the Cultural Revolution, the Cultural
Revolution, ideology, leadership, party, armed forces, techniques for action, and foreign policy. Chapter four on the
Cultural Revolution gives a brief summary and evaluation of the
upheaval. Hinton argues that the basic sociological problems,
such as student discontent and lack of opportunities for upward
mobility, were not the real causes of the upheaval. Rather the
Cultural Revolution was inspired and initiated by Mao because
he felt that the party apparatus had lost its revolutionary
momentum. The movement put pressure on the party to conform to
his line, which detailed the path that China ought to follow
to socialism.

38 HINTON, William.
Hundred Day War: The Cultural Revolution at Tsinghua University,
Monthly Review Press, New York and London, 1972, 288p.
This is a micro-study of the Cultural Revolution as it occurred
on the campus of one of the leading universities in China, the
Tsinghua University. Hinton, who also wrote Fanshen, went to
Peking in the summer of 1971 and interviewed some of the participants from the university and the adjacent neighborhood about
their involvement in the upheaval. This, then, is a narrative
account of the Cultural Revolution at an institution of higher
learning which took a leading role in the Red Guard movement
that eventually spread throughout China like a wildfire. The
book tells how the revolution arrived on campus, who was
involved and for what reasons, and how the factions based on
ideological differences developed to the detriment of the entire
movement. Finally, the account, as revealed by the participants,
shows how the students had been transformed in their ideological
thinking through their struggle in the Cultural Revolution.
This detailed account contains descriptions of the educational
system which existed before the upheaval in 1966 and the reasons
for reform in education. It delves into the political struggle
between the revolutionary students and the masses along "left"
and "right" lines. It also shows the phenomenon of the "ultra-
left" line embraced by the student leaders at Tsinghua for a

33

time and the danger the "ultra-leftists" created for the mass-
based revolution. This account helps readers from the west
to understand and differentiate the political and ideological
meanings of phrases such as "leftist," "rightist," "ultra-
leftist," "right opportunists," and "counterrevolutionary."
It also shows that Mao was the guiding force, if not spirit, in
shepherding the various contending factions into unity. After
undergoing the process of ideological struggle over the correct
line, the participants, in this case the intellectuals, were
integrated with the proletarians--peasants, workers and soldiers.

39 HINTON, William.
Turning Point in China: An Essay on the Cultural Revolution,
Monthly Review Press, New York, 1972, 112p.
This book refutes the view held by many analysts in the west
that the Cultural Revolution was a power struggle between pragmatists, led by Liu Shao-chi, and dogmatic revolutionary fanatics,
led by Mao. Instead, Hinton presents the argument that the
revolution was a class struggle over the question of who must
have control of the state power: the working class or the bourgeoisie? The book explains in Marxian terms that the Cultural
Revolution was launched to resolve the contradictions of the
Chinese people and the bourgeoisie, a prerequisite for transforming China into a totally socialistic society. This transformation must include not only the institutions, or superstructure,
but also the culture, customs, and habits of the people. Most
important of all was the need for each individual to wage a
struggle within himself to ensure that proletarian collectivism,
not bourgeois individualism, be firmly planted in the socialist
man. Class struggles, such as the Cultural Revolution, must
continue until no classes exist and until all inequalities--
privileges, careerism and individualism--are eliminated. On the
eve of the Cultural Revolution, the bourgeois ideology of privilege and careerism were prevalent in Chinese society: the former
middle, upper middle and rich peasants still had illusions about
individual property; the managers and administrators had illusions about privilege; and the intellectuals had illusions about
bourgeois practices. It was the headquarters of revisionism
that the Cultural Revolution was intended to struggle against
and to dismantle. The revolution, or class struggle, was issue-
oriented; fundamental differences existed over: agriculture,
politics-in-command, self-reliance, education, military affairs,
and foreign policy. By the late 1960's these differences, under
pressure from domestic and foreign events, had reached the point
that postponement of their resolution became impossible, and the
Cultural Revolution resulted.

40 HO, Ping-ti, and TANG TSOU, eds.
China's Heritage and the Communist Political System, China in
Crisis, Vol. 1, Book 2, The University of Chicago Press,
Chicago, 1968, 803p.
Separate annotation of articles from this book are found under
author entry in various sections of this bibliography.

41 HOOK, Brian.
"China's Cultural Revolution: The Preconditions in Historical
Perspective," The World Today, Vol. 23, No. 11, November 1967,
pp. 454-464.
In this article Hook examines historical developments in the
Chinese communist revolution which contained preconditions that
rendered it "vulnerable" to the Cultural Revolution. First was
the patriotic rather than Marxist-Leninist appeal of the revolution for the Chinese, leading to the need for a series of rectification campaigns, the latest being the Cultural Revolution.
Second was Mao's innovative strategy for mobilizing the masses
in the countryside for economic development, the so-called
"guerrilla economics." Third was the Chinese continuing
problem of preventing the revival of old attitudes and ideas,
which were encouraged by policies such as material incentives.
This problem was reflected in attacks on revisionism in the
Soviet Union. Fourth was the need to perpetuate the revolutionary fervor for succeeding generations and, thus, the necessity
to determine the form and content of education for the young.
Education reform aimed at doing away with elitism and de-
emphasizing "book learning" became a major ingredient of the
new revolution. Finally, the international situation which
existed in 1965-66 made it necessary for the Chinese leaders to
prepare the population for continued denial of China's rightful
place in the U. N., for the United States escalation in Vietnam,
and for the Sino-Soviet dispute.

42 HOOK, Brian.
"The Post-Plenum Development of China's Proletarian Cultural
Revolution," The World Today, Vol. 22, No. 11, November 1966,
pp. 467-475.
In analyzing the 11th Plenum of the 8th Central Committee of the
CCP held during August 1966, which launched the Cultural Revolution, Hook develops the thesis that it was in the interaction
between domestic concerns and foreign policy considerations that
the Cultural Revolution was conceived. The primary domestic
concern in 1966 was the tendency to restore capitalistic and
revisionistic measures in the wake of the failure of the Great
Leap and the Commune Programs. The ideologues' answer was to
wage a purification campaign, first in literature and the arts
and later in all areas, against those who had criticized the
failure of the Great Leap back in 1961-62. The major foreign
policy considerations were the sharpening of the Sino-Soviet
dispute and the United States escalation of the Vietnam War.
The Cultural Revolution was conceived at precisely the moment
when the leadership had to face the twin problems of modern
revisionism as a viable alternative to China's brand of Marxian
mass mobilization for development, represented externally by the
Soviet Union, and United States' imperialism in Vietnam. Hook
concludes: "the problem presented by modern revisionism is
likely to recur so that, in the absence of any shift in the
policies pursued by the Chinese Communist Party, the world is
likely to hear more of the Proletarian Cultural Revolution."

43 HSIAO, Gene T.
"The Background and Development of 'The Proletarian Cultural
Revolution,'" Asian Survey, Vol. VII, No. 6, June 1967,
pp. 389-404.
The central thesis of this article is that the Cultural Revolution was essentially a power struggle between two factions:
Maoists and Liuists. The crisis was triggered by the de-
Stalinization program under Khrushchev. Hsiao argues that
approval of the "secret" report in 1956 which indicted Stalin
for promotion of a personality cult by the 20th Congress of the
Soviet Union's Communist Party had a tremendous impact on Mao's
own ideological leadership. The party constitution of 1956,
enacted by the 8th Party Congress of the CCP, omitted Mao's
thought as the ideological guideline and instituted a collective
leadership, perhaps against Mao's wishes. This was the seed of
Cultural Revolution. Subsequently, Mao disagreed sharply with
Liu over a number of political and economic policies: stable
versus revolutionary development, greater institutionalization
versus more mass movements, and primacy of industrial development versus primacy of agricultural collectivization. When
Mao's original proposal for a radical commune program was
modified by the party, Mao either abdicated his chairmanship
for the state as a protest or was forced to resign. Further
divergence on policy matters developed as the Great Leap
programs failed and China had to face a disastrous economic
crisis. Mao's prestige declined as criticism on the correctness
of his policies mounted in the early 1960's. From here on the
power struggle, not only increased in tempo, but came out into
the open. Finally, Mao was able to mount an attack in the form
of the Cultural Revolution against these "rightists" who disagreed with him.

44 HSIUNG, James Chieh.
Ideology and Practice: The Evolution of Chinese Communism,
Praeger Publishers, New York, 1970, 359p.
This book is a survey of the development of the Chinese commu-
nist ideology from the May Fourth Movement through the Cultural
Revolution, 1919-1969. The last part of the book surveys the
ideology and practice of Chinese Marxism from 1949 through the
Cultural Revolution. Hsiung argues that the Cultural Revolution
was a continuation of Mao's unsuccessful campaign to purge the
bourgeois tendencies in the arts and literature during 1962-63.
The targets in the initial stage of the Cultural Revolution
were university professors and administrators, historians and
performing artists. The targets gradually spread to include
those party leaders responsible for cultural affairs. Mao's
concern for the remoulding of the Chinese mind was very obvious
at an early stage of the upheaval. According to Hsiung, a
number of fundamental issues underlay the Cultural Revolution.
These issues, or policy differences, usually involved the
interpretation of ideology or questions of ideological direction. The Cultural Revolution, thus, represented Mao's attempt
to reestablish his ideological leadership in the party. He

36

carried this to the extent of calling for the temporary destruction of the party apparatus so that it could be rebuilt.
Hsiung sees no evidence that Mao had a master plan for revolution against his own party; improvisation marked the whole
development of the Cultural Revolution.

45 HUBERMAN, Leo and SWEEZY, Paul.
"The Cultural Revolution in China," Monthly Review, Vol. 18,
No. 8, January 1967, pp. 1-17.
This article, prepared by two well known American Marxists,
offers an entirely different interpretation of the meaning of
the Cultural Revolution. The first part of the article refutes
the popular interpretation in the United States at that time
which explained the Cultural Revolution in terms of the expanding United States military action in Vietnam, China's response
to external pressures, and personal power struggles. Instead,
Huberman and Sweezy argue that the Chinese were seriously concerned about the decline in the revolutionary spirit of soli-
darity and sacrifice, not only in European socialist countries
such as the Soviet Union and Yugoslavia, but in China as well.
The growth of privilege for scientists, technicians, managers
and bureaucrats was inevitable in any technological backward
country in a period of rapid economic development. Privilege
creates vested interests and breeds the growth of individualism
and selfishness in a supposedly collective socialist society.
Unlike the Soviet Union, this article argues, China's revolution
had a large mass base which could contain the privileged party
cadres who misused "their power to promote special and private
interests." The Cultural Revolution, as one of these periodic
rectification campaigns, was waged to mobilize the under-
privileged, particularly the youth, to prevent China from
taking the road to capitalism. The Cultural Revolution, seen
in this light, is but an integral process of the Marxian
revolution.

46 HUNTER, Neale.
Shanghai Journal: An Eyewitness Account of the Cultural
Revolution, Frederick A. Praeger, New York, 1969, 311p.
This is a personal eyewitness account of the Cultural Revolution in Shanghai during the crucial early period from 1966 to
1967 by an English instructor at the Foreign Language Institute
in Shanghai. It draws most of its sources from the Red Guard
publications. Hunter views the Cultural Revolution as a
struggle for power between those holding conflicting visions
for China's future. It was mainly an ideological struggle
to establish a working-class culture. The revolution in
many respects, as Hunter sees it, was a reaffirmation by
China's youth and impoverished millions that their society
must not be controlled by the privileged elites who practiced
bourgeois ideology. It was also a revolt by the young against
the party's bureaucratic tyranny. In this sense, Hunter
describes the Cultural Revolution as a full-scale authentic
revolution.

37

47 ITO, Kikazo, and SHIBATA, Minoru.
"The Dilemma of Mao Tse-tung," The China Quarterly, No. 38,
July-September 1968, pp. 58-77.
These two Japanese observers make the point that Mao, as he
approached his twilight years, was determined to engineer the
Cultural Revolution in order to make the young generation
successor to his revolution. This analysis is based on circum-
stantial evidence that Mao with the help of his wife, Chiang
Ching, Lin Piao, and Chen Po-ta instigated the campaign. A
sketchy background of the Cultural Revolution is given by tracing events back to the Great Leap, which represented a rejection
of the Soviet Union's model for development--a model that relied
on material incentives and the creation of special classes of
elites. Since Mao's revolutionary policies ran counter to the
policies of those who controlled the party, his strategy was
to intensify the Cultural Revolution. Potential war with the
United States and the Soviet Union was one devise used to
recapture power in the party. The article reports firsthand
observations at a very early stage of the Cultural Revolution.

48 JOFFE, Ellis.
"China in Mid-1966: 'Cultural Revolution' or Struggle for
Power?," The China Quarterly, No. 26, July-September 1966,
pp. 123-131.
Joffe takes the position that the Cultural Revolution was both
a power struggle and an ideological rectification campaign. He
asks that we accept the Chinese explanation of the motives for
the revolution--it is necessary for the aging leaders to keep
the "flame" of the Chinese revolution burning by continuously
inculcating in the masses the necessary ideological outlook.
It is doubly important that periodic campaigns be waged against
the elitist attitudes and habits of the intellectuals, who
occupy positions of power in society and whose social background
was bourgeois. In this sense the campaign was truly a Cultural
Revolution to remold the minds of the cadres. As the rectification campaign intensified, the question of correct ideology,
or line, became intertwined with the problem of succession and
power. The purged top officials, such as Peng Chen, were
considered possible contenders for succession to Mao. Joffe
argues that these contenders refused to submit to criticism for
being "revisionistic" because they did not want to take themselves out of the running for succession.

49 JOHNSON, Chalmers.
"China, the Cultural Revolution in Structural Perspective,"
Asian Survey, Vol. VIII, No. 1, January 1968, pp. 1-15.
This analysis of the origin and meaning of the Cultural
Revolution adheres to the thesis that while Mao had control
in initiating the upheaval, his efforts were diverted into
"emergency salvage operations" as forces unleashed led to
uncontrolled conditions. The revolution had begun with a
debate on policy issues, but by 1967 it turned into a massive
assault on the very structure of the party. Viewed from this

38

perspective, the article proceeds to analyze the fundamental
problem of a rigid and ossified communist bureaucracy to which
the Cultural Revolution was addressing itself. Rectification
campaigns and mass-line and self-criticism devices have in the
past been the techniques for checking the growth of bureaucratism in the Chinese communist movement. These devices were
in use by 1965, when the top leadership was in disagreement on
policies and methods. Since some party leaders might subvert
the rectification campaign, Mao finally was forced, according
to this analysis, to use non-party forces--students and masses--
to correct the practices and work-style of the party. A chaotic
situation was created when the students formed factions and
fought among themselves, eventually requiring use of the military to suppress the revolutionary rebels. With the military
in control, a purge of the party cadres ensued, culminating in
the restructuring of the party.

50 JOHNSON, Chalmers, ed.
Ideology and Politics in Contemporary China, University of
Washington Press, Seattle and London, 1973, 390p.
This collection of essays and research reports on the relationship between ideology and politics in China was the result of
a conference held in 1971 and sponsored by the Joint Committee
on Contemporary China of the American Council of Learned
Societies and the Social Science Research Council. The theme
of the conference was the function of ideology in Chinese
political actions. The Cultural Revolution, as a political
action, grew out of Mao's concern with the function of ideology
in Chinese society: "ideology as the summing up of the heritage
of the past plays a prescriptive role for the present." Separate annotation of the articles from this book are listed under
author entry in various sections of this bibliography.

51 JOHNSON, Chalmers.
"The Two Chinese Revolutions," The China Quarterly, No. 39,
July-September 1969, pp. 12-29.
Johnson believes that of all the variables which serve as
explanations for causes of the Cultural Revolution, the most
important is the ideological one. Mao's preoccupation with
ideology in 1957 may be attributed to the series of unprecedented international problems which required ideological
explanations. The article presents a catalog of Mao's ideological explanations, from his speech in 1957 on the Hungarian
revolution through the ninth polemic in 1964 charging the
Soviet Union with "phoney communism." The Cultural Revolution,
viewed in this light, is the clearest example of the influence
of ideology on the functioning of a communist system. The
revolution was concerned with remoulding human beings in
accordance with an ideological image prior to constructing the
material infrastructure for the society.

52 KARNOW, Stanley.
Mao and China: From Revolution to Revolution, The Viking Press,

New York, 1972, 592p.
This book is a history of the cataclysmic events that occurred in
China during the Cultural Revolution. It is written in a narrative fashion with sources well documented in reference notes at
the back of the book. Karnow traces the origin of the Cultural
Revolution to Mao's ideology and to his leadership style. Mao's
ideology is essentially a moralistic and visionary set of principles couched in Marxist-Leninist terminology. Basic to the
ideology is his desire to perpetuate the revolution so that the
Chinese people will be cleansed of their individualistic and
materialistic desires--in other words, the creation of a new communist man. It was really Mao's persistent drive to create a new
collective man that brought him into conflict with other leaders
who also contributed to the success of the revolution but who
held different views. Several chapters are devoted to the study
of the complex and contradictory Mao, who at one time or other
was opposed by the Chinese intellectuals, technocrats, military
professionals, his own party bureaucrats, and even the poor peasants. The Cultural Revolution then, in Karnow's view, was the
last and the most intensive rectification campaign waged by Mao.
It was Mao who personally launched the Cultural Revolution and
who during the course of the Cultural Revolution oscillated
between doubt and confidence as events became uncontrollable.

53 KAROL, K. S.
"Why the Cultural Revolution?," Monthly Review, Vol. 19, No. 4,
September 1967, pp. 22-34.
This article from the American Marxist monthly was originally
the introduction to the Norwegian edition of Karol's book,
China: The Other Communism (Hill and Wang, New York, 1967).
Karol, who was born in Poland, educated in the Soviet Union
and now resides in Paris, visited China in 1965. The article
refutes the hypothesis, popular among Sinologists during the
initial period of the Cultural Revolution, that the revolution
was basically a power struggle for succession among the top
leaders. Karol argues that the Cultural Revolution was concerned with the primacy of political incentives, moral values,
and the collectivist ethics embodied in Mao's thought which
serve as the cement for the new Chinese civilization. Therefore, the upheaval called for the destruction of old customs
and beliefs. Viewed in this light, it was logical for China's
leaders, such as Mao, to insist on the establishment of a new
institutional framework prior to further industrialization so
that these moral values could be assimilated by the masses
and so that an omnipresent bureaucracy and Russian-style revisionism could be avoided. The real meaning of the Cultural
Revolution lies in the relationship, to be drastically altered
by the upheaval, between the rulers (the party) and the ruled
(the masses)--the former would have to be more responsible as
well as more responsive to the latter.

54 KAROL, K. S.
The Second Chinese Revolution, translated from the French by

Mervyn Jones, Hill and Wang, A Division of Farrar, Straus, and
Giroux, New York, 1974, 472p.
The central thesis of this book is that the Cultural Revolution
had a multiple purpose: to break away from the Soviet model
of development, to mobilize the masses for possible conflict
with foreign powers, and to proletarianize the party. The
book, therefore, dismisses some of the more popular theories
on the causes of the Cultural Revolution, including personal
animosity between Mao and Liu, personal power struggle, and
Mao's concern for succession. Karol, instead, traces the
genesis of the Cultural Revolution back to 1962-63 and the
Socialist Education Campaign. He sees the Cultural Revolution
as a manifestation of the inevitable contradictions within the
party and the dilemma in the superstructure, particularly the
role of culture and of the intellectuals. The events of 1966
are pieced together to show that Mao intended to create a new
form of state, "a commune of China." The entire Red Guard
movement and the brief experimentation in Shanghai in January
1967 are analyzed within the framework of a quest for the
"commune of China." The vicissitudes of the Cultural Revolution from the spring of 1967 to a final stabilization in 1968
are carefully analyzed with supporting documentation from
Chinese sources. Karol also presents the thesis that the
conflict in Vietnam, the Soviet invasion of Prague, and clashes
along the Ussuri River between Soviet and Chinese troops
contributed to the final phase of the Cultural Revolution.
In the last chapter, Karol offers his interpretation of Lin
Piao's fall from power. One general conclusion of the book is
that "the CCP is not like any other Communist Party, and that
it is somehow destined to follow a radically different policy
from that which was pursued by Stalin in his days ..." The
Cultural Revolution, Karol argues, shows that Mao was in full
control and that it was not a contest between the army and
civilians. Finally, the Cultural Revolution was not simply a
division of those for or against the Soviet model for development. Rather it was a "Second Revolution," which reveals that
"in Mao's eyes, the building of socialism extends through a
long historical period and depends basically on the class
struggle, on the political and productive action of the workers
themselves."

55 KIRBY, E. Stuart.
"The Framework of the Crisis in Communist China," Current Scene,
Vol. VI, No. 2, February 1, 1968, pp. 1-10.
Under the general theme that the Cultural Revolution was complex
with no single explanation, Kirby sketches areas of conflict of
the six main contending groups, each trying to further its own
interest: (1) the leadership group of the party, (2) the armed
forces, (3) the administrative and technocratic bureaucracy,
(4) the rising student generation, (5) the factory workers, and
(6) the peasants. Mao ruled autocratically and was surrounded
by a small group of close associates who helped to execute
Mao's personal policies. Not until 1958, following the failure

of the Great Leap, was this personal rule challenged. Liu
Shao-chi, the first designated successor to Mao, contended for
power representing and supported by the urban-industrial
technocrats who believed in the reliance on expertise and
efficiency. Opposing Liu's power position in the party was
the armed forces dominated by Lin Piao, who shaped the military
into Mao's loyal instrument for revolution, despite dissension
within the military on the issue of professionalism and modernization. Resentment by the bureaucratic elite of egalitarian
and mass mobilization techniques for building socialism was
another element in the struggle. The Cultural Revolution
unleashed the pent-up energies and idealism of the young, which
Kirby views as an attempt by Mao to solve problems of future
revolutionary succession and preservation of the original
revolutionary fervor for the regime. The industrial workers'
seizure of power, a la Paris Commune, might be viewed as Mao's
attempt to win over the urban proletariat, whose spokesman up
to that time had been none other than Liu Shao-chi, the man
Mao wanted to depose. Lastly, in order to complete his revolution, Mao had to win the peasants' support.

56 LA DANY, L.
"Mao's China: The Decline of a Dynasty," Foreign Affairs,
Vol. XIV, No. 4, July 1967, pp. 610-623.
This article pictures the Cultural Revolution as the "end of a
dynasty." Father LaDany develops this thesis by giving a
rough sketch of the events leading up to the Cultural Revolution, when Lin Piao and the military emerged as the dominant
force in society. To LaDany, military dominance is a sure sign
of the decline of Mao's dynasty: "Emperors assign energetic
general to defend the rights of the dynasty, and the empresses
dowagers come to the forefront." The article notes the major
domestic events which weakened Mao's dynasty from the promulga-
tion of the Great Leap and the Commune programs, through dissension at the 1959 Lushan Conference and the attacks on Mao
after failure of the Great Leap, to Lin Piao's efforts to
establish Mao's thought as the "peak" of Marxist-Leninism.
LaDany asserts that Mao--a "rejuvenated enfant terrible" who
always wants to ferment revolutions--personally directed the
Cultural Revolution. He speculates about the possibility that
Mao was really Lin Piao's captive. To LaDany, all the symptoms
of the end of a dynasty were visible in China during 1966-67,
ranging from cruel centralized power and court intrigue to
disloyal ministers, a strong general, and peasant unrest.

57 LEVENSON, Joseph.
"Communist China in Time and Space: Roots and Rootlessness,"
The China Quarterly, No. 39, July-September 1969, pp. 1-11.
The Cultural Revolution represents China's continued search for
values that would be appropriate for a revolutionary China.
From 1949 to 1957 the modern and international value of indus-
trialization was the basic objective for the regime. China
welcomed expertise and technical competence. Then Mao began to

feel that the purely "technical tasks" of the first decade were
not sufficiently revolutionary. Class struggle must be continued so that revolutionary man would end nuclear fear--this was
the explosive theme of the Cultural Revolution. The revolution
must be continued so that all search for individual satisfac-
tions would cease to exist. The Cultural Revolution was basically a continued struggle between "red" versus "expert"--man's
victory over machines, over the bourgeoisie who live by machines.
The Cultural Revolution represents the "provincial cultural
spirit."

58 LEWIS, John Wilson.
"The Cultural Revolution," China Briefing, Frank E. Armbruster,
John W. Lewis, David Mozingo and Tang Tsou, University of
Chicago, Center for Policy Studies, University of Chicago Press,
Chicago, 1968, pp. 17-22.
The basic argument advanced by Lewis is that there were real
differences among top leaders on the direction for political and
social change. During the first part of the Cultural Revolution
(1965-66), "the principal issue was: How can the revolutionary
doctrine be perpetuated in a modernizing society and what
aspects of the revolutionary tradition should be passed on to
the second generation of Communists?" The article traces the
development of the dispute over these issues back to the summer
of 1964: the attacks on art and literature, on the Young
Communist League and on the party schools. The Cultural Revolution, according to this interpretation, was interrupted in
mid-1964 as a tactical move to allow attention to be focused on
defense when the United States escalated the war in Vietnam.
Mao viewed the interruption as a deliberate attempt to prevent
his ideas from "penetrating to the lower-level cadres and the
general population." It was this suspicion cast by Mao on Liu
and other senior party officials that precipitated a power
struggle in the summer of 1966. The article briefly analyzes
the opposing concepts for development in China: Mao's
"mobilization" and Liu's "controlled society." The article
views the Cultural Revolution as a battle between two gigantic
factions.

59 LIFTON, Robert Jay.
Revolutionary Immortality: Mao Tse-tung and the Chinese
Cultural Revolution, Vintage Books, New York, 1968, 178p.
This is essentially an interpretative essay on the theme of
revolutionary immortality as it relates to the ideological
purity stressed in the Cultural Revolution. From another point
of view, it is a psychological analysis of the character of a
revolutionary leader and his political style. The Cultural
Revolution was a quest for revolutionary immortality--"a shared
sense of participating in permanent revolutionary fermentation,
and of transcending individual death by 'living on' indefinitely
within this continuing revolution." Lifton, a social psychia-
trist, argues that man needs "an assurance of eternal survival
for his self"--this is what motivated Mao to launch the Cultural

43

Revolution. What Mao dreaded was the death of a revolution, or
the inability to fulfill his vision. The Cultural Revolution,
as analyzed by Lifton in Chapter IV, represents a demand for
renewal of a socialist life, for the rebirth of a "new community," a community of immortals engaged in an eternal revolutionary process. Thus the revolution represents an effort to
mobilize the masses for revolutionary or eternal purity.

60 MAC FARQUHAR, Emily.
"China: Mao's Last Leap," The Economist Brief Booklets, No. 6,
The Economist Newspapers, Ltd., London, 1968, pp. 1-24.
MacFarquhar sees Mao's basic concern for the creation of a new
breed of revolutionary men as the main reason for the Cultural
Revolution. Mao believes it is possible to remould the Chinese
masses and cadres in his own image. A brief summary of events
from 1958 to 1968, focusing on Mao's experimentation in radicalism, is given. The Great Leap is seen as Mao's first attempt
to create a communist paradise in one giagantic step. The
program's failure to produce miracles led to serious opposition
against further experiments in "romantic radicalism." During
the post-Leap period, from 1959 to 1962, Mao saw the revival of
revisionism, and in 1963 he implemented the Socialist Education
Campaign to combat revisionism. By 1965 Mao had become convinced that the education campaign had failed to produce the
desired revolutionary spirit and, therefore, launched the
Cultural Revolution aimed at the "bourgeois reactionary thinking" prevalent among intellectuals and cadres at all levels.
The Cultural Revolution is, thus, an outgrowth of Mao's obsession with the creation of revolutionary fervor in China.

61 MAC FARQUHAR, Roderick.
The Origins of the Cultural Revolution, Volume I: Contradictions among the People, 1956-1957, published for the Royal
Institute of International Affairs and the East Asian Institute
of Columbia University by the Columbia University Press,
New York and London, 1974, 439p.
This is the first volume of a planned three-volume study on the
origins and development of the Cultural Revolution. The focus
in this volume is on the events which evolved around the
Hundred Flowers Movement during 1956-57. The book examines
"the impact of the main events of this period on the thinking,
actions, and interactions of the Chinese leaders." MacFarquhar
attributes the causes of the Cultural Revolution to "disagreement over the aims of the Chinese revolution, over how to rule
China, over how to develop China." It was an upheaval, as
interpreted by MacFarquhar, "rooted in both principled and
personal disputes." MacFarquhar points out that it is crucial
for an understanding of the origins of the Cultural Revolution
to examine the events that evolved during 1956, the year
collectivization was completed. During the ensuing five years,
the Chinese leaders devoted a vast amount of time and energy
in devising ways for "a major economic breakthrough." It was
also in 1956 that Khrushchev's de-Stalinization program began

at the conclusion of the 20th Congress of the Communist Party
of the Soviet Union. To MacFarquhar, "Khrushchev's de-
Stalinization and the consequential Hungarian revolt later in
the year raised in Mao's mind the whole question of the relationship of a communist party to the people it ruled." The book
discusses the Hungarian revolt and Mao's decision to launch a
rectification campaign, the Hundred Flowers blooming, in order
to criticize the party from without. The final chapter of the
book analyzes why blooming and contending turned into an anti-
rightist campaign. MacFarquhar portrays Mao during this period
not as a "radical" but as a "liberal" who wanted to work with
the intellectuals. Nor does MacFarquhar pictures Liu Shao-chi
as a fervent advocate of the Soviet model of development. In
MacFarquhar's view, 1956-57 was a turning point in the regime's
history: "Behind lay the optimism and disillusion of the
Hundred Flowers period which saw the emergence of the problems
that increasingly preoccupied Mao over the next decade—the
nature of the ideal communist society, the role of the Communist
Party, the pace of economic development, the validity of the
Soviet model, and the ambiguity of his own position." Thus,
"the process of fermentation of Mao's mind which determined him
to launch the Cultural Revolution was initiated by the events
of 1956."

62 MACKERRAS, Colin, and HUNTER, Neale.
China Observed: 1964-1967, Pall Mall Press, London, 1968, 194p.
The authors of this book are Australians who spent two years
as English teachers in Shanghai. They provide an inside view
of the Cultural Revolution in Shanghai. The authors describe
Shanghai during the Cultural Revolution as being in a state of
controlled chaos. The book gives a detailed description of the
twists and turns of the Cultural Revolution, including the
confrontation between the Red Guards and the workers and the
support given by the PLA to the Red Guards to end the impasse.
The authors feel that the Cultural Revolution in Shanghai was
left unfinished because the young had lost faith in the party
leaders who returned to their old positions. The experience
of the upheaval, the authors contend, resulted in indecisive
and weak leadership in Shanghai. Viewed from the authors'
perspective, the basic purpose of the revolution had not been
accomplished.

63 MICHAEL, Franz.
"The Struggle for Power," Problems of Communism, Vol. XVI,
No. 3, May-June 1967, pp. 12-21. Also in Richard Baum with
Louise B. Bennett, eds., China in Ferment: Perspectives on
the Cultural Revolution, Prentice-Hall, Inc., Englewood Cliffs,
N. J., 1971, pp. 52-59.
The Cultural Revolution is clearly a power struggle between
Mao's radical utopian communism and pragmatic, rational commu-
nism. It began in 1958 when Mao selected the mass mobilization
strategy as the method for modernizing China and discarded
previously accepted development methods. Mao was isolated and

lost power after this strategy failed in the Great Leap in 1959.
The pragmatists controlled development until the Cultural
Revolution, which represented the culmination of Mao's attempt
to regain his lost power and prestige.

64 MILTON, David, MILTON, Nancy, and SCHURMANN, Franz, eds.
People's China: Social Experimentation, Politics, Entry onto
the World Scene, 1966 through 1972, Vintage Books, A Division
of Random House, New York, 1974, 673p.
Part II of this fourth volume of the "China Reader" deals with
the Cultural Revolution. Introductory remarks to Part II by
the editors present a summary of the origin and development of
the Cultural Revolution. The editors believe that the revolution was essentially an ideological campaign to implement Mao's
concept for an uninterrupted revolution. It was also a rejection of the Soviet model for developing a socialist system.
Mao's original intent in launching the campaign was to have a
debate based on reason and argument--an educational campaign in
which cadres and masses participated--rather than a struggle
using force or violence. Other dimensions of the Cultural
Revolution discussed include concern over problems of the
bureaucratic elite, political passivity, and routinization.
The goals of the revolution, according to Mao, could only be
realized through raising the political consciousness of the
cadres and the masses. The reading selections include the
following topics: Mao Tse-tung--The Leading Rebel, Mobilization for Rebellion, Bombard the Headquarters--Correcting the
Orientation, The January Storm--Seizing Power from Below,
Liu Shao-Chi--"China's Khrushchev," Countercurrents--The Right
and the "Ultra-left," Struggle for Unity and the Great Alliance,
and Rebuilding the Party. The reading selections consist
mainly of original Chinese source material in English with some
interpretative analyses by western scholars and observers.

65 MYERS, James T.
"The Fall of Chairman Mao," Current Scene, Vol. VI, No. 10,
June 15, 1968, pp. 1-18.
Myers takes the position that the Cultural Revolution was the
result of divisions among the top leaders in China. In exploring the background of the strife, he places the burden for the
disorder on the role that Mao played in crucial decisions made
by the party prior to the Cultural Revolution. By using a
series of official documents released during the early part of
the Cultural Revolution on the purge of Peng Teh-huai at the
party's 1959 Lushan Conference, Myers argues that the roots of
the leadership's schism were the domestic economic policies of
the mid-1950's. It was precisely because Mao had been attacked
personally at Lushan that the subsequent campaign for the
glorification of Mao was launched to "apotheosize" the person
and revolutionary thought of Mao and to discredit the leading
dissenters' arguments against the policies of the Great Leap.
The Lushan Conference dealt a serious blow to Mao's power and
influence, the beginning of Mao's downfall, according to this

article. While the Lushan Conference practically placed Mao in
retirement, it catapulted Lin Piao into dominance by virtue of
his alliance with Mao. The strategy of the Mao-Lin faction was
to create a more reliable revolutionary base by organizing the
youth and indoctrinating the military. By 1965 the Mao-Lin
alliance had made its first attack against the dissident subordinates of Liu's chief lieutenants in the cultural fields.
Then the attack was gradually focused on Liu Shao-chi and the
party apparatus under his control. This article asserts that,
at least initially, Mao clearly was directing these attacks and
the Cultural Revolution.

66 NEE, Victor.
The Cultural Revolution at Peking University, Monthly Review
Press, New York, 1969, 91p.
This book describes the Cultural Revolution at Peita, Peking
University, the cradle of the May 4th student movement for
nationalism. It pieces together, from the accounts of Chinese
and foreign student participants, a coherent picture of the
struggle between the revolutionaries, who supported Mao, and
the so-called bourgeois oriented university administration, who
were close to the faction of the party's top leaders led by the
Mayor of Peking, Peng Chen, in opposition to Mao. Although the
bulk of this book concerns the struggle at Peita and the events
that finally led to the formation of a Red Guard group, the
first two chapters analyze causes for the Cultural Revolution
with particular reference to the development of an elitist
educational system. The book reviews the shifts back and forth
from professionally-technologically oriented university education to a more revolutionary and egalitarian education. From
1952 to 1956 Chinese university education reflected the Soviet
Union model, which stressed academic excellence and acquisition
of technological knowledge. Then came a period emphasizing
work study programs with stress on manual labor under the
hsia-fang movement to the countryside. The economic recovery
of 1960-1963 was accomplished by a reemphasis on professionalism
and intellectual elitism with political commitment and experience counting for less than excellence in academic work. This
emphasis on academic excellence created a dilemma for students
from the countryside because they felt intellectually inferior
in competition with those whose class origin provided cultural
and intellectual advantages for academic work. It was against
this background that the Cultural Revolution came to Peita.

67 NOUMOFF, S. J.
"China's Cultural Revolution as a Rectification Movement,"
Pacific Affairs, Vol. XL, Nos. 3-4, Fall and Winter 1967-1968,
pp. 221-234.
Noumoff argues that the Chinese communist movement has undergone
numerous rectification campaigns to solve many internal party
problems, ranging from cadres class awareness to corruption and
inefficiency. In analyzing the stages of the Cultural Revolution, he shows how it has followed the pattern established by

previous rectification campaigns: airing, counterattack, rectification, study and self-criticism. A large portion of inner party problems derived from the need to recruit hastily a large number of party members who had intellectual training but who had varying degrees of ideological commitment. The 1965-66 period seemed to have been the appropriate time for an intensified rectification campaign to transform cadres from all levels, through struggle, into committed adherents of the Chinese communist ideology. Intellectual activity must be in conformity with political action. Activities like those of the intellectuals in the 1956 Hungarian crisis would not be tolerated in China. The Cultural Revolution of 1965 was also used to solve the problem of the absence of revolutionary experience among the young and the problem of separation between the ruling party and the masses. Thus, the Red Guards were used to shake up the entrenched party bureaucracy.

68 OKSENBERG, Michel.
"China: Forcing the Revolution to a New Stage," Asian Survey, Vol. VII, No. 1, January 1967, pp. 1-15.
The Cultural Revolution, according to Oksenberg, was an "intensification" of the Socialist Education Campaign of 1962-65. The rise of the military during the Cultural Revolution and its role as a model for the nation to emulate was a continuation of the pattern that emerged in the early 1960's. The rampaging of youthful Red Guards and the appeal for ideological conformity resembled the political developments during the modernization process in other countries. Oksenberg, therefore, discounts the popular interpretation that these events were manifestations of a personal power struggle and places the Cultural Revolution in the framework of development politics. He devotes his main effort to providing insights into two major developments during the early stage of the Cultural Revolution: the problem of youth and the ascendancy of the military. The frustration of China's youth lay in the sheer numbers entering the job market. The system, at this time, was faced with the twin problems of absorbing large numbers of youths and of providing opportunities for advancement in a system where the older cadres monopolized the party apparatus. Under these conditions, careerism, status seeking and routinization developed in a supposedly revolutionary society. Thus the need for new values became increasingly important. Because the party was becoming increasingly rigidified, Mao saw the military, which by 1966 had become a model for studying and living the thought of Mao Tse-tung, as a prime instrument for the Cultural Revolution.

69 OKSENBERG, Michel, ed.
China's Developmental Experience, The Academy of Political Science, Columbia University, Praeger Publishers, New York, Washington, and London, 1973, 227p.
This book is a collection of papers presented at Columbia University in October 1972 under the sponsorship of the Academy

of Political Science and the National Committee on United
States-China Relations. In describing the book Oksenberg
states: "it explores the lessons, both positive and negative,
that may be learned from China's developmental experience
which might have a bearing on Western societies and on other
developing nations." The articles cover a wide range of topics
with particular emphasis on economic and scientific development
and social values, ideology, and social organization. Selected
entries from this book are annotated separately in the appropriate sections of this bibliography.

70 OKSENBERG, Michel.
"Communist China: A Quiet Crisis in Revolution," Asian Survey,
Vol. VI, No. 1, January 1966, pp. 1-12.
Looking into 1966 from events unfolding in 1965, Oksenberg
seemed to detect the rumbling of a crisis situation for China.
After sixteen years in power, the top leadership had aged and
had lost some of its vigor; the expansion of party membership
since 1949 had attracted many who were more interested in
furthering their own career than in the revolution; there was
more concern expressed in 1965 about the growth of bureaucratic
behavior than at any time in the past. Yet the party was faced
with a dilemma: momentum for change could only be generated by
an attack on "bureaucratic ossification," but an excessive
attack might disrupt the orderly progress of development. "The
regime's most recent solution to this problem is the establishment of offices in charge of political affairs, located in
organizations dealing with finance and trade, industry and
communications, and agriculture and forestry." This major
reorganization was modeled on the PLA's political training
apparatus. The underlying question in 1965's quiet crisis was
how to generate the momentum for revolutionary change.

71 OKSENBERG, Michel.
"Occupational Groups in Chinese Society and the Cultural
Revolution," The Cultural Revolution: 1967 in Review, Michigan
Papers in Chinese Studies No. 2, Chang Chun-shu, James Crump
and Rhoads Murphey, eds., Center for Chinese Studies, University
of Michigan, Ann Arbor, 1968, pp. 1-44.
Oksenberg analyzes the role of policy influential groups during
the early stages of the Cultural Revolution (1966-67). The
article focuses on the social science concept of aggregate
interest groups, including their interest articulation, their
ability to manipulate information and to cultivate influence at
higher levels to shape policy formulation, and their acquisition and retention of power. Seven occupational groups were
selected for the analysis: peasants, intellectuals, industrial
managers, industrial workers, students, party-government functionaries and military personnel. The analysis indicates that
the peasants influenced policy only indirectly, while industrial managers and workers affected policy swiftly. The
intellectuals were generally submissive. Students were in a
relatively strong position to influence policy, particularly

when their cause received support from the military and the
party bureaucracy. The members of the military, finally,
became the most powerful group in influencing policy because
they had the support of Mao and Lin Piao and because many held
policy-making positions in both the government and the party.
Since these groups have conflicting interests and since they
have varying degrees of influence in decision formulation,
Chinese politics may become increasingly an arena for intense
bargaining between interest groups and the central authority.

72 OKSENBERG, Michel.
"Political Changes and Their Causes in China, 1949-1972," The
Political Quarterly, Vol. 45, No. 1, January-March 1974,
pp. 95-114.
After examining the major trends in China's political development from 1949-1972, Oksenberg explores the major theories
which serve as explanations for political change, including the
Cultural Revolution, in China. One theory is that all political
changes in China for the past twenty-five years have been the
result of the conflict between Mao's ideological line versus
other less revolutionary lines. Another theory postulates the
thesis that political changes have been the result of pressure
from abroad--the Cultural Revolution was Mao's response to
United States military escalation in Vietnam. A third theory
tends to attribute China's alternate periods of mobilization
and consolidation to fluctuating economic cycles. A fourth
explanation for change is the interrelationship of the top
leaders, which is governed by the leaders' ambitions and
animosities--a personal power struggle. A fifth theory states
that once the revolution had come into power, the interests of
its leader and the political party began to diverge, resulting
in a situation where the leader made sole claim to the determination of ideology with the party reduced to a routine
bureaucracy. Finally, political change, such as the Cultural
Revolution, has been attributed to the development of divergent
interest groups in society, all bidding for a share in the
distribution of power, status, and authority.

73 PFEFFER, Richard M.
"The Pursuit of Purity: Mao's Cultural Revolution," Problems
of Communism, Vol. XVIII, No. 6, November-December 1969,
pp. 12-25. Also in Richard Baum with Louise B. Bennett, eds.,
China in Ferment: Perspectives on the Cultural Revolution,
Prentice-Hall, Inc., Englewood Cliffs, N. J., 1971, pp. 205-227.
In launching the Cultural Revolution, Pfeffer maintains, Mao
had a set of maximal goals toward which the revolution was
directed. These maximum goals included (1) the training of a
new generation of dedicated revolutionaries among the young,
(2) the creation of a new superstructure supported by a socialistic economic base, and (3) the reinstitution of mass participation. The Cultural Revolution was an authentic revolution
in that the leader intended to transform a whole culture, to
prevent the elites from becoming a special class in society

and to de-legitimize individual pursuit of material gain. In fact, what Mao wanted to accomplish in the Cultural Revolution was to establish countervailing institutions to replace the large scale organizations established under the regular party. In his attempt to transform the party, the most powerful institution in China, Mao sought to impose his own set of moral values as shared norms for the leaders, institutions and the masses. Since the Cultural Revolution involved conflicts of social values and changes, as well as attitudes and interests of individuals and groups, it was a part of the world movement to challenge established authority and entrenched bureaucratic life.

74 POSSONY, Stephan T.
"The Chinese Communist Cauldron," Orbis, Vol. XIII, No. 3, Fall 1969, pp. 783-821.
The article begins with a lengthy but seemingly unrelated discourse on the United States policy toward China and on Mao's legitimacy to rule and his credentials as a Marxist. To Possony, the Cultural Revolution was launched to restore Mao's power within the party. It was basically, so the article contends, a civil war favored by a reckless Mao, who involved the military in his contest for power. A section of the paper deals with social contradictions under the Cultural Revolution, which is an analysis of the various groups contesting for power. Another section touches upon China's relations with the United States and the Soviet Union vis a vis the Cultural Revolution. The author offers a course of action for the United States government including treating Mao, Lin Piao and the PLA as common enemies of the United States and the Soviet Union and enlisting the Chinese military on the side of the United States in order to prevent trouble and bloodshed in the world.

75 POWELL, David E.
"Mao in Stalin's Mantle," Problems of Communism, Vol. XVII, No. 2, March-April 1968, pp. 21-30.
This article examines the features of the Cultural Revolution reminiscent of Stalin's great purge in the 1930's in terms of techniques and rhetoric. The development of Stalinism is analyzed in historical perspective to provide an understanding of China's upheaval. In Powell's view, Mao found Stalin's formula for intensified class struggle very appropriate for China as socialism drew closer in 1965-66. Mao, an orthodox Stalinist, wanted to see the "class enemy" perpetuated as a myth in the Chinese revolution: "For Mao, as for Stalin, the ultimate danger to the revolution lies within the party itself-- but in the Chinese conception, the danger is one of ideological subversion."

76 PUSEY, James R.
Wu Han: Attacking the Present through the Past, East Asian Research Center, Harvard University Press, Cambridge, 1969, 84p.

This is a study of the Chinese intellectual who waged the anti-party literary campaign. An analysis is presented of Wu Han's writings, from his historical works in the pre-liberation period to his most celebrated play, "Hai Jui Dismissed from Office," which triggered the attacks against Liu Shao-chi and Peng Chen in 1966 and launched the Cultural Revolution. The book demonstrates how intellectuals, such as Wu Han, used historical allegory as a medium for citicism of the regime, its leaders and its policies.

77 PYE, Lucian W.
"Coming Dilemmas for China's Leaders," Foreign Affairs, Vol. XLIV, No. 3, April 1966, pp. 387-402.
In this three-part article, Lucian Pye presents "the prudence model." He argues that even though Chinese leaders have made mistakes and committed follies in the past, they are not "madmen." The regime "is essentially rational in seeking their goals and not prone to taking excessive risks." He argues, however, that significant changes must take place as the aged top leadership is replaced. He cites evidence that the "Chinese system is not so stable or so institutionalized as to be able to endure a major shift in leadership without significant structural change," including the reliance on mass mobilization and intensive propaganda and the rigidities which have developed in the system. Continuing problems such as conflicts between the central and local and regional authorities, the Sino-Soviet dispute, the modernization of the military, the revolutioniza-tion of organizational and managerial development also contrib-ute to instability. "A final source of potential instability in China is the passing of the revolutionary mystique and the need for the regime and the people alike to learn to live without the elation of their earlier dreams."

78 PYE, Lucian W.
The Authority Crisis in Chinese Politics, Center for Public Policy, University of Chicago Press, Chicago, March 1967. Also see Pye's The Spirit of Chinese Politics, M.I.T. Press, Cambridge, Mass., 1968.
This is the original version of an address delivered at Chicago in connection with the Center for Policy Study's China project in 1967. In this lecture Pye presented the psychological aspects of the Cultural Revolution in terms of an authority crisis. Pye treats China as a transitional society going through the process of modernization, a favored theme of scholars in development politics. China's problems of modernization were: her sense of historical greatness and the feeling of not being able to excel in those values--art of government and a high living standard--that she shared with the west. Pye sees the characteristics of Chinese politics as the reliance upon ideol-ogy, monolithic leadership style, and a strong feeling for authority, undivided authority. Pye maintains that it is the issue of authority which has become the basic problem in China's modernization process. While the Chinese feel the need for

order and authority, they must face change which is the essence
of modernization. Change in Chinese politics means political
activism--to be an angry person, to hate, and to be able to
identify the enemy. Thus, Chinese politics contains a great
deal of emotional involvement. Psychologically, Chinese
politics become a continuous conflict between emotion and
ritual, between red and expert. The Cultural Revolution, as
seen in this perspective, brought forth ritual responses which
Mao, the revolutionary, considered to be too routine. So Mao
conjured up the disorder to activate the routinized cadres and
to frighten those who might challenge his leadership.

79 ROBINSON, Joan.
"The Cultural Revolution in China," International Affairs: A
Quarterly Review, Vol. 44, No. 2, April 1968, pp. 214-227.
This article was written by a Cambridge University professor of
economics after she had completed her fifth visit to China in
1967. The meaning of the Cultural Revolution is seen through
her interpretation of some of the more important terminology
employed in the Chinese media. For instance the term "taking
the capitalist road" refers to those "rightists," the middle-
class in China, who while supporting the regime, retained a
superstructure--institutions, traditions and habits of thought--
that was "capitalistic" and elitist in orientation. The
"rightists" believed in efficiency for the organization that
they administered and in the acquisition of power along with
special status and privilege. "Class struggle" refers to
conflict between the leftists, the true socialists, and those
party leaders who supported the "rightists" and the "rightists"
themselves. Robinson then traces the initial stage of the
Cultural Revolution beginning with the attack on the president
of Peking University, which immediately spread into other
institutions. Confusion soon became the order of the day as
"rightists" counterattacked by invoking the party's authority.
Mao, as the leading leftist, then incited the masses, mostly
young students, to rebel against the party as an established
institution. Now an establishmentarian rebellion was sanctioned
by the party at the urging of Mao; this marked a full-blown
struggle in schools and factories and in cities and provinces.
At first these struggles were discussions after work, but they
soon degenerated into physical violence. Robinson criticizes
misinterpretation by many scholars about the Cultural Revolution.
To her, the Cultural Revolution was not Mao's "incoherent fanat-
icism" but a sincere attempt to re-inculcate revolutionary
collective values in Chinese society.

80 ROBINSON, Joan.
The Cultural Revolution in China, Penguin Books, Ltd.,
Harmondsworth, Middlesex, England, and Baltimore, Md., 1969
and reprinted with revised Postscript, 1970, 154p.
This book is divided into three parts: an introductory essay
on the complex origins of the Cultural Revolution, a detailed
account of the revolution as seen from the city of Shanghai,

and a selection of key Cultural Revolution documents. The
Cultural Revolution, as seen by Robinson, was really a new
revolution in that the Chinese Marxists, led by Mao, had
serious doubts about the post-Stalin Soviet model of communism.
This model demonstrated the possibility of developing a capitalistic superstructure despite the establishment of a socialist
economic base. Under such a system, power, privilege and access
to education can form the basis of class distinction. When this
happens, the class struggle ceases to exist. Chinese Marxists
feared that the unquestioned imitation by "rightists" of the
Soviet model would eventually destroy Chinese socialism. The
aim of the Cultural Revolution, as seen by this noted British
economist, was to plant the roots of socialism firmly in the
superstructure and to eliminate bourgeois tendencies already
appearing in the Chinese system. To the Chinese, Robinson
explains, it is a simple question of which path to travel:
socialist or capitalist. It was inevitable that the struggle
engulfed the party apparatus and its leaders who had the
authority to steer the regime to the "rightist" path. A new
party organ had to be formed embracing the proletarian ideology
which stresses the attitude of service to the people. The
educational system also had to be modified to assure that Mao's
proletarian views would be inculcated in the young, the successors to the revolution, who lacked practical experience making
a revolution. The Cultural Revolution was, therefore, an
authentic revolution to remold the minds of the people through
continuous class struggle in order to build a truly socialist
society.

81 ROBINSON, Thomas W., ed.
The Cultural Revolution in China, University of California Press,
Berkeley and Los Angeles, 1971, 509p.
This book consists of five case studies on the Cultural Revolution covering the 1966-67 period by China experts from the Rand
Corporation. Topics covered are ideology, theories of policy-
making, the role of a leader, foreign policy, and the revolution
in the countryside. Several generalizations emerge from this
volume: the Cultural Revolution did possess elements of a
genuine revolution, the revolution made it possible to view
Chinese politics from the inside, the internal political scene
contained common features present in many other countries--
personal rivalry and policy disputes, and ideology played a
central role during the early period of the revolution. Articles from this volume are annotated separately under author
entry in this bibliography.

82 SCHRAM, Stuart, ed.
Chairman Mao Talks to the People: Talks and Letters, 1956-1971,
translated by John Chinnery and Tieyun, Pantheon Books, A
Division of Random House, New York, 1974, 352p.
This is a collection of directives, statements, and speeches
made by Chairman Mao covering the period of 1956-1971. A large
portion were divulged by the Red Guards during the Cultural

54

Revolution. In discussing the reasons for this volume, Schram states: "Moreover, the real flesh-and-blood Mao revealed in these uncensored utterances, Rabelaisian in speech and forthright in his criticism both of himself and of others, is not only more believable, but far more impressive, than the plaster saint worshipped by some of his self-appointed disciples." This material reveals more of Mao's ideas than it does of events. It is designed to aid, not only the general public, but also China specialists by compiling material from various sources. Schram's introduction and his notes to the texts are most useful. The collection begins with Mao's 1956 speech on the ten great relationships, continues through his speech at the Supreme State Conference in 1958 and his talks with Chang Chun-chiao and Yao Wen-yuan in February 1967, and concludes with his summary of the Lin Piao affair given on his provincial tours in August and September 1971. Schram believes that the Mao of the 1960's is richer and more confident; but "at the same time, one is struck by the basic continuity and consistency of Mao's approach to politics and to life, over the past half century and more."

83 SCHURMANN, Franz.
"The Attack of the Cultural Revolution on Ideology and Organization," China's Heritage and the Communist Political System, Ping-ti Ho and Tang Tsou, eds., China in Crisis, Vol. I, Book 2, The University of Chicago Press, Chicago, 1968, pp. 525-564.
The thrust of this article on the effect of the Cultural Revolution on ideology and organization is that the Cultural Revolution was a huge purge aimed at the party structure as an organization and at the party bosses at all levels. The problem for the party was that it had grown too large and too fast. By 1962 the Central Committee had to wage an ideological indoctrination campaign to eliminate the evil tendencies of elitism, provincialism and authoritarianism. Schurmann defines an organization as a "goal oriented structure of power." An attack on the organization must entail some differences over basic issues and goals. Schurmann postulates that, in addition to domestic policy differences, foreign policy issues, particularly the Sino-Soviet dispute, played a dominant role in the Cultural Revolution. "Revisionists," in Schurmann's view, refer, not only to those who believed in orderly planning, but also to those who wished to seek collaboration with the Soviet Union so that in the event of an American attack from Vietnam, China would have Soviet nuclear protection. Additionally, Schurmann argues that since the Chinese elite relied more on pragmatic measures and material incentives than on Mao's ideology, they would eventually produce revisionistic tendencies similar to those which have occurred in the Soviet Union. "Revisionists" refers also to those who advocated a military strategy of confrontation with the United States in Vietnam rather than Mao's protracted guerrilla war.

84 SOLOMON, Richard H.
Mao's Revolution and the Chinese Political Culture, University
of California Press, Berkeley, California, 1971, 604p.
Solomon's book on Mao's revolution and its place in China's
political culture has three interrelated theses. One is that
the Chinese had always been governed by the Confucian ethics
of harmony and respect for authority. Psychologically, this
sense of respect for authority has a negative side: an
ambivalent attitude toward authority. Mao sensed resentment
toward authority and, therefore, stressed conflict. He conceived revolutions to provide an outlet for the negative side
of the respect for authority and harmony. Solomon postulates,
that, as a revolutionary leader, Mao simply channels the emotional aggression of the Chinese and focuses it on a desired
target. Mao's technique for mass mobilization is dependent on
this capacity to focus the hostility against authority. To
demonstrate the validity of the theses, Solomon presents the
findings of his interviews of mainland born Chinese and the
results of many sociological and psychological tests given to
measure their attitudes. The second thesis is that Mao is
obsessed with the remolding of the Chinese mind and institutions through mass mobilization and mass participation. Mao
is preoccupied with restructuring the Chinese political culture
because he sees this as necessary to perpetuate the 1949 revolution for succeeding generations. Finally Solomon finds there
is a continuous thread between Mao's political thinking during
the Yenan days and policies implemented after 1949 under the
party.

85 SOLOMON, Richard H.
"On Activism and Activists: Maoist Conception of Motivation
and Political Role Linking State to Society," The China
Quarterly, No. 39, July-September 1969, pp. 76-114.
This is an exploratory study of the concept of activism as a
political value and the role played by China's political
activists. Solomon argues that the Chinese Communist Party
leadership devoted time and energy to "break down the passive
and dependent quality of Confucian authority relations" and
attempted to inculcate the revolutionary values of conflict
and "open rebellion." Activism, in the form of mass agitation
and self-criticism, became institutionalized long before the
Cultural Revolution: "the belief that the controlled conflict
of criticism, both within the party and between party and mass,
is the basis for generating active political participation and
creativity, and is also the technique by which effective communication links will be established between leaders and the led."
Solomon believes that "the politics of activism" was one of
the underlying causes in the Cultural Revolution. To Solomon,
Mao viewed the Cultural Revolution as "a mass movement for
restarting the engine of mobilization and recruitment which
would bring the positions of leaders a new generation of political activists; a way of revitalizing a party and government
system he saw as increasingly bureaucratic in its style of work,

and unresponsive to his own methods and goals."

86 SNOW, Edgar.
The Long Revolution, Vintage Books, New York, 1973, 267p.
Although this book is an account of Snow's trip to China in
1971, it provides insights and interpretations on events in
China. Snow's views on the essence of the Cultural Revolution
in Chapter 3 are worth noting. Snow believes that the primary
aim of the Cultural Revolution was to make the Chinese Communist Party, which had increasingly become bureaucratized, more
proletarian. It was Mao's strong feeling that to build a new
culture without any bourgeois or feudal tendencies, it was
necessary to tear down the party and purge the top party
personnel, who were mainly responsible for the development of
these tendencies. It seems evident from Snow's conversation
with Mao that the latter had reached his decision in January
1965 to launch a rectification campaign to purge top party
leaders who had introduced revisionistic measures into the
economic system. Mao began to wield his enormous personal
prestige in the purge with the objective of recapturing the
party's authority in order to direct the regime's revolution.
The rise of a new class of bureaucratic elite in China would
prevent the completion of the revolution. All economic and
technological measures must serve revolutionary politics and
goals. To Mao the revolutionary goals could only be achieved
when the successors to the revolution had experienced the
meaning of struggle and revolution. Snow sees the Sino-Soviet
dispute and the United States escalation in Vietnam as secondary issues to the struggle over policies between Mao and Liu
Shao-chi. The final aims of the Cultural Revolution were
essentially Marxian: "the complete liberation of man from
hunger, greed, ignorance, war and capitalism." This book not
only includes a detailed account of events which occurred
prior to the Cultural Revolution, but also includes those
which followed it. A unique feature of the book is the series
of personal interviews with Mao and Chou En-lai, which reveal
valuable insights about the Cultural Revolution and its causes.

87 STARR, John Bryan.
"Conceptual Foundations of Mao Tse-tung's Theory of Continuous
Revolution," Asian Survey, Vol. XL, No. 6, June 1961,
pp. 610-628.
This is essentially a theoretical discussion on the meaning of
Mao's concept of continued revolution. Starr points out that
this concept can be traced to Trotsky's theory of permanent
revolution but "is actually directed toward a very different
set of circumstances." Mao's significant innovations in the
theory of continued revolution are examined. Starr lists the
Socialist Education Movement of 1963 and the Cultural Revolution of 1966 as the most important example of the practical
implications of this theory. Starr points out three aspects
of the Cultural Revolution which are particularly important to
the theory of continued revolution: the seizure and

redistribution of individual and institutional power, the
actual experiencing of class struggle, and the creation of new
political institutions.

88   STARR, John Bryan.
Ideology and Culture: An Introduction to the Dialetic of
Contemporary Chinese Politics, Harper and Row, New York, 1973,
300p.
Starr takes the approach that there are many parallels between
political problems in China and problems in political development in general. He examines China in terms of the nature of
ideology, political life, and political style. The Cultural
Revolution represents a new campaign in the political style of
China. Numerous campaigns prior to the Cultural Revolution
had the committed involvement of the masses in tackling certain
problems. But the Socialist Education Campaign of 1963-65, the
one preceding the Cultural Revolution, failed to involve the
masses in substance: "The masses had learned how to live
through one without becoming involved." The Cultural Revolution
was a movement of three parts: a power struggle to eliminate
those top leaders who disagreed with Mao's views, a real
cultural upheaval to eliminate the superstructures considered
bourgeois, and a learning experience for its participants on
the making of a revolution.

89   STARR, John Bryan.
"Revolution in Retrospect: The Paris Commune through Chinese
Eyes," The China Quarterly, No. 49, January-March 1972,
pp. 106-125.
This article examines the use of the Paris Commune of 1871 as
a model for organizational form and for mass participation in
Chinese political thought during the early stage of the
Cultural Revolution. The article traces the development of
Mao's use of the Paris Commune model in his social theory for
China from 1956 to 1964, when the ninth polemic on Khrushchev's
"phoney communism" was written. According to Starr, the
relevance of the Paris Commune is that for Mao it is a precedent
for the Cultural Revolution--the whole Paris Commune episode
was an experiment in mass participation for power seizure and
decision-making. The short-lived Chinese experimentation with
the new political structure during the Cultural Revolution in
the formation of the "Shanghai People's Commune," "Peking
Commune," and "Harbin People's Commune" is examined to show
the common features of these two movements one hundred years
apart: "Both sought to destroy the existing state structure
and to rebuild a new one, and in both cases, the ideal for the
new structure was the same: it was to be a structure which was
highly responsive to its constituents and which would thereby
serve to break down the alienation of state from society typical
of the old order."

90   TANG TSOU.
"The Cultural Revolution and the Chinese Political System,"

The China Quarterly, No. 38, April-June 1969, pp. 63-91. Also in Richard Baum with Louise B. Bennett, eds., China in Ferment: Perspectives on the Cultural Revolution, Prentice-Hall, Inc., Englewood Cliffs, N. J., 1971, pp. 191-204.
The Cultural Revolution, according to Tang Tsou, was guided by Mao's vision to make a truly egalitarian society where the rulers and the ruled became indistinguishable in terms of policy-making, power, and privilege. It was a revolution "from the bottom to the top" which contained a certain degree of spontaneity and which, by focusing on the cult of Mao, set out to establish a new standard of revolutionary behavior for other leaders. Mao, the supreme leader, saw the party as being bipolarized in a class struggle in which correct ideology and revolutionary morality must prevail. Since the revolution was aimed at the radical transformation of man, its first targets were the intellectuals, who are the bearers of knowledge. The other major targets were the party and government bureaucrats. Red Guards were used for the attack; and the military, for seizing power. The end result of the Cultural Revolution was not only destruction of the party organization but serious damage to regional party authority and loss of confidence among the leaders in their own institutions.

91 TANG TSOU.
"The Cultural Revolution - I," China Briefing, Frank E. Armbruster, John W. Lewis, David Mozingo and Tang Tsou, The University of Chicago, Center for Policy Study, University of Chicago Press, Chicago, 1968, pp. 9-15.
Tang Tsou argues that the Cultural Revolution was initiated and directed by Mao to recover his control over the party. Since the party in 1965-66 was under the control of leaders who believed in modernization and pragmatism, Mao was compelled to employ non-party forces, such as students, to destroy and then to reorganize the party to reflect his radical views. The Cultural Revolution, from the perspective of China's development since 1949, may be viewed as one cycle among many cyclical shifts in policy and program. Tang Tsou offers two main explanations for Mao's loss of control over the party. "One is that the domestic and foreign policies of Mao were intimately related to his thought." While Mao's thoughts were successful for guerrilla war, "they no longer suit the needs of a modernizing, industrializing society, and they do not reflect the aspiration of the people for stability, routinization and relaxation of tension." The other explanation is the bureaucratization of the party and decline of power for the "charismatic leader." Tang Tsou sees China's political system functioning most effectively when the "influence of the charismatic leader was on the decline." He points out that, following the failure of the Great Leap and commune programs, it was the pragmatists in the party who stabilized the economy. The article presents Mao as the chief architect of the Cultural Revolution, upon which he set two limits beyond which no rebellion was to be permitted: an open civil war and serious disruption of the economy.

92 TANNENBAUM, Gerald.
"China's Cultural Revolution: Why It Had to Happen," China in
Ferment: Perspectives on the Cultural Revolution, Richard Baum
with Louise B. Bennett, eds., Prentice-Hall, Inc., Englewood
Cliffs, N. J., 1971, pp. 60-66. Also see Tannenbaum's The Great
Proletarian Revolution: What Really Did Happen in China,
Eastern Horizon Press, 1969, pp. 1-27.
Basic to China's problem is the relationship between the economic base and the cultural superstructure. The new economic
base did not insure a corresponding cultural superstructure.
The socialist base would always be in danger of destruction if
the cultural superstructure--ideology, arts and literature,
social thought, customs and habits, and education--developed
bourgeois tendencies. China's crisis was essentially a crisis
in culture and a conflict between proletarian and bourgeois
lines. The struggle was, therefore, inevitable as the system
evolved because in building a new culture, the old one, the
result of thousands of years of class ideology, must be
destroyed. The young, as successors to the revolution, must
learn about revolution by participating in it.

93 TEIWES, Frederick.
"A Review Article: The Evolution of Leadership Purges in
Communist China," The China Quarterly, No. 41, October-December
1970, pp. 123-135.
This article analyzes the three main inner-party power struggles
of the Chinese Communist Party: The 1954 Kao-Jao affair, the
1959 Peng Teh-huai dismissal, and the 1966 Liu Shao-chi case in
the initial phase of the Cultural Revolution. Liu's case was
wholly different from the two previous purge cases in that the
Cultural Revolution's purges were not limited to policy disputes
involving only a few top-level leaders. It was a general house-
cleaning campaign at all levels. Liu Shao-chi was not purged
because he challenged Mao's authority but rather because he
misused the party apparatus to subvert the implementation of
Mao's goals. The Cultural Revolution was mainly a struggle to
reject all policies, past and present, which did not reflect
the radical side of Mao's ideology. Teiwes attempts to prove
that it was the growing gap between Mao's perspectives and the
party's operation that caused the Cultural Revolution to erupt.
What made the Cultural Revolution so unique was that it engulfed
the entire party apparatus and the leadership with it.

94 TERRILL, Ross.
"The Siege Mentality," Problems of Communism, Vol. XV, No. 2,
March-April 1967, pp. 1-10.
Terrill sees the Cultural Revolution as a reaction to, or fear
of, "U. S. imperialist aggression" threatening the Chinese
revolution. The upheaval in China evoked the "siege mentality"
and determination that the struggle be waged against "the twin
evils of 'revisionism and imperialism.'" Terrill analyses the
dual menace in terms of the Sino-Soviet rift. China was also
fearful of United States escalation in Vietnam, and the

Cultural Revolution was "the Maoist fashion of girding China's loins to face possible armed struggle with the U.S." Terrill lists and analyzes considerations that support his thesis; "for the Chinese Communist leaders believe that the threat at the gate, linked as it is in the minds with the dreaded class threat to the revolution, points a dagger at the heart of all that China has struggled for since the Opium War."

95 TRAGER, Frank N., and HENDERSON, William, eds.
Communist China, 1949-1969: A Twenty-year Appraisal, New York University Press, New York, 1970, 356p.
Fifteen China scholars contributed a total of fourteen articles appraising the progress and problems of China for the twenty-year period, 1949-1969. Separate annotations of all fourteen articles are entered under individual author in this bibliography.

96 UNION RESEARCH INSTITUTE.
CCP Documents of the Great Proletarian Cultural Revolution, 1966-1967, Hong Kong, 1968, 692p.
This book is a compilation of one hundred and twenty-two official documents issued by CCP central authorities and ten issued by the Peking municipal authorities during the turbulent years of 1966 and 1967. The issuing authorities include the Central Committee, the Military Affairs Council and the Cultural Revolution Group as well as the State Council. The collection is published in bilingual form so that scholars can check the Chinese text for possible omissions of nuances in the English translation. Contained in this collection is a wealth of original source material on the origin and development of the Cultural Revolution. It is a valuable reference if used in conjunction with analyses of events and developments for the period.

97 VOGEL, Ezra F.
"The Structure of Conflict: China in 1967," The Cultural Revolution: 1967 in Review, Michigan Papers in Chinese Studies No. 2, Chang Chun-shu, James Crump and Rhoads Murphey, eds., Center for Chinese Studies, University of Michigan, Ann Arbor, 1968, pp. 97-125.
Vogel analyzes the conflicts within the Chinese communist movement by using the Cultural Revolution as a case study. His basic premise is that the communist movement had long been sustained by an elan of unity which transcended all differences. The unity could be maintained for a time even with mistakes made in policies and with differences and varying interests within the leadership. But as soon as the revolutionary elan began to fade, these basic cleavages would emerge. The erosion of elan was hastened by several basic policy discords among the top leaders: the speed of collectivization, the extent of mass mobilization, and the degree of independence from the Soviet Union. In each of these cases Mao seems to have insisted on the correctness of his policies over the resistance of his

colleagues. The failure of the Great Leap in 1959 merely hardened the opposition's stand. From this perspective, the Cultural Revolution was the culmination of disputes between Mao and his colleagues. The attacks launched by Mao during the initial phase of the revolution were part of his attempt to regain control over the party. Vogel analyzes the nature of the development of factions within the party. Mao's strategy during the Cultural Revolution was to purge the leaders by non-party means and to rebuild a new party organization at all levels by utilizing the military.

98 WALLER, D. J.
"China: Red or Expert?," <u>The Political Quarterly</u>, April-June 1967, pp. 122-131.
The article analyzes the underlying causes of the Cultural Revolution by focusing on two non-constitutional checks on the power of an authoritarian party: the army and the bureaucratic-intellectual complex. China has been troubled by the contradiction between "political reliability," or "red," and "technical knowledge," or "expert." Anti-party dissent by the experts is channelled through the system of non-constitutional checks, the military and the bureaucracy. The conflict of red versus expert in the military appeared in two areas. The first was between veterans of the Long March who were more at home with guerrilla warfare and the officers who had been exposed to modern professional military techniques. The second concerned control by the party over the military. The dissent by Peng Teh-huai, who was subsequently purged at the 1959 Lushan Conference, is seen basically as a protest by a professional military officer against the party's ruinous policies. At the level of bureaucracy, the conflict between red versus expert was between the line men (supervisory party cadres and the less educated) and the staff men (professional and technical non-supervisory cadres and the well educated). In the line-staff conflict, the party supported the professional's position until 1955. Then it shifted its emphasis from "reliance to professionalism" to "politics-in-command." The bias in favor of the line culminated in the Great Leap when the professionals and technicians, predominantly middle level cadres, were bypassed in order to link the top policy-makers directly with the masses. Thus, the Cultural Revolution was a continuation of the earlier policy of excluding the experts from power and influence.

99 WYLIE, Ray.
"Revolution within a Revolution?," <u>China After the Cultural Revolution</u>, A Selection from <u>Bulletin of the Atomic Scientists</u>, Vol. XXV, No. 2, February 1969, Vintage Books, New York, 1970, pp. 29-32.
The Cultural Revolution, seen by this Canadian observer who was employed by the Chinese government to teach English at the time of the upheaval, was "a revolution within a revolution" for the purpose of preserving the original character of Mao' revolution. The struggle for power was essentially a struggle over policy.

Purge became necessary so that Mao's supporters could be in a
position of power to implement the correct line. Most important
to Mao was the need to curb the power of the bureaucratic elite
and to restore the guerrilla ethics of mass line and egalitarianism. This required dismantling and then restructuring the
party. Wylie includes a discussion of economic and social
reforms of the Cultural Revolution: greater university student
participation in decision-making in education, abolition of
payment by piecework, and improvement of cultural and social
facilities in the countryside.

100 WYLIE, Ray.
"The Meaning of the Cultural Revolution," China and Ourselves:
Explorations and Revisions by a New Generation, Bruce Douglass
and Ross Terrill, eds., Beacon Press, Boston, 1970, pp. 30-48.
Wylie searches for the meaning and origin of the Cultural
Revolution by examining Maoist thought and policy. He traces
Mao's major concern that China develop her own revolutionary
path to socialism back to 1925 and through the 1930's, when
Mao opposed the influence of the Soviet trained party leaders
and their policies. Thus by 1959, according to Wylie, Mao
felt the need to rely less on the Soviet Union after almost a
decade of close cooperation. The break with the Soviet model
and "the Maoists' desire to establish their intellectual and
organizational independence from the Soviet Union was both a
direct cause and a major theme of the Cultural Revolution."
Wylie explains that Mao has always seen the revolution as a
vehicle to serve the peasants, the majority of the Chinese
people. The Cultural Revolution was, therefore, Mao's attempt
to "direct the revolution back to its rural origins." Wylie
uses the changes in the programs for medical education in China
to illustrate this thesis of reorientation to rural origins.
He also argues that the Maoist desire to prevent the growth of
special classes in Chinese society was another major objective
of the Cultural Revolution. The abolition of rank and insignia
in the military and the subsequent nationwide campaign to
emulate the PLA represented Mao's attempt "to extend egalitarian
principle to that part of society which is generally regarded
as inherently anti-egalitarian." Lin Piao's work in the PLA
prior to the Cultural Revolution is seen by Wylie as a "pilot
project" and "an integral part of the Cultural Revolution."
Thus the Cultural Revolution was launched to accomplish a set
of well established goals, among which were "independence from
foreign--especially Soviet--control, orientation toward the
peasantry, and maintenance of an egalitarian ethos."

101 YANG, C. K.
"Cultural Revolution and Revisionism," China's Heritage and the
Communist Political System, Ping-ti Ho and Tang Tsou, eds.,
China in Crisis, Vol. 1, Book 2, The University of Chicago
Press, Chicago, 1968, pp. 501-524.
Focusing on the issue of revisionism in the Cultural Revolution,
Yang develops the hypothesis that the struggle was over control

of the party, over policies and, most importantly, over the
goals for the Chinese revolution. The stage for the struggle
was set between the mid-1950's and the mid-1960's in conflicts
over policies and goals between a radical Mao and a pragmatic
Liu Shao-chi. Liu's supporters in the cultural fields mounted
an attack against Mao's radical Great Leap policies. The
central issue prior to 1965 was whether revisionism, the scaling
down of the idealistic goals of communism, should be permitted.
By 1965-66 the struggle had shifted to a seizure of power by
the radicals and the purging of party leaders. Behind the shift
was the idea that revisionistic ideas are intellectual products
implanted in minds of the masses by carriers, the intellectuals
and party leaders. By removing the carriers through purge,
revisionists among the masses would lose their support. The
article has a good discussion on the main issues of revisionism:
material incentives as promoters of individualism in a collective society, the exclusive dominance of politics over all other
matters, the red versus expert controversy, liberalization of
party control, and promotion of traditional culture. In sum,
the Cultural Revolution represents the culmination of a series
of unresolved issues between the charismatic leader and his pragmatic dissenters on the final goals of the Chinese revolution.

CHAPTER II

THE CHINESE COMMUNIST PARTY: BUREAUCRATISM, LEADERSHIP

DISSENSION AND THE CADRE PROBLEM

The items annotated in this chapter deal with three major
areas of the Chinese communist system closely related to the
Cultural Revolution: the factional disagreement among the top
leaders within the party hierarchy, the party structure, and the
cadre system. There is general agreement among China scholars
that a major factor which precipitated the Cultural Revolution
was the factional dispute among top party leaders. Many observers see this dispute as closely bound up with the crucial
questions of bureaucratism of the party organization and the
controversy over efficiency and professionalism versus the
revolutionary mass-line approach. Some China scholars have
related the loss of revolutionary elan, particularly among the
party's basic-level cadres, frequently attributed to hasty
recruitment and deficient ideological training of cadres soon
after liberation, to the party's bureaucratism.

Entries in this chapter include examinations of leadership
in China in terms of style, control, decision-making, and upward
mobility. The roles played by Mao, Liu Shao-chi, Lin Piao,
Chou En-lai and others before and during the Cultural Revolution
are analyzed in a large number of the works. These entries
offer explanations on why and how a highly cohesive and united

65

group of revolutionary leaders became bitter rivals, hurling epitaphs at the purged officials, such as "freaks," and "counterrevolutionary." Analysis of the party, its structure at the various levels, and the role of its cadre are also included in this chapter. The theme of the function of bureaucratism and the nature of communism in China's modernizing process is examined from a number of points of view. Several articles on the party elite pattern and conflicts within it are also placed in this chapter.

102 BAUM, Richard.
"Elite Behavior under Conditions of Stress: The Lesson of
'Tang-chuan Pai' in the Cultural Revolution," Elites in the
People's Republic of China, Robert A. Scalapino, ed., University
of Washington Press, Seattle and London, 1972, pp. 540-574.
This study deals with the strategies and tactics for survival
developed by the lower and middle level rural cadres of the
party while under attack by non-party elements during the
Cultural Revolution. The article begins with an examination
of the Red Guard groups formed during the period from the
Central Committee plenum, which launched the revolution in
August, to the end of 1966. The attitude of the provincial and
basic level authorities toward the urbanized Red Guards was
that of resentment. They treated the efforts of students from
the major universities located in the urban centers to "link up"
with rural youth as an intrusion. Moreover, in many provinces
the party leaders recognized the agitation aroused by the Red
Guards as a threat to their established authority. Their
defense was to form separate and counter Red Guard groups made
up of local rural youth. Various other tactics were used to
counter the invasion by Red Guards from urban areas: evasion,
suppression, and even co-optation. The study provides a good
sample of illustrations to show how these tactics were actually
employed by the established party leaders in the provinces. As
a result of these activities, the rural cadres became reluctant
to assume any leadership responsibilities for fear of continued
criticism and repudiation. Thus, when the rural party cadres
were under attack, they discovered that their "self-interests"
were no longer congruent with the "class-interests."

103 BAUM, Richard, and TEIWES, Frederick C.
"Liu Shao-chi and the Cadres Question," Asian Survey, Vol. VIII,
No. 4, April 1968, pp. 323-345.
One of the major charges levelled against Liu Shao-chi was his
erroneous cadres policy instituted before the Cultural Revolution. This study analyzes the cadres problems at the basic
level as revealed during the Socialist Education Movement,
which preceded the Cultural Revolution. These problems, involving some thirty million basic level cadres, included: difficulties in the implementation of the mass-line principles, deviant
behavior, special privileges, declining morale and tensions.
Efforts by the regime to strengthen the mass line in rural work
are analyzed, particularly the work teams, led by higher party
officials, sent down to the rural communes to spot check the
basic cadres work performance and the political education and
work attitudes of the cadres. The initial formula for correcting the mistaken behavior of the basic cadres was persuasive
education. Then a campaign of criticism and dismissal was
launched to eliminate unreliable cadres at the basic level.
Baum discusses the various directives for a cadres policy during
the Socialist Education Campaign, particularly the directive
issued by Liu in September 1964 and the one issued by Mao in
early 1965. Baum concludes that the alternating treatment

between harshness and mildness of the basic level cadres
produced uncertainty and demoralization of the cadres on the
eve of the Cultural Revolution.

104 BRIDGHAM, Philip.
"Factionalism in the Central Committee," Party Leadership and
Revolutionary Power in China, John W. Lewis, ed., Cambridge
University Press, Cambridge, 1970, pp. 203-233.
This study investigates the nature and scope of factionalism
within the Central Committee of the Chinese Communist Party in
order to gain insights on the Cultural Revolution, which
Bridgham views as the "most momentous of these factional
struggles." The first portion of the article is devoted to a
review of the 1953-55 Kao Kang affair and the dismissal of
Peng Teh-huai in 1959 in light of new disclosures by the Red
Guards during the Cultural Revolution. The second part describes in detail Mao's suspicion about the top leaders loyalty
to his revolutionary ideas and his decision to wage a gigantic
rectification campaign to cleanse the whole party by employing
instruments outside of the established party machinery. In
Bridgham's analysis, factionalism within the party in China was
motivated by considerations of policy, power, and personal
rivalry. These were present in all the three party struggles
described in the article.

105 CHAI, Winberg.
"The Reorganization of the Chinese Communist Party, 1966-1968,"
Asian Survey, Vol. VIII, No. 11, November 1968, pp. 901-910.
This study describes the disintegration and reorganization of
the Chinese Communist Party in the midst of the Cultural
Revolution. The control of the party was placed in three
established institutions: the Military Affairs Committee, the
State Council, and the Central Cultural Revolution Group. A
list of members in each of the three organizations is given.
Changes in the provinces and other local levels occurred all
over China in varying manners, ranging from peaceful to bloody
turnovers. Red Guard groups usually served as "storm troopers"
in bringing about the downfall of the existing party and government machinery, resulting in the formation of revolutionary
committees with the military in control. A large scale purge
was also conducted in all party and government institutions,
including the Central Committee. In 1968, Chai concluded, the
Cultural Revolution weakened the party as an institution, which
might lead to more instability for the regime. This study
includes a brief discussion on Mao's vision of a "model cadre,"
which would serve as an example for all to émulate.

106 CHANG, Chen-pang.
"The Present and Future Situation of the Chinese Communist
Party and Administration," Chinese Communist Affairs, Vol. 5,
No. 5, October 1968, pp. 15-28.
The main task of the Cultural Revolution was to attack leaders
of the party such as Liu Shao-chi. The attack then spread to

68

other party and government cadres. A detailed list of the widespread purges within the party and government apparatus is given
in this study. The destruction of the party's top machinery is
demonstrated by a list of top leaders purged from 1966 to 1968.
The formation of revolutionary committees to replace the regular
party machinery and the difficulties involved in establishing
them are also described. The rebuilding of the party was to
begin right after the formation of temporary revolutionary committees in the provinces by convening a new party congress to
legitimize the remolded party.

107 CHANG, Parris H.
"Mao's Great Purge: A Political Balance Sheet," Problems of
Communism, Vol. XVIII, No 2, March-April 1969, pp. 1-10.
After summarizing the vicissitudes of the Cultural Revolution
through the fall of 1968, when revolutionary committees had
been established in all the provinces, Chang presents the view
that the large scale purge had both disrupted and undermined
the party machinery and its authority. The purging of cadres
was carried out in a Stalinistic fashion by labelling the
purged officials as traitors, spies and counterrevolutionary.
A detailed description of the purge revealed a thirty percent
loss among Politburo members and more than a fifty-six percent
loss among Central Committee members. An account and figures
are given for the regional and provincial level officials. The
purge during the Cultural Revolution is contrasted to Stalin's
purges. Unlike Stalin's bloody purges in the 1930's, the
Chinese made little use of secret police and did not phsycially
liquidate the purged individuals. Rather, the Red Guards
seized power from provincial and local officials in many areas.
Frequently the Red Guard attacks were not aimed at any particular individuals. The balance sheet of the Cultural Revolution
purge includes a high degree of upward political mobility, the
paralyzing effect on the party as an institution, the ascendency
of the military and Mao's continued reliance on a coercive
instrument for control, a new relationship of bargaining, and
the emergence of negotiation between the central and provincial
authorities.

108 CHANG, Parris H.
"Provincial Party Leaders Strategies for Survival during the
Cultural Revolution," Elites in the People's Republic of China,
Robert A. Scalapino, ed., University of Washington Press,
Seattle and London, 1972, pp. 501-539.
This is a study of the provincial party leaders' struggle for
survival under the onslaught of the Red Guards during the
Cultural Revolution. The first portion deals with the provin-
cial leaders' perceptions about the launching of the Cultural
Revolution from the center. Then an analysis of the strategies
employed by the provincial leaders to fight off the attack is
presented. The concluding portion discusses the provincial
party leaders' sources of power and the structure of authority
in China's political system. The perception of the Cultural

Revolution by the provincial leaders varied according to the
stages of the upheaval. In the spring of 1966, most of them
were puzzled by the events occurring at the center and maintained a noncommittal stance. As the attacks intensified, most
leaders at the provincial level felt a sense of insecurity,
and their strategies were those of evasion, diversion and
deception. Typically during this period, these provincial
leaders instituted their own purges of "rightists" scapegoats
in order to show obedience to Peking. They made pretense of
self-criticism within the party and generally used the traditional "work teams" to contain the conflict. By the time the
top leaders at the center, such as Liu Shao-chi, had been purged
through the activities of the Red Guards, they sensed their
imminent downfall and began to devise a strategy for survival:
they formed and recruited their own Red Guards as a counter-
measure, thus "waving the red flag to oppose the red flag." The
strength of the provincial party leaders came from their cohesiveness as a group, their control of the media, and their
traditional authority associated with their position as party
heads. The article concludes with the observation that as long
as Mao remains the "fountainhead of the legitimacy," the
provincial leaders can only devise a strategy to defend themselves because, in the final analysis, Mao defines what the
rules of the game are at any given moment.

109 CHANG, Parris H.
Radicals and Radical Ideology in China's Cultural Revolution,
Research Institute on Communist Affairs, Columbia University,
New York, 1973, 103p.
This booklet gives a detailed account of the factional infighting along ideological lines of leaders and masses, focusing on
the radicals and their brand of ideology during the Cultural
Revolution. Chang also presents, for the benefit of students
and researchers of this confused and complicated aspect of the
Cultural Revolution, profiles of radical leaders from Chen Po-ta
and Chiang Ching down to Wang Li and Kuan Feng. Chang attributes the growth and development of radicalism in China to
socio-economic inequalities and injustices and the outcry for
righting these grievances in the Chinese social system. Since
these grievances were present in society, the radical elements
of the leadership simply exploited the discontent to suit their
particular purpose. The seemingly legitimate grievances of the
students were channeled into Red Guard protests and hostility
against the party and government establishment during the
Cultural Revolution. Chang believes that radicalism in China
may revive periodically if grievances and injustices are not
corrected. Radicalism may again play an important political
role in China, as it did briefly during the Cultural Revolution.

110 CHANG, Peter.
"Liu Shao-chi and the Cultural Revolution," Asian Survey,
Vol. XL, No. 10, October 1971, pp. 943-957.
This essay analyzes the reasons for Liu Shao-chi's downfall and

the causes for the Cultural Revolution. Chang reconstructs the events beginning with the debate at the 10th Plenum of the 8th Central Committee in 1962 through the Red Guard attack against Liu's subordinate, Peng Chen, in April 1966. Using the Chinese media and Red Guard posters, Chang compiled a list of alleged crimes committed by Liu Shao-chi, including his repudiation of class struggle, his promotion of economism by opposing Mao's policy of agriculture collectivization, his support of the purged Marshal Peng Teh-huai, and his marriage into a bourgeois family. Details are also given on the self-criticisms made in the midst of the Cultural Revolution by both Liu and his wife, Wang Kuang-mei. Chang argues that the controversy, or "feud," between Mao and Liu was over the basic question of whether priority should be given to the implementation of revolutionary programs. This essay focuses on the divergent views of the two top leaders on political and economic policies for China.

111 CHINA NEWS ANALYSIS.
"Reconstruction of the Communist Party," No. 790, February 6, 1970, pp. 1-7.
This issue examines in detail the process of party rebuilding during the Cultural Revolution. The rebuilding of the civilian party machinery was performed in the main by the party committees of the military. The article describes how the troops of No. 8341 of the central force in Peking became the model for party building by successfully resolving the difference of rival factions. The principles of collective leadership in the party and the warnings to mass organizations not to "stand above the party" are covered.

112 CURRENT SCENE, The Editor.
"Lin Piao: A Political Profile," Vol. VII, No. 5, March 10, 1969, pp. 1-16.
This is a biographical study of a top level leader who played a very important role in the Cultural Revolution. It gives a comprehensive study of Lin Piao's career during 1928-1968. Sketches are given of Lin's lieutenants, including Huang Yung-sheng, Wu Fa-hsien, and Li Tso-peng. All of these men occupied positions of power during and at the end of the Cultural Revolution. The study also speculates on the murkiness of Lin's relationship with Mao and other top leaders.

113 CURRENT SCENE, The Editor.
"Lin Piao and the Cultural Revolution," Vol. VIII, No. 14, August 1, 1970, pp. 1-14.
This is a two-part analysis of Lin Piao and the role that he played in the Cultural Revolution. Part one deals with Lin's activities prior to 1966, and part two concerns his role from 1966 to 1970. From an analysis of Lin's appearances, speeches and orders for the period of the Cultural Revolution, the editor perceives a strong indication that Lin and Mao had a seemingly abiding personal relationship in which the former exhibited his loyalty and reverence for the latter. Outside

of the confines of the military, Lin Piao first showed himself
at the early stages of the Cultural Revolution as a polemicist
and agitator. Later Lin shifted his attitude to that of
moderate in relation to the disruptive behavior of the Red
Guards and to that of a demanding commander of his military
subordinates insofar as discipline was involved. In his relation with Premier Chou, Lin showed an attitude of "sweetness
and sourness"; while at the same time, the military extended
its responsibilities in the management of state affairs at the
expense of the State Council. Within the PLA, Lin showed
concern over the purges of his lieutenants but never once
risked his life to save his falling colleagues when purges
extended into the military ranks.

114 CURRENT SCENE, The Editor.
"The Cultural Revolution: Act III - The Maoists against Liu
Shao-chi," Vol. V, No. 6, April 15, 1967, pp. 1-10.
This essay presents a list of issues on which Mao Tse-tung and
Liu Shao-chi differed, as revealed by editorials of the media
and publications of the Red Guards. These contentious issues
included: (1) the concept and the interpretation of "democratic centralism," (2) the work-method employed by the work
teams dispatched by Liu to implement the August 1966 decision
of the Central Committee, (3) the alleged attempt by Liu to
exercise control over the ideology and organization of the
military, (4) evaluation of the Great Leap Program of 1959,
(5) Liu's desire, as alleged by Maoists, to encourage "individualism," and, finally, (6) the concept and applicability of
the "people's War of Liberation" as a guide for foreign policy.

115 DITTMER, Lowell.
"Mass Line and Mass Criticism in China: An Analysis of the
Fall of Liu Shao-chi," Asian Survey, Vol. XIII, No. 8, August
1973, pp. 772-792.
Dittmer views the Cultural Revolution "as an attempt to unite
criticism and self-criticism with the mass line by opening
inner-Party struggle to mass participation." It is, in a
sense, a study of the role of mass criticism in the concept
of mass line. The first portion summarizes the origin and
development of the mass line concept and its actual application during the Cultural Revolution, i.e., Red Guards and
their posters. The second portion of the study is a content
analysis of press criticisms against Liu Shao-chi from January
1967 to October 1969. Dittmer describes the patterns of
criticism, innovation and diffusion in the mass criticism
campaign against Liu Shao-chi. His conclusion is that the
Cultural Revolution has increased vertical communication
between hierarchical levels but has failed to achieve consensus between the elites and the masses. (As this bibliography
was going to press, a book length version of this article was
published. It is entitled Liu Shao-chi and the Chinese Cultural
Revolution: The Politics of Mass Criticism, University of
California Press, 1975, 400p.)

116 DITTMER, Lowell.
"The Cultural Revolution and the Fall of Liu Shao-chi," Current
Scene, Vol. XI, No. 1, January 1973, pp. 1-13.
This article provides a succinct summary of events which led to
the official purge of Liu Shao-chi in 1968. It examines two
interrelated questions: why was the attack on Liu Shao-chi
escalated in the fall of 1968 after he had made self-criticism
of his erroneous policies and why had it taken so long to depose
of Liu, who for practical purposes ceased to play any role in
policy-making at the end of 1966. The study shows that Mao had
forgiven Liu in early October 1966 but then changed his mind,
apparently under the influence of the radicals in the Central
Cultural Revolution Group, which had become his advisory body.
The voices of moderation, which should have come from Liu's
supporters in the provinces and in the State Council of the
central government, did not surface because of these supporters'
preoccupation with fending off the Red Guard attacks against
themselves. Liu, Dittmer argues, in the end became "a convenient symbol against which every grievance could coalesce" and
"the scapegoat for events in the party's past that seemed embar-
rassing in the light of the revolutionary ideals of the present."

117 DOMES, Jurgen.
"Party Politics and the Cultural Revolution," Communist China,
1949-1969: A Twenty-year Appraisal, Frank N. Trager and
William Henderson, eds., New York University Press, New York,
1970, pp. 63-93.
This article, which treats the Cultural Revolution as one of
the four most important conflicts over basic policies within
the Chinese Communist Party, analyzes the implication of party
politics on the Cultural Revolution. The unresolved conflicts
of 1958-59 and 1961-62 precipitated a new crisis within the
party over the major policies of cultural regimentation, educational reform, ideological diversity and economic incentives.
A detailed analysis is provided on the confrontation inside the
party between those who sought modification of these fundamental
policies and those who supported the correctness of Mao's
approaches to these policy matters--in essence the drama of the
Cultural Revolution, which produced a split within the party.
It was this division within the party that finally paved the
way for a breakdown of the party authority all over China. The
Cultural Revolution, as seen by Domes, also brought about significant changes in resolving intra-party disputes. These
changed included the symbols and terminology used by the
contenders, ad hoc organizations employed, and the rise of the
military as a new type of leadership organization. The Cultural
Revolution, Domes argues, cannot be regarded as a victory for
Mao because the upheaval has produced a new power coalition in
the party: central and regional military leaders, the old
administrative cadres, and the radical elements of the party.

118 FUNNELL, Victor.
"Bureaucracy and the Chinese Communist Party," Current Scene,

Vol. IX, No. 5, May 7, 1971, pp. 1-14.
The central thesis of this article is that Mao, like Stalin, promoted and expanded the vast bureaucracy under the party for the management of state affairs. Mao's attack on the party structure during the Cultural Revolution was not, in Funnell's view, to make it less bureaucratic but to exercise his control over the apparatus. To gain this control he was willing to employ instruments and forces outside the party. This article contains a discussion of an inherent conflict between bureaucracy and communism in the process of modernization. The concept of the Leninist party as the sole initiator of programs for achieving social and economic progress compels it to be identified closely with the bureaucratic machine of the state. The inevitable growth of the bureaucratic elite tends to promote the existence of a special class in society with power, prestige and security. In this sense, Lenin's "centralism" must be equated with "bureaucraticism." Bureaucratic organizations are the most suitable organizational models for the revolutionaries. As bureaucrats' and technocrats' authority increases with industrialization, not only are they rewarded with special privileges and status, but they are drawn into the party. The rapid growth of party membership in both the Soviet Union and China occurred at the beginning of their first Five-Year Plan periods. The article contains information and statistics on the growth of the Chinese party membership and the cadre system.

119 HARDING, Harry, Jr.
"Maoist Theories of Policy-making and Organization," The Cultural Revolution in China, Thomas Robinson, ed., University of California Press, Berkeley and Los Angeles, 1971, pp. 113-164. In this treatise, Harding argues that the Cultural Revolution represents a struggle between the opposing views of Mao and Liu on theories of policy-making and organization. In one section of the article, a theoretical analysis is made to illustrate differences as well as convergences of policy-making, as conceptualized by Mao and his opponents. The content of a policy is essentially influenced by the character of the policy-making process. The dichotomy between pragmatism and dogmatism appears in political, social and economic issues facing China. The contention between elitism and mass line is usually present in technical-managerial issues. In another section, Harding argues that a major objective of the Cultural Revolution was to rectify and reform the Chinese Communist Party. The article illustrates examples to show that organizational restructuring was undertaken during the Cultural Revolution: the new party constitution of 1969 and the creation of the revolutionary committees as temporary party apparatus. Evidence is produced to demonstrate that on the eve of the Cultural Revolution, Mao sensed that the party had become institutionalized, had bogged down in bureaucratic details, had lost faith in mass-criticism as a means of control, and relied heavily on those who possessed technical managerial skills for recruitment. Mao's remedy, as

revealed by the changes introduced during the Cultural
Revolution, was to establish unified leadership in the form
of revolutionary committees to assume both party and state
functions. Party discipline was placed in the hands of the
masses, and party recruitment had to be based on social class
origin.

120 HSU, Kai-yu.
"The Chinese Communist Leadership," Current History, Vol. 57,
No. 337, September 1969, pp. 129-136.
This article analyzes the forces, or groups, which have provided leadership for China since the revolution in 1911, the
way these forces have been controlled, and the reasons for
periodical realignment among these forces. Of these forces at
play in Chinese politics--the party and government machinery,
the military, the intellectuals, and the mass organizations--
the intellectuals have always been considered the dominant
force in remolding Chinese society and have formed the backbone
of the leadership for the Chinese Communist Party since its
inception. Successful leadership in China requires the ability
to keep these forces together in delicate balance. Whenever a
major decision is made, adjustments must be made to maintain
this balance. Adjustments take place in the form of party
rectification campaigns. The Cultural Revolution, then, is
seen as a pattern of grouping and regrouping of the collective
leadership in China. The pattern of periodic reform, Hsu
argues, will most likely continue in the future.

121 KLEIN, Donald W.
"A Question of Leadership: Problems of Mobility Control and
Policy-making in China," Current Scene, Vol. V, No. 7, April 30,
1967, pp. 1-8.
This article deals with the question of leadership in the
Chinese Communist Party in terms of mobility and control.
Problems within the party stem from the rapid recruitment of
members in the 1950's at the time when the First Five Year Plan
was launched and functional specialization became the norm in
order to provide the regime with needed skilled personnel for
administration and management. At the same time the central
authority promoted the second echelon personnel in the provinces to important positions at the center, leaving a gap
between the top and the lower level leaders. The intellectuals,
the men in the middle, thus, became bureaucrats in central and
provincial administrations. The pattern of leadership in China
prior to the Great Leap Forward was one of stability and cohesiveness. The Great Leap Program of 1958-59 altered this
pattern as the party tightened its control over the vast
administrative apparatus and reversed the trend toward further
functional specialization. The crash program launched in
1958-59 also prevented the orderly buildup of the party in
terms of upward mobility for the lower level young leaders. As
a result, by the 1960's stagnation had developed and policy-
making was limited to a very few at the top.

122 KLEIN, Donald W.
"The State Council and the Cultural Revolution," The China
Quarterly, No. 35, July-September 1968, pp. 78-95.
This study of the impact of the Cultural Revolution on the
State Council, the administrative organ of the Chinese government, is based mainly on the author's own file of leadership
and personnel changes in the State Council. This essentially
statistical study of some 366 ministers and vice-ministers
shows the degree, as well as the extent, of purges of these
top experts and technocrats in China. Nearly half of the 366
ministers and vice-ministers were missing from the public view
from 1966 to 1968, presumably purged or undergoing rehabilitation. Non-party ministers and vice-ministers seemed to fare
better as the Cultural Revolution turmoil intensified. There
was apparently no large scale attempt by Lin Piao to "pack"
the State Council with his military lieutenants during 1966-68.
Similarly, there is no evidence that regional leaders packed
the State Council with their men. Klein's general conclusion
from his study of the Cultural Revolution's impact on the State
Council is that the Chinese central civil bureaucracy is quite
institutionalized.

123 KLEIN, Donald, and HAGER, Lois B.
"The Ninth Central Committee," The China Quarterly, No. 45,
January-March 1971, pp. 37-56.
General comments are given about the characteristics of the
Central Committees of the Chinese Communist Party from 1945-1956
in this article. Specific analysis on the Ninth Party Congress
of 1969 at the conclusion of the Cultural Revolution forms the
bulk of this study. Membership profiles in terms of members'
association with the revolution, education, age, native province
or region, foreign travel, sex, national minority, and worker
or peasant are presented with detailed charts and statistics.
Comparative figures are given on the membership representation
in the 8th and 9th Central Committees in terms of senior officials in charge of various organizations, such as the State
Council, the military, revolutionary committees, Communist
Youth League, federations of trade unions, and foreign affairs
specialist. The study concludes: "There is little to indicate
that the hypothetical 'brilliant young administrator and
activist' who reached maturity in the past decade has now
emerged to hold crucial posts. On the contrary,... the Ninth
Central Committee members are fairly elderly and have served the
Communist movement for many years."

124 LEWIS, John W.
"Leader, Commissar, and Bureaucrat: The Chinese Political
System in the Last Days of the Revolution," China's Heritage and
the Communist Political System, Ping-ti Ho and Tang Tsou, eds.,
China in Crisis, Vol. 1, Book Two, University of Chicago Press,
Chicago, 1968, pp. 449-481.
The thesis of this paper is that Mao's ideal political system
can be best described as a "primitive political system"

unsuitable for a modernizing society in the Weberian sense.
While Mao as a charismatic leader demanded "irrational compul-
sions and emotional commitments," the local political commissar
had to learn how to make his operation workable and to control
his masses. The article has a detailed discussion on the origin
of the Mao-Liu rift, which stemmed from their different experiences and responsibilities during the guerrilla days of the
party. While Mao emphasized the importance and the capability
of the masses, Liu, the political commissar, had personal knowledge of the limitations of the masses. While Mao perceived his
role as an inspirer and saw the rigidity of bureaucracy, Liu had
responsibility for effective organization and discipline. The
Cultural Revolution is seen by Lewis as Mao's opposition to
Liu's approach to the party's role in the revolution and the
party apparatus. Thus, the initial attack launched in the
Cultural Revolution was aimed at the cultural and educational
areas to foster proper attitudinal change away from the entrenched concept of rational organizations. After the initial
stage, Mao's attack centered on the purges of the political
commissars. The rising power of the party organization had
become, in Mao's view, a potential for counterrevolution. The
Cultural Revolution was Mao's method of postponing the process
of industrialization. The upheaval was Mao's attempt to revive
charisma of the leader. It prolonged the polarization of the
leader and his political commissar.

125 LEWIS, John Wilson, ed.
Party Leadership and Revolutionary Power in China, Cambridge
University Press, Cambridge, 1970, 422p.
The eleven essays in this volume were originally presented as
conference papers at Ditchley Park, England, in July 1968. The
first group of papers deal with the development of the Chinese
Communist Party in the changing environments from the early days
of defeat and frustration through Mao's role in the 1930's to an
analysis of the party as a totalitarian system, a monolith.
Mao's relationship with the party and his changing concept of
party morality are some of the themes in this section. The
second group of papers deals with ideology, intra-party motivation and elite factionalism. The third group contains essays
which describe the party in Chinese society since 1949. The
last two essays deal with the problems of autonomy within the
government structure, the State Council, and the party-army
relationship from the perspective of the Cultural Revolution.
Selected entries from this book are annotated separately in the
appropriate sections of this bibliography.

126 LINDBECK, John M., ed.
China: Management of a Revolutionary Society, University of
Washington, Seattle and London, 1971, 391p.
This is a collection of studies on the relationship between
authority and the masses, policy-making at the central and
provincial level, economic management, the legal and educational
systems, the management of foreign affairs and the role of the

military. Selected entries in this collection are annotated
separately in the appropriate sections of this bibliography.

127 MEHNERT, Klaus.
Peking and the New Left: At Home and Abroad, China Research
Monographs No. 4, Center for Chinese Studies, University of
California, Berkeley, 1969, 156p.
This booklet written by Mehnert for the Center for Chinese
Studies at Berkeley explores the rise and demise of the ultra-
left movement during the Cultural Revolution. Relying essentially on the Red Guard documents from the Hunan "Sheng-wu-lien,"
Mehnert reconstructs the development of the ultra-left movement,
its relationship with the May 16 Corps, and the final indictment
by the leadership of the new establishment of old government-
party cadres and the military under Chou En-lai which branded
the ultra-left Red Guard group and the May 16 Corps as "counterrevolutionary." The book analyzes the reasons for the attack
mounted by the ultra-leftist group against Chou and the military
in 1968 as "the rule of the bureaucratic bourgeoisie." It gives
a detailed analysis of the reasons for the leadership's shift of
policy from its initial encouragement of the leftist trend to a
suppression of ultra-leftists. The finer subtleties and nuances
of what is "left," "right," "ultra-left," and "counterrevolutionary" are explained in the context of the vicissitudes of the
Cultural Revolution. The ultra-left's ideas about China as a
"new Commune," based on the Paris Commune model, is also analyzed. Mehnert does not agree with the theory that the Red
Guard movement in China was a part of the world-wide New Left
movement because the Red Guard movement lacked the quality of
spontaneity: "They did not rise of their own volition; they
were mobilized by one part of the establishment (Mao Tse-tung,
Lin Piao, Chiang Ching) against its other part (Liu Shao-chi and
a large segment of the power holders in Party, administration,
industry, and education)." The Cultural Revolution, concludes
Mehnert, is a "revolution from above."

128 MYERS, James T.
"The Fall of Chairman Mao," Current Scene, Vol. VI, No. 10,
July 15, 1968, pp. 1-18.
This is a study of Mao's role in the breakdown of authority
during the Cultural Revolution. Myers attributes the initial
leadership division to the dissension on policy issues among top
leaders in 1959 at the Lushan Conference. Mao's policies and
programs were attacked by Peng Teh-huai. Mao's supporters
launched a subsequent campaign to repair the damage done to
Chairman Mao's image. However, Myers argues, Mao's status as
omnipotent leader had been damaged. It required a leader like
Lin Piao to repair that damage. Lin rebuilt the "Cult of Mao"
in the 1960's through the military machinery under his control.
There were two basic objectives for a Mao-Lin alliance: to
develop a new revolutionary mass base and to legitimize Mao's
thought as the basis for any future political action by destroy-
ing the opposition within the party. A step by step account is

given in this paper showing Mao's personal involvement in the planning and execution of the Cultural Revolution. The Cultural Revolution was Mao's frontal attack against the party leaders who opposed his views and policies.

129 NATHAN, Andrew J.
"A Factionalism Model for CCP Politics," _The China Quarterly_, No. 53, January-March 1973, pp. 34-66.
This study places decision-making and dissension of the Chinese leadership in a conceptual framework, a factionalism model for inner party politics. The elite conflicts during the Cultural Revolution are examined within the framework of this model to investigate the mobilization of resources for the struggle, the type of rules employed in these conflicts, and the organizational constraints on political behavior. Based on a set of characteristics of factional politics from the model, Nathan concludes that since 1968 there have been many conflicts and changes at the highest level of the political system: "they indicate not that the Cultural Revolution remains unsettled, but that China remains in the pre-Cultural Revolution pattern of factional conflict at the center."

130 NEUHAUSER, Charles.
"The Chinese Communist Party in the 1960's: Prelude to the Cultural Revolution," _The China Quarterly_, No. 32, October-December 1967, pp. 3-36.
According to Neuhauser, the basic cause for the Cultural Revolution lay in the Maoists' perception that the party was bureaucratized and had lost its revolutionary elan. Underlying this basic cause were the cadre problems: hasty recruitment and deficient ideological training for the basic-level cadres, bureaucratic abuses among the middle-level cadres, and superficial response to national campaigns by the middle and upper level cadres. Interwoven with these internal party problems was Mao's desire to reassert his personal authority over the party machine at all levels. The stress on organizational virtues such as order, discipline and routine in the 1960's prompted the party leadership to embark on rectification and reeducation campaigns to eradicate these tendencies. Emphasis on ideological purity, the appeal to revolutionary successors, and campaigns to emulate military heroes were all aimed at the rejuvenation of the party. The article examines situations in which party policies were opposed to key elements within the party and the party machinery was used by top leaders to oppose Mao's wishes. The Cultural Revolution was launched with the party as the chief target, Neuhauser concludes.

131 NEUHAUSER, Charles.
"The Impact of the Cultural Revolution on the Chinese Communist Party Machine," _Asian Survey_, Vol. VIII, No. 6, June 1968, pp. 465-488.
This article contains a detailed catalog of ills of the Chinese Communist Party and the damage done to its structure and morale

by the Cultural Revolution. It lists the purges inflicted
upon party personnel from the Politburo to the basic level.
Neuhauser asserts that the Cultural Revolution was aimed at
the party machine because of the problems within the party.
Some of these problems, such as bureaucratic inertia and the
emphasis by lower party committees on bureaucratic efficiency
and pragmatism, are analyzed to support the contention that the
party's organizational problems were the major issues in the
initial stages of the Cultural Revolution. As attacks were
mounted against the party, it attempted to fend off these
attacks. Extra-party instruments were employed as the party
machinery became increasingly unreliable in carrying out its
own purge. When the Red Guards began their wanton destruction
of the party, local party cadres in order to protect themselves
and the authority of the party counterattacked by beating up
the students and by organizing their own Red Guard group.
Factional disputes and infighting finally resulted in the
military involvement to restore order. The role of the military
was to help rebuild the party through formation of the revolutionary committees and to facilitate the reconciliation among
the various factions.

132 OKSENBERG, Michel.
"The Institutionalization of the Chinese Communist Revolution:
The Ladder of Success on the Eve of the Cultural Revolution,"
The China Quarterly, No. 36, October-December 1968, pp. 61-92.
Also see "Getting Ahead and Along in Communist China: The
Ladder of Success on the Eve of the Cultural Revolution," Party
Leadership and Revolutionary Power in China, John W. Lewis, ed.,
Cambridge University Press, Cambridge, 1970, pp. 304-347.
This article is concerned with the meaning of the institutionalization of the Chinese Communist Revolution. From interviews
of refugees from mainland China, Oksenberg shows that a clear
pattern of career and ladder of success had been institutionalized by the party and government and that unwritten "rules of
the game" for advancement and for achieving career status had
developed. The four stages for determining career in terms of
organizational affiliation, education, special skill, occupation
selection, and pursuit of ambition and security are examined.
The article also examines factors in the socio-economic background and the skills required to achieve personal goals of
political survival, security, and power. It illustrates how a
careerist in China develops an "operational code" for survival
and advancement. Oksenberg concludes by stating that by 1965
China was no longer a revolutionary society because by initial
contact with political subsystems and a careful selection of
education and occupation, a careerist could very well predict
the outcome of his life. Chinese careerists by 1965 had established political power, high income and security as life goals.
A ladder of success in a supposedly revolutionary society had
been established. Party campaigns for rectification and reeducation were looked upon by the careerists as disruptive,
and they developed techniques to subvert them. The Cultural

Revolution with the party as its target was seen as Mao's
attempt to develop new weapons for reestablishing revolutionary
fervor in the party as old style campaigns became less effective.
It was, according to Oksenberg, the erosion of revolutionary
elan among the party members that the Cultural Revolution was
trying to arrest: "Far from being enthusiastic agents of social
change, many CCP members could be expected to use their political skills and limited power to defend the system against
radical effort to change it."

133 ROBINSON, Thomas W.
"Chou En-lai's Political Style: Comparisons with Mao Tse-tung
and Lin Piao," Asian Survey, Vol. X, No. 12, December 1970,
pp. 1101-1116.
This is an essay on the role of Premier Chou during the first
year of the Cultural Revolution and his political style. A
brief description is given of Chou's role in each of four phases
during the first year of the Cultural Revolution: the Red
Guard ascendency (August-December 1966), the January Revolution,
"February adverse current," and the Wuhan Incident (July 1967).
Robinson portrays Chou's role as being "chief problem-solver,
trouble shooter, negotiator, organizer, administrator, guide-
advisor to revolutionary groups, and local enforcer of Central
Committee policy." In performing these varied roles, Chou
pursued the goals of settling disputes and providing direction
for revolutionary groups. Chou employed different tactics to
attain these goals, including his ability to move with the tide
and to place himself in a position of executing as well as
making policies. Robinson also compares Chou's political style
with those of Mao and Lin and speculates on Chou's future after
Mao.

134 ROBINSON, Thomas W.
"Chou En-lai and the Cultural Revolution in China," The Cultural
Revolution in China, Thomas W. Robinson, ed., University of
California Press, Berkeley and Los Angeles, 1971, pp. 165-312.
This article represents the most comprehensive analysis of the
role of Chou En-lai, the leading cadre in government in the
Cultural Revolution. The activities of the Premier in handling
many problems of the Cultural Revolution are analyzed. Chou is
pictured here as a person who can be flexible, resilient, and
realistic. Although he stayed away from the debates in the
initial stage of the Cultural Revolution, he joined the Mao-Lin
side as soon as he saw it emerge as the predominant faction.
For his support of the Mao-Lin faction, Chou extracted certain
concessions from them: exemption for the scientists and technicians from participation in the upheaval and recognition of the
necessity for production to continue unimpeded. The bulk of
the article deals with Chou En-lai's activities during 1966-69.
Chou, Robinson concludes, was seen by Mao and Lin as "their
chief problem-solver, troubleshooter, negotiator, organizer,
administrator, guide-advisor to revolutionary groups and local
enforcer of Central Committee policy." Chou's perception of his

role might be to see that disputes were settled and that the goals of the Cultural Revolution were implemented. The paper also draws two major conclusions about Premier Chou's participation in the Cultural Revolution: to prevent disruption in the bureaucratic, economic and scientific establishments and to establish himself as an "indispensable person." Chou's effectiveness was due in large part to his enormous personal experience in bureaucratic politics and diplomacy and his ability to persuade the contending factions to either reach a compromise or to retract their planned activities. He is "the archetype of the bureaucratic politician."

135 ROBINSON, Thomas W.
"Lin Piao as an Elite Type," Elites in the People's Republic of China, Robert A. Scalapino, ed., University of Washington Press, Seattle and London, 1972, pp. 149-195.
While most elite studies are aggregate elite analyses, this study on Lin Piao is intended as a case study on the political style, philosophy, and working relationships of one leading decision-maker in China. It seeks to examine the elements that distinguished Lin Piao and to compare his political style with those of Mao and Chou En-lai. Elements which were unique to Lin Piao include his political radicalism, his psychological search for a substitute father figure, and his ability to make himself stand out and be recognized. Although he spent time in the Soviet Union, Lin saw defects in the Soviet system and questioned the desirability of modeling China after it. His political style is described as reserved but deliberate and calculating. Robinson concludes that the content of Lin Piao's political views followed very closely those of the party in all instances. Changes in Lin's ideological orientation usually came after these changes were accepted in the party. Lin was a model son in his relationship with Mao and a supportive close colleague in his relation with Chou. With his military superior, Lin was subservient but competitive. He expected his subordinates to be loyal to him and noncompetitive.

136 SCALAPINO, Robert A., ed.
Elites in the People's Republic of China, University of Washington Press, Seattle and London, 1972, 671p.
This is a collection of scholarly works on Chinese elites: how they manipulate power and how they make and execute policies. Included in this book are essays on the Chinese communist political elite at the national level; Lin Piao as a typical member of the top political-military elite; several studies on provincial leaders and political leaders in urban centers; several studies on the importance of special elites in the government and party, and elite behavior under conditions of stress. ·Selected entries from this book are annotated separately in the appropriate sections of this bibliography.

137 SCALAPINO, Robert A.
"The Transition in Chinese Party Leadership: A Comparison of the Eighth and Ninth Central Committees," Elites in the People's

82

Republic of China, Robert A. Scalapino, ed., University of
Washington Press, Seattle and London, 1972, pp. 67-148.
This is by far the most comprehensive study of the leadership
pattern of the Chinese Communist Party. By using available data
on the 37 members of the 8th Central Committee (1956-1959) and
the 9th Central Committee (1969-1974), Scalapino provides vital
information about the leadership pattern in terms of age, socio-
economic background, educational level attained, career pattern,
geographical representation, and Soviet influence. Several
general conclusions are reached in this study of the Chinese
elites: they were mainly men who came from China's interior
and rural areas, they were less well educated than most modern
elites, their role-orientation has been predominantly
administrative-cadres of a generalist type, those who were
close to Mao were trained in the Soviet Union during the Stalin
era, and, finally, they have reached advanced age and soon
will have to depart from the scene. The data in this study
also reveals the extreme dependence upon Mao for direction,
the limited diversity among elites at present in terms of their
background and experience, the continued presence of a strong
military role in government and party, and the continued fear
of specialists (intellectuals), which even the Cultural Revolution could not remove.

138 SCHRAM, Stuart R.
"Mao Tse-tung and Liu Shao-chi, 1939-1969," Asian Survey,
Vol. XII, No. 4, April 1972, pp. 275-293.
This is a study about the ideas, political styles, and the
cooperation and rivalry between Mao and Liu. Schram analyzes
the differences in views between Mao and Liu, which dated back
to the Yenan days, on the role of the worker, the role of the
party organization, and on their attitudes toward the Soviet
Union and the Soviet model for development. On the question of
the role of workers and peasants, Schram points out that Liu,
unlike Mao, has always looked upon the worker to provide leadership over the peasantry. This difference, Schram argues, is
rooted in the two men's personalities as well as their revolutionary experiences. While Schram portrays Liu as an organizational man, he sees Mao as one who believes in personalized
leadership. Their knowledge about the Soviet Union has provided
the basis of their differences in attitude toward that country.
The study also examines the factors underlying the Mao-Liu
alliance and its fateful rupture during the Cultural Revolution.

139 SCHRAM, Stuart R.
"The Party in Chinese Communist Ideology," Party Leadership and
Revolutionary Power in China, John W. Lewis, ed., Cambridge
University Press, Cambridge, 1970, pp. 170-202.
This essay discusses the nature of the party, the locus of power
in the party and the relationship of the party to other institu-
tions and groups as perceived by Mao and Liu Shao-chi. It
begins with a survey of the history of the Chinese Communist
Party from 1935 to the 1960's. According to Schram, Mao's

experience with the party led him to see it as "a soul or para-
site" living in the body of the army. This basic perception
of the party resulted in the subsequent subordination of the
party's development to armed struggle--the only form of class
struggle according to Mao. Liu, on the other hand, perceived
the party's organization and discipline as basic to the development of a Leninist party. As Mao gradually moved away from
Leninist orthodoxy on key issues such as organization and
leadership over mass line techniques, workers over peasantry,
technical elite over rank-and-file, material over moral factors,
he became convinced that the party structure and hierarchy
must be destroyed and built anew so that it would obey his
will. Mao's perception of the party as highly "leader-centered"
is amply evident, not only in the events during the Cultural
Revolution, but also in the 1969 new party constitution, which
urged establishment of a direct link between the individual
party members and the Chairman or the Central Committee. Schram
concludes that Mao's perception of the party, as described
above, was based on his experience, not as a Leninist intriguer
who had organized a minority for power seizure, but as a
guerrilla fighter who had involved a large segment of the masses
in a political struggle.

140 SCHWARTZ, Benjamin I.
"The Reign of Virtue: Some Broad Perspectives on Leaders and
Party in the Cultural Revolution," Party Leadership and
Revolutionary Power in China, John W. Lewis, ed., Cambridge
University Press, Cambridge, 1970, pp. 149-169. Also see
The China Quarterly, No. 35, July-September 1968, pp. 1-17.
The main thesis of this essay is that the Cultural Revolution
was a conflict between the party and its leader and that this
conflict is related to some larger perspectives. Mao, in
Schwartz's analysis, wrecked the party deliberately during the
Cultural Revolution, but he could not possibly discard the
party. The party, Schwartz argues, is, and must be, endowed
with moral virtues. The party, in the mind of Mao, must also
serve the supreme leader. The issue here, which has its intellectual origin in the works of Rousseau and Marx, is that of
the leader versus the institution. It is the moral leader who
ensures the "reign of virtue" for the institution. Mao as the
charismatic leader is the "fountainhead" of the proletarian
dictatorship; this dictatorship is shared by many groups and
institutions in addition to the party. The Cultural Revolution
represents Mao's attempt to impose his moral virtues on the
party: "Maoist virtue, one might say, was to play the role of
a kind of collectivistic Protestant ethic." Finally, the
article presents the view that the language of the Cultural
Revolution owes more to the Chinese cultural perspective than
to either Rousseau or Marx.

141 VAN GINNEKAN, Jaap.
"The 1967 'Plot of the May 16 Movement,'" Journal of Contemporary China, Vol. 2, No. 3, 1972, pp. 237-254.

This article discusses the activities of the ultra-leftist
movement during the Cultural Revolution to show the conflict
between three leaders in the upheaval: Lin Piao, Chen Po-ta,
and Chou En-lai. It gives an account of the origin and implication of the May 16, 1966, circular in relation to the ultra-
leftist movement. The brief take-over of the Ministry of
Foreign Affairs by the ultra-leftists and their attack on
Chen Yi and Chou En-lai are explained in terms of the complex
power relationship which existed at the time. The article
also analyzes the rise of the ultra-left group and the brief
rise to power of Wang Li in the Cultural Revolution Group. The
ultra-left's attack mounted by the mass media under their
control is described in detail. Van Ginnekan pictures Chou as
"the partisan of reconciliation" vis a vis his attitude toward
the ultra-leftists. Lin Piao, on the other hand, is viewed by
Van Ginnekan as "identifying himself with the ultra-left" in
the hope of strengthening his own position as Mao's successor.
He also sees Chou as the one who masterminded Lin Piao's final
downfall; Van Ginnekan concludes by stating: "In the 'ultra-
leftist' episode, he (Chou) must have concluded that Lin
underestimated the danger coming from this side, that he was
not able to give a correct assessment of the internal and
external political situation, and that he was, therefore, not
the appropriate person to succeed to Mao as the leader of the
Party."

142 VOGEL, Ezra F.
"From Revolutionary to Semi-Bureaucrat: The 'Regularization'
of Cadres," The China Quarterly, No. 29, January-March 1967,
pp. 36-60.
This article gives a comprehensive description of the revolutionary cadre in China and his growth and development into a
bureaucrat as the regime became stabilized and activities
multiplied. The factors which shaped the cadre who was a
leader in the revolutionary cause into "an official in a formal
bureaucratic organization" were many, but most important was
the need for "regularizing" the work of the cadres to confront
and solve complex administrative tasks and problems. By 1955
a rank system for work assignments for cadres had been instituted; it was based on the acquisition of technical skills and
the time when the cadres had joined the revolution. As economic
activities accelerated, a shortage of cadres developed. This
made it necessary to set up cadre training schools to prepare
young people with some education to staff the organs of the
government. In order to encourage young people to enter government service as a career, a system of salary scales was promul-
gated along with the rank system for cadres. Recruitment and
promotion rules were also instituted in the late 1950's. By
1960 one could sketch the typical career pattern for the major
groups of cadres in China. Thus, on the eve of the Cultural
Revolution, the cadres as bureaucrats and administrators were
more committed to efficiency and orderly transition of tasks
than revolutionary enthusiasm and vision.

143 WHYTE, Martin King.
"Bureaucracy and Modernization in China: The Maoist Critique,"
<u>American Sociological Review</u>, Vol. 38, No. 2, April 1973,
pp. 149-163.
This paper analyzes the relationship between bureaucracy and
modernization in the light of recent events in China, particularly the Cultural Revolution. Whyte examines the controversy
over whether the Maoist model for "nonbureaucratic development"
is the most suitable to meet the demands of the developing
societies or whether this Maoist model is "a romantic and
irrational approach" not suitable for the process of modernization. The nature of the Maoist critique of bureaucracy, the
features of the alternative Maoist organizational ideal, and
the extent of anti-bureaucratic feeling in the Maoist model are
discussed in the article. Whyte argues that the Chinese seem
to object to the emphasis on technical competence and resist a
higher degree of specialization. They also challenge "the
Weberian emphasis on the autonomy of bureaucratic organizations."
Whyte points out that the main concern of the Maoists "is with
maximizing (human) inputs rather than with getting the most
return from limited inputs." The Cultural Revolution represents
a frontal attack on the growth of bureaucratization in China.
Whyte concludes that "the Maoist ideal does not seem to be
totally irrational or contrary to human nature or the demands
of industrialization," but the model is not "a panacea for all
organizational problems."

CHAPTER III

THE RED GUARD AND THE YOUTH MOVEMENT DURING

THE CULTURAL REVOLUTION

In the West the Red Guard movement represented a dramatic
aspect of the Cultural Revolution. A popular image was one of
the rampaging and unruly students bent on overturning the
establishment, as personified by the Chinese Communist Party.
It appeared that the authorities had lost control or that Mao
had gone mad and sent millions of young students to make
revolution in the streets. At the beginning of the Cultural
Revolution, these students were adulated by the Maoists as
"Little Generals" who wanted to gain revolutionary experience
to prepare themselves as successors to the revolution.

The entries in this chapter present a gamut of interpretations and analyses on the purposes, causes, activities and
eventual fate of the Red Guards. Explanations for the rise of
the Red Guard movement include generational politics, the
Marxist theory of alienation, manipulation of the young in the
power struggle by leaders, a reaffirmation of the ideals of a
Maoist society, and a massive reaction against the past and
influences from the West. Included in this chapter are items
which relate personal experiences in the Red Guard movement and
the participant's perception about his role in the Cultural
Revolution and about Chinese society. Values gained from this

mass movement of youth in terms of political awareness and youth participation in politics are discussed in other entries.

Finally, a number of entries examine the military intervention to halt Red Guard factional infighting and to return students to schools, the sending down of Red Guard members and their leaders to the countryside, the disillusionment by the Red Guards about the system and their ill-fated cause.

144 BENNETT, Gordon A., and MONTAPERTO, Ronald N.
Red Guard: The Political Biography of Dai Hsiao-ai, Anchor
Books, Doubleday and Co., Inc., Garden City, N. Y., 1972, 258p.
This is a most revealing personal account of the Cultural
Revolution as told by a student participant to two American
China scholars. It tells how the Cultural Revolution came to
a middle school in suburban Canton in early May 1966 when the
school principal, a party cadre, initiated a tightly controlled
criticism campaign in response to Peking's call for revolution.
The criticism meetings usually amounted only to "slogan shouting." The local party cadres seemed to provide revolutionary
initiative for the purpose of placing the campaign in their
control for their own protection. The controversy about the
dispatching of work teams to schools and factories is described
in detail. When the Red Guard units were formed after August
1966, factionalism developed along "conservative-progressive"
lines. The split was heightened by the confusing manner of
admitting students into membership based on the criteria of
revolutionary elements. The account then provides firsthand
information about (1) the effect of the movement on students
engaged in exchange of revolutionary experience, which included
free tours of China at the state's expense, (2) the power
seizure in January 1967, (3) the implication of the military's
intervention and suppression of the Red Guards, and (4) the
disillusionment that followed military control all over China.
The student summed up his final disillusionment: "...I was
actually being attacked and suppressed... It seemed they had
used me and then cast me aside when I had ceased to be of value
to them. My bitterness knew no bounds." Finally he decided to
escape from Canton, seeking refuge in Hong Kong.

145 CURRENT SCENE, The Editor.
"Mao's Revolutionary Successors: Part II - Youth to the
Countryside and Back Again," Vol. V, No. 16, October 2, 1967,
pp. 1-8.
This article deals with the 1957 program for sending educated
youth to the countryside and its relationship to the Red Guard
movement which expanded into the rural areas during the Cultural
Revolution. The program for sending educated youth down to the
countryside was designed to relieve scarce resources for production not for the education of a large number of youths who
had completed primary level education. Urban educated youth
under the program became "cultured peasants." When the Red
Guard movement was launched, many of these "educated peasants"
in the countryside joined the ranks and abandoned their jobs in
communes for the cities. The end result was that many of them
became wanderers, and some of them took advantage of the situation to attack party officials, particularly the local party
officials who had sent them down to the countryside, whom they
blamed for their plight.

146 CURRENT SCENE, The Editor.
"The Revival of the Communist Youth League," Vol. VIII, No. 5,

March 1, 1970, pp. 1-7.
This article is devoted exclusively to the activities during
1968-69 to revive the demised communist youth organization, a
victim of the Cultural Revolution. This revival of the youth
organization indicated completion of its internal rectification
campaign, a part of the overall party rebuilding program in the
post-Cultural Revolution period. The article reports indications of the reasons for the purge and dismantling of the
organization, based on monitored provincial radio broadcasts and
press articles. These include deficient ideological training
among the League's leadership and members and the study and
recreation programs, controlled by Liu Shao-chi, which were
detrimental to the class struggle.

147 FUNNELL, Victor C.
"The Chinese Communist Youth Movement 1949-1966," The China
Quarterly, No. 42, April-June 1970, pp. 105-130.
This study of the development of the Chinese Communist Youth
League examines the reasons for the rectification campaign
within the youth organizations in China during the Cultural
Revolution. The history, organization and work of the Communist
Youth League are discussed to give background for the problems
which developed prior to the upheaval. These problems included
overaged members, lack of stable and experienced leadership,
size of membership, poor social composition of the League's
membership, and "bureaucratic fossilization" of the organization.
The fate of the Youth League was tied closely to that of the
party: "the League was in the classical situation that has
sometimes faced the Party in the past. If it was ripe for
rectification, the Cultural Revolution provided a drastic
answer."

148 GITTINGS, John.
"A Red Guard Repents," Far Eastern Economic Review, July 10,
1969, pp. 123-126.
This is an account of the vicissitudes of a famous Canton Red
Guard leader, the ultra-left Wu Chuan-pin, the Cohn-Bendit of
the Red Flag movement at Chungshan University. Gittings tells
the story of how Wu, as leader of the radical left students,
was caught in the cross currents of the upheaval when Peking
decided in 1967 to halt all factional violence being committed
in the name of the Cultural Revolution in China. Wu subsequently became a symbol of Red Guard unity and repented his
past "sins," being an ultra-leftist.

149 HEASLET, Juliana Pennington.
"The Red Guards: Instruments of Destruction in the Cultural
Revolution," Asian Survey, Vol. XII, No. 12, December 1972,
pp. 1032-1047.
This article attempts to give all the necessary information as
well as insights on the Red Guard movement. It is Heaslet's
thesis that the Red Guard movement was created by Mao and Lin
Piao as a political weapon outside the established party

apparatus to destroy their opponents in the party. The movement began in the limited confines of Peking schools and the Peking University. The movement did not, like the Cultural Revolution itself, spread to the provinces until the August (1966) plenum of the Central Committee. The article first gives a detailed description of the four categories of Red Guards formed after August, and then discusses the organization of the Red Guards in terms of their goals, their control of the movement, and their accomplishments. There was clearly no organizational unity nor any set guidelines for control. Red Guard accomplishments, in Heaslet's opinion, were largely negative: discrediting eighty percent of the Central Committee members and practically dismantling the party machinery. However, the movement did create or arouse the political awareness in the young, an awareness which may in the future enable the young to have a larger role in China's political process.

150 ISRAEL, John.
"The Red Guards in Historical Perspective: Continuity and Change in the Chinese Youth Movement," The China Quarterly, No. 30, April-June 1967, pp. 1-32.
This essay first analyzes the problems of organizing the youth encountered by the CCP from 1949 to 1967, particularly the serious troubles within the Young Communist League. The internal crisis of the party and the search for a way of passing on to the young the revolutionary experience led to the birth of the Red Guard movement in 1966. Israel traces the early development of the Red Guard groups in middle schools and universities and analyzes the encouragement they received from the Cultural Revolution Group in Peking. Then the author gives a summary account of the Red Guards action, behavior and targets of attack during the early stages of the Cultural Revolution. He also analyzes the way in which the Red Guard movement was being manipulated in the power struggle and the development of factionalism within the movement as the upheaval intensified. In discussing historical precedents for the Red Guard movement, Israel cites the Hitler Youth, the Boxers of 1901, and even the KMT's New Life movement as counterparts. He concludes that the movement was a gamble to "spare China a grey, managerial bureaucratic fate; a final effort to prove that charisma, ideology and youthful zest could triumph over political prudence and economic incentives; a crude, terrible, yet high-minded attempt to rescue the permanent revolution from an agonizing death."

151 KEN LING.
The Revenge of Heaven: Journal of a Young Chinese, Ballantine Books, New York, 1972, 438p.
This is another personal account of a Red Guard participant in the Cultural Revolution written in a colorful narrative. Although the accuracy of details has been questioned, the book reveals China in the midst of a gigantic revolution which seemed to be ruled by selfish men, including the otherwise idolized PLA soldiers. The outline of Ken Ling's (pseudonym)

account follows closely the events of the Cultural Revolution
which began with big character posters criticizing the local
party cadres and teachers in schools. By manipulating his
fellow students, Ken Ling emerged as a rebel leader who led the
attack against the provincial party secretary. He then made
contact with other groups in Peking and had his share of train
travel at the state's expense. Upon his return from his
travels, he led the seizure of power and was engulfed in factional infighting. There was much bloodshed in these struggles.
After the military intervened and suppressed the Red Guard
movement, he became disillusioned and finally fled to the
Nationalist held offshore islands.

152 LEADER, Shelah Gilbert.
"The Communist Youth League and the Cultural Revolution,"
Asian Survey, Vol. XIV, No. 8, August 1974, pp. 700-715.
This study is an attempt to find out the reasons for the purging
and dismantling, during the Cultural Revolution, of the Communist
Youth League, a vital mass organization in China, and for its
subsequent reorganization with new leaders. Membership recruitment and selection as well as leadership style prior to the
Cultural Revolution are discussed. During the Cultural Revolution doubts about the Communist Youth League's reliability as a
successor to the revolution were cast for three reasons: faulty
recruitment of youth from dubious class background, the bureaucratic lethargy of the organization, and an aging leadership
slow or reluctant to respond to warnings and criticisms. The
Communist Youth League was restructured and rebuilt with particular emphasis on careful selection of its leaders, recruitment
of women for the organization, and a new membership drive.
Leader concludes that the Communist Youth League before the
Cultural Revolution was "a stagnating organization in need of
dynamic reform."

153 LONDON, Marian, and LONDON, Ivan D.
"China's Lost Generation: The Fate of the Red Guards Since
1968," Saturday Review World, No. 30, 1974, pp. 12-15 and 18-19.
Two social scientists from Brooklyn College of the City University of New York pieced together this vivid description of the
fate of the Red Guard students from interviews with student
refugees in Hong Kong. After the central authorities had
ordered the Red Guards to cease further factional infighting
and to return to school in 1968, the worker-peasant-soldier
propaganda team took charge and assigned students to work in
the countryside or in the communes. Summaries and verbatim
excerpts of interviews with students who were sent down to work
alongside of the peasants are presented. One obvious shock for
the urbanized youths was "the paucity and deprivation of the
peasant diet." Another was "the physical strain of peasant
labor." The article also reports the reactions of the peasants
toward the educated urban youths: old peasants were resentful
of the young students who would consume part of the already
meager provisions in the villages, and the younger peasants were

baffled by the presence of these high school and university students. The interviews revealed that these Red Guard students who were sent to the countryside developed two types of reactions: one was that of "total rejection of politics as contemptible, merciless, and dangerously unpredictable," and the other was "an unideologized obsession with power for its own sake." In the authors' opinion, the Red Guard students thought, while participating in the Cultural Revolution, that they were playing an important political role for China's future; "it never occurred to them that it was precisely their own future that they had forfeited."

154 MITS, F. T.
"Mao's Revolutionary Successors: Part I - The Wanderers,"
Current Scene, Vol. V, No. 13, August 15, 1967, pp. 1-7.
This is a study of China's youth who withdrew from participation in any political affairs--another implication of the Cultural Revolution. Analysis of newspaper accounts from China, particularly from cosmopolitan areas such as Shanghai, revealed a new breed of youth who emerged during the Cultural Revolution: the wanderers, or the Chinese hippies. These wanderers included young students who took part in the Cultural Revolution but made mistakes or got "burned." Many of the wanderers were urban-oriented young people who were afraid of being sent down to the countryside or to some remote part of China like Sinkiang. So, they withdrew and became loiterers in the parks, on the streets and on school campuses. Thus the Cultural Revolution may have created a new generation of young people who no longer have any enthusiasm for revolution.

155 MONTAPERTO, Ronald N.
"From Revolutionary Successors to Revolutionaries: Chinese Students in the Early Stages of the Cultural Revolution,"
Elites in the People's Republic of China, Robert Scalapino, ed.,
University of Washington Press, Seattle and London, 1972,
pp. 575-605.
This is a case study of a student leader who participated in the Cultural Revolution as a Red Guard. The article examines the factors which influenced and determined Red Guard behavior and the impact that the upheaval had on the Red Guard's perception of Chinese society. Using data from interviews with a student informant, Montaperto concludes that students' perception of the party had changed from seeing it as an institution to seeing it as a collection of personalities. The participating students considered their attacks on local party committees as something acceptable and sanctioned by a higher authority. They were motivated in the main by political idealism and a sense of duty to the party and the nation which sustained them. Their willingness to be involved in the revolution was also influenced by factors such as the benefits derived from participation, the recognition of students as a social class and the access to centers of power. Montaperto points out that the study revealed that the Cultural Revolution prepared the youths in China for a

93

new political style of action, direct participation in politics.

156 MONTAPERTO, Ronald N.
"The Origins of 'Generational Politics': Canton 1966," Current
Scene, Vol. VIII, No. 11, June 1, 1969, pp. 1-16.
Essentially this account of a student Red Guard leader in Canton
describes the erosion of the party's authority as an established
institution. From the account a picture of personalized leadership emerges when party discipline and leadership rested upon
Mao in 1966. (A lengthier version of Dai Hsiao-ai's activities
is contained in the book coauthored by the writer of this
article; it is annotated in this section of the bibliography.)
This article focuses on how the provincial authority was brought
down by the Red Guards, who by now had perceived that they were
receiving direct communications from the Chairman, the party
authority. It would appear from this account that, at least
temporarily, the top leaders, mainly the Cultural Revolution
Group led by Mao and Lin, had linked directly with the masses
without the involvement of the middle level leaders, the provincial and local party authorities.

157 PRAHYE, Prabhakar.
"Why Red Guards?," China Report, Vol. 3, No. 1, December 1966-
January 1967, pp. 4-8.
This article traces and analyzes the activities of the Red
Guards during the summer and fall of 1967 to reveal the underlying reasons for the movement. The targets for Red Guards
were both past traditions and western influence: "Their pasting
the Maoist slogan on the face of the Buddha statue is matched by
their invasion of the Sacred Heart Convent and shouting the
slogan; 'get out, foreign devils.'" Prahye sees the Red Guard
as an instrument used by Mao to shake up the party apparatus and
to instill "revolutionary will" among the young. The Red Guard
movement is viewed as "Mao's substitute for the Long March and
the Civil War."

158 WILSON, Richard W., and WILSON, Amy A.
"The Red Guards and the World Student Movement," The China
Quarterly, No. 42, April-June 1970, pp. 88-104.
The Red Guard movement is evaluated in terms of the Chinese
socialization process and western concepts in social sciences
theory. Topics discussed concerning the Red Guard movement are:
composition, goals and values, and style. The role of youth in
the Chinese socialization process and value formation are analyzed within the framework of western social theory and the
western cultural milieu: youth, alienation, and resentment.
Although the authors question the applicability of western
social theory "as analytical tools for the study of Chinese
society," they argue, nevertheless, that the Red Guard movement
can fit into the theoretical constructs. The Red Guards'
loyalty to the supreme leader and his values characterizes them
as "normative transgressive groups organized from above into a
norm-oriented movement." The authors do not assess the Red

94

Guard movement as an expression of "alienation": "Rather the Cultural Revolution witnessed a committed and forceful, albeit unruly and contentious, affirmation by Red Guard youth of their vision and of their ideals of the Maoist society."

CHAPTER IV

THE ROLE OF THE MILITARY IN THE CULTURAL REVOLUTION

The entries annotated in this chapter include the major interpretations and theories by China scholars on the participation and complex political role of the People's Liberation Army (PLA) in the Cultural Revolution. As some of the entries in this chapter point out, even though there was unprecedented disruption in the party organization during the Cultural Revolution, the Chinese Communist Party as a political institution remained intact within the military. It was the party within the military that spearheaded the ideological rectification campaign in 1959, when Lin Piao took over control of the armed forces; and it was the PLA that popularized the intensive study of Mao's thought and printed millions of copies of the Quotations from Chairman Mao in 1964. In one sense the party has functioned, in Stuart Schram's words, as "the ideological mentor" of the army.

A number of the entries in this chapter discuss the fact that the initial role of the PLA in the Cultural Revolution was a limited one, involving leadership in the ideological assault against the Liu Shao-chi group and basic logistic support for the Red Guards. The order for the PLA to actively intervene in the Cultural Revolution on the side of the revolutionary groups, issued by the central authorities in January 1967, placed the

96

PLA in an extremely delicate and difficult position. Several
works discuss the lack of specific instructions and the lack of
definition of revolutionary group in this order, which resulted
in confusion, mistakes and criticism against the PLA. Several
items analyze some military commanders' opposition to PLA
involvement in local political struggle for power; factionalism
within the PLA system; the problems and implications of the PLA
regional and district commands being tied to provincial and
local party establishments; and the disunity caused by the
active intervention within the military as well as conflict
between the military and the masses.

Other items in this chapter provide analysis and interpretation on the PLA activities in the provinces, its use of force
in suppressing Red Guard groups, the exercise of military control
in the provinces, and the emergence of military dominance in
provincial politics. Analysis is also included on developments
related to the military's role during the Cultural Revolution,
such as the ultra-leftist attacks against the PLA, which resulted
in the purge of the May 16th group; the dispatch of PLA dominated
worker-peasant propaganda teams to factories, schools and the
countryside to exercise control; the military's task in consoli-
dating power; the military's management of economic and production activities; the PLA's role in the process of rehabilitating
veteran cadres; the role of the PLA main force as final arbiter
in the Cultural Revolution; and the changing relationship between
the military and the party as the result of the PLA's involvement
in the Cultural Revolution.

97

159 BENNETT, Gordon.
"Military Regions and Provincial Party Secretaries: One Outcome of China's Cultural Revolution," The China Quarterly, No. 54, April-June 1973, pp. 294-307.
This is essentially a quantitative study of some 158 party secretaries appointed to the provinces during 1971, in terms of their provincial/regional identification prior to the Cultural Revolution, in order to test some of the hypotheses popularly held by a number of China scholars about the Cultural Revolution. By utilizing quantitative methods, including the construction of a provincial localism index, this study yields several "unexpected findings." One of the findings is that a large proportion of the new provincial secretaries were recruited from outside their own provinces and regions. This casts doubts on the popular assumption that there has been an erosion of central authority since the Cultural Revolution. A second unexpected finding is that there was less "intervention" from outside in the larger regional units during the Cultural Revolution, but subsequently these larger units suffered stronger purges in late 1971. With respect to the PLA, this study indicates that "PLA loyalty systems were apparently the most prominent unit of localism evident in the selection of new provincial Party secretaries."

160 BRIDGHAM, Philip.
"Mao's Cultural Revolution in 1967: The Struggle to Seize Power," The China Quarterly, No. 34, April-June 1968, pp. 6-36.
In this detailed account of the turbulent events of 1967, Bridgham describes the reasons for the military's intervention in the Cultural Revolution in January 1967. The conditions of chaos and disorder, created by factionalism among the revolutionary rebels, finally forced the central authority to order the army to intervene. The PLA's main tasks were to fill the power vacuum created by the dismantling of party and government organizations in the provinces and to supervise economic production. In addition, the PLA was to provide ideological training in universities and schools and, thus, to exercise control over the students. Bridgham analyzes the three sets of actors on the Cultural Revolution stage: the mass organizations, the rehabilitated cadres and the military. Bridgham describes Mao's manipulation of these groups to achieve his objective: the establishment of new institutions. When the military provided too much stability and order, a resurgence of the left was encouraged. When the left became too unruly, the military was again commanded to restore order. Thus, by the end of 1967, the military in effect was in control of China and was uneasy in the governing role entrusted to it.

161 BRIDGHAM, Philip.
"Mao's Cultural Revolution: The Struggle to Consolidate Power," The China Quarterly, No. 41, January-March 1970, pp. 1-34.
Bridgham offers the interpretation that Mao, after having been convinced that "most old cadres still do not understand the

Cultural Revolution," issued the call for seizure of power by
the revolutionary masses from below. It was not Mao's intention to have the mass organization groups actually exercise the
power once they seized it--he wanted only a "hard core" to
represent the reformed party. The article presents an account
of "the adverse February current," which was branded as counterrevolutionary and the "destructive phase" of the Cultural
Revolution, when the revolutionary masses were unleashed.
Bridgham then analyzes the events of the summer and fall of
1967 to show the appearance of the ultra-left waging assaults
against the military. Bridgham also gives an analysis of the
difficulties in the formation of revolutionary committees in
the provinces, the dispatch of worker-peasant Mao thought
propaganda teams to schools and universities to restore law
and order, and the introduction of a number of radical social
and economic experiments reminiscent of the Great Leap period.
Finally, Bridgham assesses the Ninth Party Congress and the
problem of the military in terms of placing new constraints on
the military.

162 BURTON, Barry.
"The Cultural Revolution's Ultra-left Conspiracy: The 'May 16
Group,'" Asian Survey, Vol. XI, No. 11, November 1971,
pp. 1029-1053.
This article examines one of the episodes during the Cultural
Revolution when the People's Liberation Army was attacked by
the so-called "ultra-left," disguised as the "May 16 Group."
The episode began with criticism of the military regional
commanders' unwillingness to give support to the directives of
the Cultural Revolution Group of the Central Committee. As
the criticism campaign intensified against the PLA in the
summer of 1967, a sudden policy shift reversed the situation
giving the PLA complete political control at all levels in the
country. By utilizing Red Guard publications, Burton attempts
to substantiate the charge that Mao, at the outset, really
wanted to conduct a purge within the PLA regional commands.
But as the campaign "to drag out" the PLA regional commanders
intensified, so did the pressure exerted by the military on the
central authority to back off from the criticism lest a revolt
by the generals at the provincial level erupt. Burton argues
that a compromise was then worked out to preserve both Mao's
status and the integrity of the PLA by purging the so-called
"ultra-left May 16 Group," made up of radicals who controlled
the party's media for a time, and the PLA's chief of staff,
Yang Cheng-wu. This study shows how the regional PLA commanders assumed political power during the vicissitudes of the
Cultural Revolution.

163 CHANG, Parris.
"Changing Patterns of Military Roles in Chinese Politics,"
The Military and Political Power in China in the 1970's,
William W. Whitson, ed., Praeger Publishers, New York, 1972,
pp. 47-70. Also see Orbis, Vol. XVI, No. 3, Fall 1972,

pp. 780-802.
Chang assumes initially that the military, after many years of
political education and ideological work under Lin Piao's
guidance, envisaged only a limited role in the Cultural Revolution, such as providing logistical support for the Red Guards.
He argues that the military's professional commanders were
opposed to the army's involvement in the intra-party struggle
from the beginning. In fact, local commanders and political
commissars tended to side with the established party authorities
in the struggle since many of them had maintained personal and
organizational ties with the local party power-base throughout
the years. The Wuhan Incident in July 1967 was a good example
of this contention. When the local military units stood aloof
from the factional battle waged by contesting groups for power
seizure, the radicals in the Cultural Revolution Group instigated a campaign of "dragging out" the "reactionary clique"
within the PLA. They raided the military arsenals and started
riots which culminated in armed clashes in many provinces,
including the celebrated Wuhan Incident. Realizing that there
was danger that the society might completely disintegrate, the
military was allowed to use its coercive power to restore order.
These events finally catapulted the PLA into the dominant position in politics: the conservative minded local military
commanders replaced the provincial party power in managerial
and supervisory roles in the economy. It was now the military
rather than the party which served as the locus of political
power, contrary to a long standing dictum of Mao that the gun
should never control the party. This changing role of the
military, in the author's judgment, might bring about further
conflicts and rivalries for China's power groups.

164 CHIEN, Yu-shen.
China's Fading Revolution: Army Dissent and Military Divisions,
1967-68, Centre of Contemporary Chinese Studies, Hong Kong,
1969, 405p.
This book brings together from many sources--official press,
radio broadcasts, and Red Guard publications--the events which
unfolded after the July 1967 Wuhan Incident, the defiant act
staged by regional and provincial military commanders against
the central authorities in Peking. The central thesis of this
book is that the Chinese military is faction ridden and that
regional military commanders tend to support the entrenched
local political powers against radicalized militant rebel
organizations, such as the Red Guards. Events after the Wuhan
Incident in the provinces seemed to indicate the upsurge of the
"rightists" as a countercurrent. This rightist movement in the
provinces would thwart any attempts at consolidation made by
leaders at Peking. Defiance at Wuhan quickly spread to other
provinces such as Szechwan, Kwangtung and Kweichow. In many
instances the military in the provinces simply stood aloof from
the factional fights among the radicals making the revolution.
In other instances the military was pitted against the Red
Guard extremists in open battle. It was under these conditions

of chaos and the gradual erosion in the cohesiveness of the
military in September 1967 that a policy reversal was made
entrusting the task of consolidation and party-rebuilding to
the military. This instantly created a new military elite in
power, which in cooperation with the moderate civilian elite
dominated the political scene and prevented a dangerous civil
war in China. The appendixes contain very useful source material on the Cultural Revolution, including Central Committee
directives and excerpts of important speeches by leading
figures in the Cultural Revolution. The glossary at the end
of the book is a valuable reference tool which gives probable
meanings and interpretations for current terms and slogans used
by the Chinese official media.

165 CHINA NEWS ANALYSIS.
"Military Rule," No. 655, April 14, 1967, pp. 1-7.
Using Chinese media sources, Father LaDany of the Hong Kong
based China News Analysis provides details of the military
take-over in China in the spring of 1967. The military exer-
cised its power through the new temporary revolutionary comit-
tees, which in most cases were controlled by the military
commanders and political commissars. In certain areas the
military was on the horns of a dilemma in giving support to the
contending factions in the civil strife. Detailed accounts of
four northern provinces--Heilungkiang, Kirin, Shansi, and
Hupei--are given to show how the PLA operated and how it
manuevered to gain political control.

166 CHINA NEWS ANALYSIS.
"Decline in the Prestige of the PLA," No. 664, June 16, 1967,
pp. 1-7.
This article is a digest of press reports on the activities of
the military in many sectors of society: schools, factories,
and coal mines. It includes a description of the PLA's role in
giving support to production by entering factories and attempting to help organize temporary revolutionary committees. The
dilemma of the military in distinguishing which group to support
among the mass organizations is described. This difficulty
resulted in resentment and opposition to the army among the
masses.

167 CHINA NEWS ANALYSIS.
"PLA Soldiers in Politics," No. 751, April 4, 1969, pp. 1-7.
This issue of China News Analysis presents a vivid picture of
how the military leadership ensures that its troops do not
become tempted by material desires. A survey of the media in
China revealed that the military leadership was aware of the
temptations soldiers could fall prey to in administering the
economy and government agencies. Soldiers were subject to
criticism and reeducation to ensure that they were incorrupt-
ible. Generally the troops were accompanied by the political
control cadres. Often so many soldiers were out engaging in
support of the left work that the barracks were practically

empty. Frequently public meetings were held by the soldiers
to permit masses to come forward to criticize the incorrect
behavior of the soldiers. Continued indoctrination of the
soldiers was instituted to keep them humble. Selective reports
from several provinces are given in this issue to show the
strained relationship which developed between the army and the
mass organizations as the military assumed more of a leadership
role in the Cultural Revolution.

168 CHINA NEWS ANALYSIS.
"Army Rule: Part I - Inner Party Relations," No. 707, May 10,
1968, pp. 1-7.
The soldiers who engaged in political and economic activities
during the Cultural Revolution were the party members of the
PLA who provided guidance and control for the military. The
thesis presented in this issue is that the success or failure
of the revolution rested on the shoulders of a small number of
party members within the military. It is these party members
who could obtain the loyalty of the ordinary troops. Thus
inner party relations between party cadres and soldiers became
crucial. Evidence, culled from the Chinese media, of the party
cadres attempts to maintain good relations with the common
soldiers is given in this issue. These reports also indicate
the gap which existed between the party cadres and the common
soldiers within the military organizations.

169 CHINA NEWS ANALYSIS.
"Army Rule: Part II - Personnel Changes," No. 708, May 17,
1968, pp. 1-7.
This issue, written in the spring of 1968 and based on Chinese
media sources, indicates that new personnel appeared in many of
the provinces where revolutionary committees were established
with the help of the military. These personnel changes represented the dispatch of centrally controlled army units to
troubled provinces where local party apparatus tended to associate closely with the regional command forces. This issue
also makes a study of those leaders in power who appeared in
the traditional May Day parade in Peking. The information on
the central and provincial political and military powers listed
in this issue provide valuable source material on the leadership in China in 1968.

170 CHINA NEWS ANALYSIS.
"Army Rule: Part III - Soldiers in the Maze," No. 710, May 31,
1968, pp. 1-7.
The first section of this issue is a digest of the PLA activities in various provinces. Based on articles in the People's
Daily, a detailed picture is presented showing how the military
tried to resolve the infighting among Red Guard factions. The
military exhibited patience and tact under tremendous pressure.
On the whole, these reports seemed to show that the troops were
restrained in these non-military activities. The second section of this issue deals with the question of dissension within

the military. The selective digest of the media gives the impression that there was widespread friction within the army over treatment of the rebels who created disorder in the provinces.

171 CHINA NEWS ANALYSIS.
"Army Rule: Part IV - In Factories," No. 711, June 7, 1968, pp. 1-7.
Case studies of the military's involvement in resolving conflicts within a number of heavy industries are given in this issue. In all these cases there were disturbances in the industrial plants, and the military was called in to lend support to one group against another and to restore order. Labor discipline was maintained primarily because of the military's presence in the plants. The military who entered the factories, on occasion, had to use heavy-handed tactics to oust uncooperative workers; sometimes mass trials were conducted by the military in the factories to resolve labor discipline. There were also conflicts between the trade unions and the soldiers on many managerial problems.

172 CHINA NEWS ANALYSIS.
"Army Rule: Part V - In the Villages," No. 712, June 14, 1968, pp. 1-7.
This issue illustrates the activities of the military in rural areas during the Cultural Revolution. One section contains a digest of reports of these military activities in the provinces of Shangtung, Hunan, Shansi, Hupei, Kiangsi, and Honan. Large numbers of regular troops stationed in various regions were dispatched in roving teams to the villages. Frequently the PLA troops, who controlled the provincial and local revolutionary committees, sent members from these newly formed committees to the villages along with the soldiers. In many instances resentment and distrust of the military developed in villages.

173 CHINA NEWS ANALYSIS.
"Army Rule: Part VI - In Schools," No. 715, July 5, 1968, pp. 1-7.
Political and military training was the major task of the PLA soldiers who were sent to the universities, colleges and schools during the Cultural Revolution. In addition, the military was to check on the political stands of the teachers and the party cadres in the schools. Soldiers assigned to schools were responsible for maintaining discipline and instituting work assignments for students. A section of this issue provides background material on the schools prior to the Cultural Revolution. A digest of Chinese media reports illustrates the PLA's management of the schools, from kindergartens through universities.

174 CHIU, S. M.
"China's Military Posture," Current History, Vol. 53, No. 313, September 1967, pp. 155-160.

The main topics of this article are the organizational and
doctrinal aspects of the PLA. It touches upon the political
control system within the PLA and the areas of discontent. The
article also deals with the role of the PLA in the Cultural
Revolution. Chiu argues that the PLA was, in effect, under
Mao's control and was the decisive factor in the Cultural Revolution. It was largely due to the PLA's support that Mao was
able to push through the Central Committee the resolution that
launched the revolution in August 1966. Chiu also postulates
that Mao originally wanted to keep the military out of the
upheaval for fear of escalating violence. Chiu predicts that
because the PLA has played a dominant role in the Cultural
Revolution, it will most likely emerge as a powerful instrument
in Chinese politics.

175 DESPHANDE, G. P.
"The PLA and the Cultural Revolution," China Report, Vol. 3,
No. 3, April-May 1967, pp. 12-16.
The major objective of this article is to describe the role of
the PLA in the early stages of the Cultural Revolution.
Desphande characterizes the rise of Lin Piao in 1959 as a
"watershed" in the role of the military in Chinese politics.
The development of the PLA since 1960 has been to mold it into
a "predominantly political body." The article gives a brief
sketch of the PLA intervention in January 1967 and a description of the factions within the military at that time. Writing
in 1967, Desphande concludes that "a very large section of the
PLA, if not the whole of it, seems to be behind Mao and may
continue to support him."

176 DOMES, Jurgen.
"The Cultural Revolution and the Army," Asian Survey, Vol. VIII,
No. 5, May 1968, pp. 349-363.
Mao's order for the military to intervene in the Cultural Revolution in January 1967 was dictated by the deteriorating conditions throughout China as a result of the radicals seizure of
power and the strong resistance to the radicals in the provinces. Four distinct stages of the military's intervention are
analyzed. In the initial stage of intervention, January to
August 1966, the military was called upon to demonstrate in
support of rebel organizations and to give logistic support to
the Red Guards. During the second stage, August to January
1967, the regional military commanders revealed their reluctance to get involved; they tried to maintain a semblance of
neutrality in intra-party conflicts. In the third stage, the
first half of 1967, the PLA's reaction was ambiguous to Mao's
call for PLA intervention in local politics with primary
responsibility for maintaining the peace. By the fourth stage,
July 1967 to 1968, the military had gained control in the
provinces through active intervention. The military had
enhanced its influence and power to the extent that it helped
to shape subsequent events of the Cultural Revolution, and the
center of authority was forced to rely on PLA support. Domes

sees this development as the emergence of a new regionalism in China, under which compromises and new accommodations will have to be made by the central authority in respect to regional demands. Thus, for the first time in Chinese communist history, Mao's dictum that the party must control the guns was completely reversed.

177 ELMQUIST, Paul.
"The Internal Role of the Military," The Military and Political Power in China in the 1970's, William W. Whitson, ed., Praeger Publishers, New York, 1972, pp. 269-289.
The Chinese military as a political leadership force is analyzed in this essay. Elmquist presents the thesis that the PLA's political program is supportive of the party with no discernible distinction between the two institutions since 1959. From that time to the Cultural Revolution, the military's political role involved three tasks: participation in political and party reform, lending support to political revolution, and supervising and administering the emerging government. The article summarizes the politicization of the PLA from 1959 to 1972 and describes the PLA's preparation for civil government in the 1960's. The Cultural Revolution provided the PLA with actual experience in civil administration. However, the order for the military to intervene in the Cultural Revolution ushered in a new phase of its political mission, under which the military, not only shouldered the burden of government, but also asserted political leadership to insure that the Cultural Revolution reached a conclusion. It was the latter role that caused confusion within the military as reflected in its behavior in the factional squabble, ranging from a neutral stand through choosing sides to finally supporting Maoist rebels by imposing military control on the provinces. The article also discusses the party's control system in the PLA and the military's strength in the party. Elmquist concludes that future leadership disagreements and styles of political control in the military might be factors that would strain the party-military relationship.

178 FETOV, V.
"The Army: A Reliable Supporter of Mao," Reprint from the Soviet Press, Vol. IX, No. 4, August 22, 1969, pp. 15-25.
This represents the Soviet Union's view of the Chinese military role in the Cultural Revolution. Fetov points out the existence of factionalism and contradiction within the Chinese military. A list of army clashes is given to support the view that the military in the provinces was not always loyal to Mao or to the central authority in Peking. Generals stationed in the provinces were not always sure how to react to Peking's directives and often were not able to distinguish which Red Guard groups were for Mao. It was possible under these circumstances for anti-Mao leaders in the military to exploit the situation to the detriment of Mao's causes. This led to Mao's purge of army officers in 1968. With the military's

intervention in local affairs, the PLA encountered resistance
and resentment which aggravated the conflicts between the army
and the people.

179 GITTINGS, John.
"The Cultural Revolution and the Chinese Army: A Study in
Escalation," The World Today, Vol. 23, No. 4, April 1967,
pp. 166-176.
In this article Gittings argues that the original intention of
the leadership was not to involve the military in the Cultural
Revolution. The August 1966 party's directives shielded the
army from the struggle to come. Also the military's professional officers wanted more military training and less political
work--an indication of dissension within the military. According to Gittings analysis, until the third week of January 1967,
the PLA was following a policy of "nonintervention," ordered
perhaps by Lin Piao and the Military Affairs Committee. Mao's
final decision to have the military intervene in local affairs
would in the long run promote disunity within the PLA ranks.
Almost prophetically Gittings saw the possibility that the
military leadership in the provinces would lend support to the
established authorities instead of rebel groups, if regional
commands did respond to the order to act, because these commands
had maintained close ties with the local party structure over
the years.

180 GITTINGS, John.
"The Chinese Army's Role in the Cultural Revolution," Pacific
Affairs, Vol. XXXIX, Nos. 3 and 4, Fall and Winter 1966-67,
pp. 269-289.
According to Gittings, the ascendency of the military during
the initial phase of the Cultural Revolution and the presence
of dissension within the PLA ranks merely dramatized the ongoing
conflict between the party and army over their respective
priorities. Since 1964, the army has been a model for political
education and ideological work. In fact, Gittings maintains,
the entire ideological content of the Cultural Revolution was
practiced by the military before the revolution was officially
launched. The PLA continued to set the pace by its success in
political work in the summer of 1966 and became the most popular and prestigious organization in the nation. But Gittings
sees in this relationship between the party and army a new
phenomenon: with an increase in political prestige, there also
goes an increased measure of political interference by the
party. What Mao had invoked during the initial phase of the
Cultural Revolution was not the military power but its "charismatic myth." Mao in this case simply sought support among his
military colleagues to attain the goals of the revolution of
which the PLA was the living embodiment. It was, Gittings
argues, in the interests of both Mao and the military leadership not to have the PLA seize power. The correctness of this
argument was proven by the PLA's reluctance to intervene in
January 1967, according to Gittings. Active intervention would

strain the military's relationship not only with the party but
with the people as well.

181 GITTINGS, John.
"Reversing the PLA Verdicts," Far Eastern Economic Review,
No. 30, July 25, 1968, pp. 191-193.
This article is a summary of a longer paper given at the
Ditchley (England) conference on the party-army relationship
during the Cultural Revolution. Here Gittings makes the case
that the intensification of frictions between the party and
army might promote regional military factions comparable to
the historical warlord period. Looking at Chinese political
development in 1968, Gittings saw a triangular relationship
developing between the army professionals, the orthodox party
supporting Liu Shao-chi, and the radical party under Mao. In
such a situation, it might be possible for the army professionals to join forces with the party bureaucrats to oppose the
Maoist revolutionaries. At the same time the army contained
elements of diversity which would contribute to the further
strained relationship with the party.

182 GITTINGS, John.
"Army-Party Relations in the Light of the Cultural Revolution,"
Party Leadership and Revolutionary Power in China, John Wilson
Lewis, ed., Cambridge University Press, Cambridge, 1970,
pp. 373-403.
This article raises questions about the generally assumed
harmonious relationship between the army and the party in the
aftermath of the Cultural Revolution and the military's role
in it. The Leap Program and its ultimate failure revealed the
personal disagreements within the leadership. The Cultural
Revolution seems to have brought these rivalries and emotions
into the open. These frictions were the outgrowth both of
personal rivalries and of the dual control systems by the party
over the army prior to 1966. In analyzing the events of the
Cultural Revolution, Gittings finds the military's behavior
ambiguous but not disloyal to the leadership. The army did not
attempt to take over the country despite the political power
entrusted to it. In many instances, the military exhibited a
moderating influence on various contending groups during the
Cultural Revolution. In essence a triangular relationship
between the PLA, the party and Mao's ideologists emerged from
the Cultural Revolution. This triangular relationship was a
confusing one in many respects. Frequently alliances of convenience were formed between these elements which could yield
many different permutations. In this state of uncertainty, the
military refrained from staging a coup.

183 JOFFE, Ellis.
"The Chinese Army in the Cultural Revolution: The Politics of
Intervention," Current Scene, Vol. VIII, No. 18, December 7,
1970, pp. 1-25.
This is a comprehensive study of the military's role in the

Chinese Cultural Revolution. The survey of the military activities in politics begins with a discussion on the process by which the military was brought into politics by the leaders of the party. It covers the complicated process through which power was accumulated by the military during the height of the Cultural Revolution. The army was brought into the political arena in the 1960's because it had established the revolutionary qualities and elan so lacking in an increasingly bureaucratically oriented party. Mao might have planned as far back as 1965 to use the military as support for his attack on the ossified party. But before Mao could rely on the PLA, it had to rid itself of those officers who adhered to the professional line of military thinking. When the Cultural Revolution came, the military leadership, as distinct from the military organization, was on the side of Mao's cause and voiced its political views and launched attacks against the party through its organ, the Liberation Army Daily. Mao rewarded the military for its support by elevating the PLA's prestige and stature. The dissidents within the army welcomed the military's increased popularity in the hope that concessions could be obtained from the party in the stormy days to come. In the initial phase of the revolution, the role of the military was ambiguous: it provided the logistic support for the Red Guards, but its local commanders also used the occasion to restrain the militant youth. There was then evidence of a rift between Maoists in command of the revolution and the military leaders over the question of intensification of the revolution by power seizure. It was the failure of Maoist rebels to seize power in the provinces that prompted Mao to order the military to intervene in local revolutionary activities to aid the rebels. But instead of intervening, Joffe argues, the PLA played the role of a mediator seeking compromises from the contending factions. The PLA success in this role resulted in the formation of a new organ of power: the Revolutionary Committees, based on the alliance of rebel organizations, the veteran cadres, and the military. When the reluctant partners in the alliance refused to cooperate, the military imposed its rule and placed the locality under military control, thus insuring order and stability. In the process of providing a stabilizing influence, the PLA encountered difficulties and criticisms, which resulted in attacks on the military by the radicals in 1967 and 1968. As bloodshed and disorder became widespread, the Maoist leadership finally permitted the PLA to use force to restore order and to compel warring groups to reach compromises on the new political structure under which the PLA acquired dominant influence and power.

184 JOFFE, Ellis.
"The Chinese Army Under Lin Piao: Prelude to Political Intervention," China: Management of a Revolutionary Society, John M. Lindbeck, ed., University of Washington Press, Seattle and London, 1971, pp. 343-374.
The Cultural Revolution has demonstrated once again the power of

the military and brought serious consequences for the party's
authority over the military. The changes in the relationship
between the party and the army and the roots for these changes
are the subject of this article. Joffe points out that the
PLA did not intervene in politics on its own initiative, nor
against the wishes of the political leaders. It was a series
of complicated events outside of the military, including the
leadership's distrust of the party, that finally thrust the
military into prominence. Mao, on the eve of the Cultural
Revolution, turned to the army when he encountered resistance
from the established party apparatus, which had failed to fulfill its revolutionary role. Joffe analyzes the reason for
choosing the army in the early 1960's to eliminate power centers
of the party. In order to obtain the military's support, Mao
first had to eliminate the opposition within the army. The
leadership of Lin Piao was the key factor in making the PLA a
revolutionary model. Lin Piao seemed to be able to achieve a
balance among the factions within the military. In 1965 when
the U. S. escalated the war in Vietnam, however, professionally
oriented officers began to agitate for higher priority for
weaponry development. Once the top leadership decided to follow
the policy of "people's war," opposition from the professionally
oriented faction of the PLA was immediately eliminated by the
purging of Lo Jui-ching, the Chief of Staff, in November 1965.
This cleared the path for Mao to launch his attack against the
party, backed by the military, which then seemed to be united
under Mao and Lin Piao.

185 JOFFE, Ellis.
"The Chinese Army After the Cultural Revolution: The Effects
of Intervention," The China Quarterly, No. 55, July-September
1973, pp. 450-477.
This is a tentative assessment of the military's political role
in the aftermath of the Cultural Revolution. Joffe first summarizes the events in the PLA's rise to become "a powerful
force in national policy-making councils" during and since the
Cultural Revolution. He then discusses the effect of the PLA
intervention during the Cultural Revolution on internal politics
of the military: the division between the army high command in
Peking and the regional commanders and the splits and groupings
within the PLA along regional, functional, political and personal lines. The post-Cultural Revolution consolidation of
power also made an impact on military politics: as the PLA
gained power on the national scene, its internal unity went
through a process of erosion, which finally resulted in the
Lin Piao affair in 1971. Joffe advances the hypothesis that
Lin Piao and his military leaders who fell with him "were
caught at the center of powerful currents which, though conflicting, converged at a certain point to sweep the Lin Piao
group off the political scene." Joffe concludes that inspite
of the purge of the PLA high command, the military "remains a
central and highly influential element in the coalition that
stands on top of China's power structure."

186   JOHNSON, Chalmers.
"Lin Piao's Army and Its Role in Chinese Society: Part I and
II," Current Scene, Vol. IV, Nos. 13-14, July 1 and 14, 1966,
pp. 1-10 and pp. 1-11.
This is a two-part essay on the role of the military in Chinese
society. Part one deals with the leaders' pervasive belief in
the implementation of revolutionary concepts, such as "guerrilla
mentality," "Great Leap Forward," and "people's war." The use
of these concepts in building a new society, Johnson argues,
compelled the Chinese army to shift its development from professionalism to guerrilla, or people's war, footing. Opposition
to the "guerrilla mentality" within the army resulted in the
purge and reorganization of the military and placed Lin Piao
in a dominant position to reshape the army. Lin Piao introduced
reform measures to permit a greater degree of political control
by the party over the military and increased ideological indoctrination of the troops. The second part of the essay focuses
on the manner by which the military became a model, or school,
for the nation to emulate in ideology and in work style.
Johnson comments that on the eve of the Cultural Revolution,
the military was more politicized than ever before: "To say
that there is an expansion of PLA political activities within
the army and society is also to say that there is an expansion
of Party activities within the army and society." The article
includes a catalog of non-military activities engaged in by the
PLA on the eve of the Cultural Revolution.

187   JORDAN, James D.
"Political Orientation of the PLA," Current Scene, Vol. XI,
No. 1, November 1973, pp. 1-14.
This article describes the Chinese military's political and
ideological make-up as a people's army. The ideological guide
for the PLA is the application of Mao's mass-line concept and
constant class struggle. Modernization for a people's army
began in the early 1950's and accelerated after the Korean War
in 1953. In its effort to develop a professionalized army,
the PLA used the Soviet model with rank designation, field of
specialization, and pay scale differentiations, all a departure
from the concept of a people's army. As professionalization of
the army gained momentum, political control deteriorated. Moreover, a class distinction emerged simultaneously within the
military ranks in 1959. These contradictions came to a head
when Peng Teh-huai, Defense Minister and spokesman for military
professionalism, was purged. The purge marked a return to the
original mass-line concept in the PLA under the control of
Lin Piao. By the eve of the Cultural Revolution, the bulk of
the armed forces had received intensive political and ideological training and were ready to participate, at least on the
ideological front, in the upheaval. Jordan argues that at this
time, the only intent was to use the PLA in ideological battles.
However, when the radicals intensified their attack on the
party apparatus, regional military units sided with the established authority with whom they had maintained a close

association over the years. Under these circumstances, main
PLA forces, as distinct from forces under regional commands,
were sent out to restore power for the Maoists. It was the
employment of these main forces of the PLA that finally restored
Mao's power in the provinces. In this sense the PLA was loyal
to Mao's ideals.

188 MUNTHE-KAAS, Harald.
"Problems for the PLA," The Far Eastern Economic Review,
October 5, 1967, pp. 39-43.
This article discusses the problems which the military had to
face once it intervened in local politics during the Cultural
Revolution. Part of these problems arose as a result of "lack
of clear and firm directives from their superiors in Peking."
The confusing directives from Peking to regional PLA commands
are analyzed. Failure to implement the vague directives, however, would throw the military into the dangerous position of
being subject to criticism by the Red Guards. Munthe-Kass
discusses the number of high PLA commanders and commissars who
had to either make self-criticism or be purged. A summary of
the PLA activities during 1966-67 is given to show the varying
methods and techniques employed by the military in carrying out
the assigned tasks, including both establishment of direct
alliances and direct military rule. As lawlessness reached
unprecedented proportions, Peking was forced to issue the
September 5 order compelling the PLA to employ arms to restore
order. These activities, Munthe-Kaas points out, created
resentment in the Red Guard groups and led to "army-people
antagonism." Munthe-Kaas concludes that the PLA must use a
combination of persuasion and force to restore order and discipline but "that this cannot be achieved while the flame of
the Cultural Revolution is still being fanned."

189 NELSEN, Harvey W.
"Military Forces in the Cultural Revolution," The China
Quarterly, No. 51, July-September 1972, pp. 444-474.
This article presents an analysis of the role in the Cultural
Revolution of the PLA main forces, which are controlled directly
by the Military Affairs Committee in Peking and are responsible
for national defense. These main forces are distinct from the
regional forces, under the provincial military district commands, whose general tasks are to organize and train the militia
and to administer conscription and demobilization for the PLA.
It was the regional forces that were ordered by Mao and Lin to
intervene to support the troubled rebel organizations in the
power seizure struggle in January 1967. Nelsen presents evidence to show that the main forces, a total of 36 army corps,
were not involved in the Cultural Revolution until March 1967,
when they were ordered to intervene in local power seizure
activities after the regional forces had failed to implement
Mao's orders to support the rebel organizations. After the
July 1967 Wuhan meeting, the involvement of the main forces
intensified to such an extent that they were in fact seizing

control of military districts. It was through the loyal action of the main forces that the Cultural Revolution was a success from Mao's point of view. Thus, these main forces, controlled centrally from Peking, serve as the base of national political power in China. This, according to Nelsen, seems to invalidate the popular theses about regional warlordism along the lines of field armies and about the "red" versus "expert" controversy, since the prevailing main forces were the most professional units and the most loyal to the central authority.

190 NELSEN, Harvey W.
"Military Bureaucracy in the Cultural Revolution," Asian Survey, Vol. XIV, No. 4, April 1974, pp. 372-395.
The main purpose of this article is to evaluate the performance of the "military bureaucracy," defined by Nelsen as "the hier-archical structure of the PLA administrative organization as opposed to troop units," during the Cultural Revolution. Nelsen's thesis is that "China has been and remains today a bureaucratic state," despite efforts made during the Cultural Revolution to simplify or reduce the size of party and govern-ment apparatus. Nelsen estimates that about half a million PLA personnel engaged in civil administration during the Cultural Revolution. A detailed survey of regional and district (provincial) level PLA administration of the party and govern-ment is given in this article to show the party-PLA ties. For instance, Nelsen finds that the military regions had more powers than the military districts and that a large majority of the leaders from the regional commands "neither flew to the assistance of the party secretaries during the 1967 dismissals, nor attempted unilaterally to establish their own empires after military control was consolidated." But at the military district level there was a relationship of interdependence which existed between the leaders from the military district commands and the more conservative provincial party apparatus. Nelsen also discusses the policies initiated by the Cultural Revolution Group in Peking to secure "responsiveness and obedience" from the regional and provincial bureaucracy. Peking, or the center, employed a variety of techniques to achieve this responsiveness and obedience: dismissal from office, additional supervision in the form of central investigation commissions, transfer of political authority directly to the center, and the more drastic use of main force units controlled directly by Peking. Nelsen concludes that "throughout the Great Proletarian Cultural Revolution, except for a few powerful military region commands, most of the military bureaucracy in the provinces still identified itself and its interests with those of the Party apparatus."

191 OKSENBERG, Michel.
"Occupational Groups in Chinese Society and the Cultural Revolution," The Cultural Revolution: 1967 in Review, Michigan Papers in Chinese Studies No. 2, Chang Chun-shu, James Crump and Rhoads Murphey, eds., Center for Chinese Studies, University

of Michigan, Ann Arbor, 1968, pp. 1-44.
A section of this article discusses the role of the PLA in the
Cultural Revolution. Oksenberg takes the position that it is
misleading to describe the situation in China in 1967-68 as a
military seizure of power. He offers four reasons why this was
not so: (1) the PLA was closely identified with the party,
(2) the purge of some PLA leaders, (3) the reluctance of some
military leaders to assume political roles in local matters, and
(4) the continued survival of many high government and party
officials under attack. The PLA, however, did increase its
power and prestige during the Cultural Revolution. The reasons
for this were many, including Mao's and Lin's confidence in the
PLA and the vigor and elan that the PLA had been able to maintain throughout the years.

192 PARISH, William L., Jr.
"Factions in Chinese Military Politics," The China Quarterly,
No. 56, October-December 1973, pp. 667-699.
This study is concerned primarily with the field army loyalty
system, or factions in Chinese military politics. The intent
of the article is to raise questions about the popular view
that the Chinese military is faction ridden. The article
presents evidence that from 1949 up to the middle of 1967
there was very little competition in the field army system for
political power and for assignments to various military regions.
It was only during the chaotic period of the Cultural Revolution
when normal administrative procedures were discarded in the
upheaval that there was strong evidence of military appointments
by Lin Piao in favor of his own field army (the 4th). Even
these appointments were limited to central level positions with
little change at the regional and provincial levels. Thus, the
loyalty system of the Chinese military did not at any time
during the Cultural Revolution pose a real threat to the central
authority. Parish proposes a modified version of the theory of
bureaucratic politics as a possible explanation of the Chinese
military's behavior prior to and after 1967. The theory of
bureaucratic politics argues that when there is an effective
structure, group conflict will be mediated by that structure
to produce the disappearance of conflicts among groups. But
when the bureaucratic structure is weakened and accepted procedures are abandoned, individual initiative increases to
encourage reliance on people whom leaders in power have known
and trusted in the past. China prior to 1966 was governed both
politically and militarily by bureaucracies which relied on a
set of established rules and conventions. This bureaucratic
structure was weakened during 1967 by the Cultural Revolution.
Thus, the behavior of Lin Piao in placing officers of his own
4th Field Army in positions of importance at the center fits
into this theory.

193 POWELL, Ralph L.
"The Increasing Power of Lin Piao and the Party-Soldiers in
1959-1966," The China Quarterly, No. 34, April-June 1968,

pp. 38-65.
The rise of the military in Chinese politics prior to and during
the Cultural Revolution is viewed as an inner-party struggle
over ideology and policy with the military as a determining
factor in the outcome. Lin Piao had increased his influence
over Mao by shaping the PLA into a loyal group for Mao's cause
and by infiltrating the party and government. A detailed
description is given in this article on the manner by which
Lin Piao gained his control over the military and the party,
from the 1959 purge of Marshal Peng Teh-huai to 1968. Powell
argues here that Lin Piao first introduced reform within the PLA
to allow party control over the corps and, at the same time, to
make accommodations to the professionally oriented officers.
Then a program of political-ideological work was introduced in
the military. By 1963 the PLA was deemed sufficiently pure
ideologically for nationwide emulation. Thus, when Mao decided
to launch the Cultural Revolution (a purge and premature succession struggle, according to Powell), the entire PLA apparatus
was placed under Mao and Lin's disposal. By mid-1966, Lin Piao
had consolidated his power and influence to such an extent that
there was a significant increase of party-soldiers in the
Politburo. As the upheaval intensified in January 1967, the PLA
became the only effective organ left to replace the disrupted
party machinery and, therefore, emerged as the instrument for
power in China. In 1968 Powell saw difficulties in the years
ahead: problems in dislodging the soldiers from power, the
likelihood of disunity within the military, and the reemergence
of regionalism.

194 POWELL, Ralph L.
"The Party, the Government and the Gun," Asian Survey, Vol. X,
No. 6, June 1970, pp. 441-471.
The Cultural Revolution was a rectification campaign aimed at
rebuilding the party in line with Mao's ideology. In this
process of restructuring the party, the PLA as party-soldiers
played a very important role. This study points out that it was
the party apparatus within the PLA that served as a nucleus for
rebuilding the party during the Cultural Revolution. A catalog
of PLA activities, including propagandizing Mao's teachings and
organizing political work conferences, are presented in this
article as evidence of the role that the party committees within
the PLA played during the Cultural Revolution. The military
officers also played the leading role in the organization and
formation of the revolutionary committees to replace temporarily
the party establishment. A detailed analysis is given of the
9th Party Congress in 1969 and the significance of the new party
consitution. A clear pattern of rapid ascendency of PLA senior
officers in provincial and central governmental affairs emerged.
This was reflected in these senior officers representation on
the provincial revolutionary committees and the Central Comit-
tee. Yet, Powell points out, the Chinese military is not an
independent element of power. These senior officers must
operate within a system which they helped to shape. Once in

positions of power, they are not very likely to withdraw grace-
fully. Thus, the party still controls the gun only because
the military officers control the party.

195 POWELL, Ralph L.
"The Power of the Chinese Military," Current History, Vol. 59,
No. 349, September 1970, pp. 129-133 and pp. 175-178.
Two essential tasks were entrusted to the military during the
chaotic days of the Cultural Revolution: military control,
involving martial law powers, and political training of students
in schools. In addition, military personnel were dispatched to
factories and other economic units to ensure uninterrupted
production. The military controlled and supervised the communication and transportation networks. They were also responsible
for supervising the young students, many members of the Red
Guards, who were sent down to labor on military farms. But, the
most important and far-reaching activities of the military
during the Cultural Revolution were in the political field.
Since the military control committees assumed power in the
provinces to maintain law and order, they controlled the political situation as well. In 1968, of the 29 provincial level
revolutionary committees, 19 were chaired by active senior PLA
officers. The military also increased their power in the new
Central Committee of the party in 1969.

196 POWELL, Ralph L.
"Soldiers in the Chinese Economy," Asian Survey, Vol. XI, No. 8,
August 1971, pp. 742-760.
The most significant aspect of the military intervention during
the Cultural Revolution was its supervision over agriculture and
industry. The military had neither experience nor skill in
managing complex economic production and, therefore, had to rely
on the skilled cadres. With decentralization of industries, the
regional military commands actually became supervisors for the
industries located within their respective regions. As new
revolutionary committees began to emerge, the military turned
over the direct supervision to these political bodies, with the
military usually retaining a guiding role. In agriculture, PLA
units were called to render support on the farms or to serve as
propaganda teams to boost production. Without this intervention
in the economy by the military, there would have been widespread
economic disruption.

197 POWELL, Ralph L., and YOON, Chong-kun.
"Public Security and the PLA," Asian Survey, Vol. XII, No. 12,
December 1972, pp. 1082-1100.
A major role played by the PLA during the Cultural Revolution
was assumption of the judicial and police functions normally in
the hands of the public security bureaus at the various levels
of government. This paper provides ample information on the
involvement by the military in the seizure of control and the
operation of the police organs for the purpose of keeping law
and order. A key preliminary step in the power seizure process

for the Maoists was to have the PLA seize the more conservatively oriented public security organs prior to the program of
purge and rectification. In this the PLA played a crucial role.
The PLA not only seized the functions of the police but also
supervised their reorganization to eliminate elements hostile
to Maoist principles. In performing the role of a police force,
the PLA experienced difficulties in carrying out investigations
of counterrevolutionary activities, arresting criminals, stopping riots, supervising prisons and directing traffic control.
In addition to these police functions, the PLA was called upon
to assist in the downward transfer to the countryside of
millions of students, intellectuals and government-party officials. The regime's success in restoring order in the latter
part of the Cultural Revolution must be attributed to the PLA's
involvement in this public security work.

198 ROBINSON, Thomas W.
"The Wuhan Incident: Local Strife and Provincial Rebellion
during the Cultural Revolution," The China Quarterly, No. 47,
July-September 1971, pp. 413-438.
Robinson, a researcher at the Rand Corporation, has pieced
together quite a complete account of the Wuhan incident, the
defiance by the Wuhan military region against the central government during July and August 1967. Many factors, such as
competition for power between the local party, the military
and Red Guard groups, the autonomous status of the regional and
provincial military and party apparatus, and the socio-economic
status of the contending groups, contributed to the final
military showdown at Wuhan. The use of the military units
controlled centrally by Peking to restore order in Wuhan marked
a change in course of the Cultural Revolution and eventually
catapulted the centrally controlled army units into the dominant position in the political struggle of the Cultural Revolution and its aftermath.

199 S. S.
"Army's Role in the Cultural Revolution," China Report, Vol. IV,
No. 2, 1968, pp. 27-32.
This is an Indian specialist's view of the role of the Chinese
military in the Cultural Revolution. The article asserts that
Mao had decided long before the Cultural Revolution to use the
army as an instrument for ideological rectification. The
intensive political indoctrination campaign conducted within
the military was preparatory to the launching of the Cultural
Revolution. When the time arrived for political action, the
military was employed to "browbeat" Mao's rivals, but there
was no intent to destroy the party apparatus. The article
gives a good summary of the events that finally catapulted the
military into a dominant position in Chinese politics during
1967-68. The July 1967 Wuhan incident, when the authority of
the central government was challenged by the regional commanders, is viewed as a turning point in Mao's relationship with
the military. The regional and provincial military commanders

were substantially opposed to Mao's revolutionary excesses. Without the compromises made by the central authority with the regional military power China might have had a civil war.

200 SHERIDAN, Mary.
"The Emulation of Heroes," The China Quarterly, No. 33, January-March 1968, pp. 47-72.
This is a study of the method and meaning of campaigns to emulate PLA heroes during the Cultural Revolution. Sheridan traces the origin of emulation of heroes to Confucian education. A detailed description is given of the succession of PLA hero emulation campaigns from 1963 to 1966. The diaries of PLA heroes, such as Lei Fang, Wang Chieh, and Liu Ying-chun are analyzed. These diaries reveal, not only the evolution of the ideal hero-type, but the military education system as well. The PLA heroes embrace the desired revolutionary values of "self-lessness," "fearlessness," and "endure suffering and pain." Hero emulation was a very important aspect of the Red Guard movement, a movement to transform society by inducing change in the character of its young people, the successors to the revolution. It is, as Sheridan contends, an attempt at "planned behavior."

201 SIMMONDS, John D.
"The New Gun-Barrel Elite," The Military and Political Power in China in the 1970's, William W. Whitson, ed., Praeger Publishers, New York, 1972, pp. 93-113.
Mao would have never launched the Cultural Revolution unless he was sure that he was in a position to conduct the necessary purges of powerful figures. By tracing key events that preceded the 1966 Cultural Revolution, Simmonds attempts to substantiate the thesis that a series of appointments and dismissals were made during the three year period from 1963-1966 with the intent (1) to strengthen Mao's control of the central military machine, (2) to weaken non-Maoist political power in the north, central, south and southwest regions, and (3) to consolidate power in the loyal military districts in the eastern regions. Thus, in the summer of 1965 when the military reorganization was completed, the stage was set for Mao to launch the Cultural Revolution. By 1971, the military elite which had emerged during the Cultural Revolution seemed to be dominated by regional military power figures associated with the original Fourth Field Army system.

202 SIMS, Stephen A.
"The New Role of the Military," Problems of Communism, Vol. XVIII, No. 6, November-December 1969, pp. 26-32.
This article assesses the Chinese military's capacity for political leadership and analyzes the major functions carried out by the military during the 1950's and 1960's. Sims discusses the military cadres' administrative and technical skills in economic production, in reclamation projects of wasteland near the disputed regions along the Sino-Soviet frontier, in water conservation and flood control and in mining and railroad construction.

117

In addition, he examines the Chinese military's role in political education. By the mid-1960's the PLA had established a
reputation as a revolutionary model for Chinese society. The
potential strength of the military in its influence in local
political and administrative structures through demobilized
military personnel who hold leadership positions is discussed.
Sims concludes that as an influential force in Chinese politics,
the military might be in a position to replace the party as the
ruling group. Because of the military's experience in managing
a large part of the Chinese economy, its cadres have become
competent governors and administrators. Sims also notes that
with increased power and influence, the military may be in a
position to bargain for a larger allocation of scarce resources
for modernizing its fighting capacity, which could have harmful
effects on the Chinese economy.

203 TEIWES, Frederick C.
Provincial Leadership in China: The Cultural Revolution and Its
Aftermath, China-Japan Program, Cornell University, Ithica,
N. Y., 1974, 165p.
This book analyzes changes in provincial personnel from 1967 to
1973 in order to examine the pattern of provincial elites in
China. Teiwes divides the period under study into four distinct
stages of development: The initial formation of provincial
revolutionary committees, the development of provincial elites
from 1969 to the end of 1970, the formation of new party provincial committees under the party rebuilding program, and the
changes wrought by the demise of Lin Piao. Teiwes illustrates
many comparable areas in the provincial elite pattern for the
stages of development. Throughout the book, Teiwes focuses on
the theme of the resurgence of provincial localism. His conclusion is that the total number of members of the provincial elite
assigned to their native provinces or remaining in the same
provinces for a length of time is much smaller than it was in
the pre-Cultural Revolution days. In short, this book is a
quantitative aggregated elite study on provincial localism.

204 TING WANG.
"The Emergent Military Class," The Military and Political Power
in China in the 1970's, William W. Whitson, ed., Praeger
Publishers, New York, 1972, pp. 115-132.
This article is a study of the power, status and authority of
the military commanders and officers during 1970-71. In 1971,
large numbers of military officers held powerful positions at
all levels: at the center of the party, in the government at
Peking, and at the provincial level. In fact, local commanders
and commissars monopolized party, government and military positions at the expense of Maoist radical ideologists. The consequences of the emergence of this new military class could be
(1) to legitimize the leadership status of the military over the
party and government, (2) to continue the present party-
government-military unified leadership for governing China,
(3) to shift to a more flexible but conservative orientation of

the unified leadership, and (4) to have a situation where the military elite supports Chou En-lai.

205 WANG, James C. F.
"The Political Role of the People's Liberation Army as Perceived by the Chinese Communist Press in the Cultural Revolution," Issues and Studies, Vol. X, No. 8, May 1974, pp. 57-71.
By employing the contingency content analysis technique to generate data systematically from 136 editorials of the army's organ, the Jiefang Jun Bao (Liberation Army Daily) for the years 1966-69, Wang attempts to analyze the manner in which the PLA was employed as an instrument for rehabilitating the mistaken cadres and for rebuilding the party structure during the Cultural Revolution. Rehabilitation of cadres took the form of study sessions, transfer to the countryside for manual labor and/or political reeducation in May 7th Cadre Schools. In its role of helping to rebuild the party, the PLA soldiers often mediated between the various contending factions in the revolutionary committees. This study also reveals that the PLA representatives on the revolutionary committees frequently became the sole source of judgment and power.

206 WHITSON, William W.
"The Concept of Military Generation: The Chinese Communist Case," Asian Survey, Vol. VIII, No. 11, November 1968, pp. 921-947.
Although this article does not deal with the role of the military in the Cultural Revolution, it is, nevertheless, a useful background article for understanding the military's role in Chinese politics. By using the concept of military generations, characterized by prevailing political circumstances, military styles and ethics, Whitson has classified the PLA into ten military generations from 1923 to 1967. Each military generation is analyzed in terms of the political crises for the period, the views of society on the military's role, and the responsibilities entrusted to the men who entered the military during each period. For example the seventh military generation entered the armed forces during the Korean War when emphasis was placed on military technology and combat performance. In contrast, the ninth military generation entered the armed forces during the early 1960's when emphasis was placed on mass mobilization and the increased authority of the political commissar. Through biographic research of 500 officers, Whitson estimated that in 1966, when the Cultural Revolution was launched, 96% of the military elite in China had entered the army before 1936, or belonged to the first three military generations. In short, it was these men from the first three military generations who had acquired privileged status and elite positions that dominated the party-military controversy over military style and ethics. The Cultural Revolution, viewed in this light, was but a continuation of that controversy.

207 WHITSON, William W.
"The Field Army in Chinese Communist Military Politics," The
China Quarterly, No. 37, January-March 1969, pp. 1-30.
In this article Whitson establishes the thesis that the military
elites of China still belong, or are loyal to, one of the five
field army systems and that key appointments within the military
commands at the central and regional levels since 1950 have been
made so as to maintain balanced representation of these five
major army systems. The article first gives a detailed study of
the evolution of the five field armies, dating back to 1927 when
the peasant army was originally organized in the Ching Kanshan
mountains. An important point was made that for over two
decades these field armies have remained in the locales in
which they first settled at the end of the civil war in 1949.
Military officers still maintain close ties with their senior
commanders from their respective field army systems. There has
been a surprising degree of stability of military personnel
within the military regions which have been dominated by a
certain specified field army system. This development of
regional predilection based on the field army system contains
the seeds for regional "warlordism." Whitson's study shows
that even the Cultural Revolution did not affect the informal
balance of power among the field army loyalty systems. Whitson
sees PLA factionalism as based on interpersonal relationships
associated with the field army systems among the military elite.
He concludes that the military's behavior during the Cultural
Revolution was to a large extent governed by factional considerations and personal loyalties.

208 WHITSON, William W.
"The Military: Their Role in the Policy Process," Communist
China, 1949-1969: A Twenty-Year Appraisal, Frank Trager and
William Henderson, eds., New York University Press, New York,
1970, pp. 95-122.
The key thesis in this essay is that China, after twenty years
of experience, finally in 1970 settled down to a conservatively-
oriented and routinized administration. For twenty years the
military commanders have successfully frustrated the attempts
of the party ideologues to radicalize the society. Whitson
reviews the interplay between the professionals and the ideologues in China's policy process from 1949-1966. He argues that
massive pressure was applied by the regional commanders on the
central administration because of recklessness and excessiveness
of the radicals in the Cultural Revolution. The regional commanders were able to persuade Mao and others in the central
administration to make a shift in policy in the midst of the
upheaval primarily because of two factors: (1) the commanders'
informal loyalty and their collective power and prestige in
the regions and (2) high priority for war-preparedness against
possible external threat. Once these arguments were accepted
by the central administration in the fall of 1967, professional
military opinions on policy became decisive enough to change
the entire course of the Cultural Revolution. The Cultural

Revolution's final outcome rested with the joint power of the regional military and party administrators. The future of China's political development, in Whitson's view, may well rest with this power system.

209 WHITSON, William W.
The Chinese Communist High Command: A History of Military Politics, 1927-69, Frederick A. Praeger, New York and London, 1971, 638p.
Although the bulk of this book deals with the development of military politics, Chapters 7 and 8 are devoted to a study of the role of the military leaders in the Cultural Revolution. In Chapter 7, Whitson discusses the involvement of PLA leaders in the upheaval from 1965-67. He divides the Cultural Revolution into five periods; each period involved a political and propaganda offensive phase and a counteroffensive, on conservative, phase. The involvement of the military leaders in each period and phase is analyzed in full. Thus, during the offensive phase of the first period of the Cultural Revolution (November 1965 - May 1966), only the political commissars of the PLA were involved. In the second phase, the counteroffensive, of the first period (June - August 1966), only the General Political Department of the PLA was involved. PLA activities during the offensive phase of the second period (August - mid-September 1966) were under the control of the General Political Department. It was during the counteroffensive phase of the second period that the PLA's Cultural Revolution Group was formed. In the offensive phase of the third period (December 1966 - January 10, 1967), the ambiguous role of the PLA was revealed when the political commissars in Peking lent support to the Left while the PLA in the provinces remained inactive. The military's direct participation and intervention came in the counteroffensive phase of the third period. Chapter 8 goes on to describe the fourth period (April 1, 1967 - mid-March 1968) and the fifth period (mid-March - October 1968). The role of the military during these latter periods and phases became more complex, according to Whitson's analysis. He, thus, traces PLA activities over five years, from 1964, when the PLA was first introduced into the civil administrative structure, to the end of 1968, when China had become a "garrison state."

210 WHITSON, William W., ed.
The Military and Political Power in China in the 1970's, Praeger Publishers, New York, 1972, 390p.
This is a collection of essays written by contributors associated with the United States intelligence-defense community. These essays cover the military's role in Chinese society, the power of the professional commanders, the organization of military power in China, and Chinese military strategies and tactics. Several of the essays on the PLA during the Cultural Revolution contain good summaries of contemporary events in China's political development. Separate entries are made in this bibliography on articles from this book.

211 YAHUDA, Michael B.
"China's Military Capabilities," Current History, Vol. 57,
No. 337, September 1969, pp. 142-149 and 182.
The bulk of this article deals with the Chinese military's
defense capabilities in terms of its combat readiness and development of modern weaponry, such as the nuclear and missile
programs. However, in the introductory part of this article
Yahuda discusses the civil role of the army in the Cultural
Revolution. He describes the Chinese military as a power in
the political system and the custodian of Mao's ideological
thought. The military was used during the early stages of the
Cultural Revolution as a political instrument, particularly when
the rectification campaign seemed to be disintegrating. It was
at this time that the military, as the only national organization still functioning, was ordered to intervene. As the party
apparatus was restored, the full political participation of the
military would eventually be reduced, predicted by Yahuda.

CHAPTER V

THE REVOLUTIONARY COMMITTEES IN THE PROVINCES

There is no evidence that a deliberate plan was envisaged
by the revolutionary groups in the Cultural Revolution to provide
some sort of temporary power structure after the seizure of power
had taken place. It is even highly doubtful that a temporary
power structure was a part of Chairman Mao's grand design for
the Cultural Revolution. The mere fact that there was no uniform
term for the temporary power structures formed after the power
seizures in January 1967 demonstrates the spontaneous and confused state of development. The term revolutionary committee
was first used by the Heilungkiang Provincial Red Rebel Revolutionary Committee for the "Three-in-One united power seizure."
This new provisional power structure, which served as a model
for all, was made up of representatives of the following groups:
(1) mass revolutionary rebel groups (Red Guards and other rebel
organizations of the peasants and workers), (2) military district
command of the PLA and militia, and (3) Maoist revolutionary
cadres, including of course officials and bureaucrats from the
former party and government administration who had repented or
were acceptable to the PLA. Representatives of all three groups
had to be included in order to organize any provisional revolutionary authority in provinces, cities, factories, commerce and
education. This "Three-way Alliance" was workable, according to

editorials, because the masses trusted the PLA.

While the Central Cultural Revolution Group stressed that
the revolutionary committees as "provisional organs of power"
must have "proletarian authority" by accepting representatives
of the mass organizations, the key element in the formation of
the revolutionary committees was the PLA. Thus, the role of
the PLA in these temporary power structures is a focal point in
entries annotated in this chapter. Many point out that the
success in the formation of the revolutionary committees was
dependent upon the PLA's active intervention on behalf of the
Maoists in Peking. The issue of confrontation between the
military in power in the provinces and the central authority is
analyzed in several items in terms of the degree of regional
obedience to the center in Peking and the techniques employed
by the center to obtain obedience from the regional military
bureaucratic power structure. Biographic and aggregate studies
of the nature and composition of leadership in the provincial
revolutionary committees are presented in several of these
entries.

212 BAUM, Richard.
"China: Year of the Mangoes," <u>Asian Survey</u>, Vol. IX, No. 1,
January 1969, pp. 1-17.
On July 28, 1968, Chairman Mao reportedly issued an ultimatum to
the leaders of the various Red Guard factions stating that they
would be subject to external control measures if they did not
cease using physical violence in settling their own disputes.
Soon a propaganda team, made up mostly of military elements, was
dispatched to Tsinghua University to impose discipline and to
restore order on campus. To memorialize the work of the propaganda team, Mao presented a basket of mangoes, a "treasured
gift," to members of the team. This gesture signaled the end
of the Red Guard movement; thereafter, provincial and local
military authorities were placed in charge of "reeducating" the
students with military supervision and control on all campuses
throughout China. This article describes the rise of the
provincial and local military authorities in the revolutionary
committees, a scheme of power-sharing among three elements of
the society--the military, the repentant government and party
cadres, and the mass organizations--to replace temporarily the
party's function in the provinces. Based on a study of the
leaders appointed to these committees in some 23 provinces,
Baum notes the appearance of a large number of politically
"moderate and conservative" leaders appointed to provincial
committee chairmanships in early 1968. This article indicates
that a high percentage of these "conservative" provincial
leaders were regional and provincial military commanders or commissars. Thus, the PLA was a "stabilizing force" in Chinese
society.

213 BENNETT, Gordon A.
"China's Continuing Revolution: Will It Be Permanent?,"
<u>Asian Survey</u>, Vol. X, No. 1, January 1970, pp. 2-17.
In reviewing the events in China for the year 1969, Bennett
points out Mao's continued push for the involvement of the
masses in politics and the rise of a new "militarized elite" in
the provinces. This new militarized elite, which controlled
the revolutionary committees, is conservatively oriented.
Powerful regional commanders in the east and northeast, who had
been tough in dealing with the Red Guards, now occupied leading
positions in the provincial revolutionary committees. This
article analyzes the process carried out in local areas for
"liberating," or rehabilitating, the cadres who committed errors
during the Cultural Revolution. Party rebuilding efforts and
economic and educational reforms are also discussed as a part
of this 1969 annual review of China.

214 CHANG, Parris H.
"The Revolutionary Committee in China - Two Case Studies:
Heilungkiang and Honan," <u>Current Scene</u>, Vol. VI, No. 9, June 1,
1968, pp. 1-37.
Out of the chaos and conflict in China during the Cultural
Revolution, the revolutionary committees emerged as "major

institutions of local power and administration as well as
official links with the central government in Peking." These
two case studies of revolutionary committees in two different
provinces provide a close look at the nature of these organizations and demonstrate how political power at the local level was
taken away from the established party machinery by a coalition
of forces: military, rebel and rehabilitated government cadres.
These two case studies also reveal the focal issues of the struggle in the Cultural Revolution. In the case of Heilungkiang,
once open rebellion against the provincial party and government
had been launched, a host of other "rebels" joined the cause, not
for ideological reasons, but simply because of economic and
social grievances. Demobilized and transferred soldiers, who had
been sent to the province to farm the virgin land of the northeast, peasants, and industrial workers each formed their own
organizations and demanded better deals. Clashes became frequent
as Red Guard students battled the workers in factories. Strikes,
which also usually involved clashes between the various Red Guard
groups and workers, increased in number. The article describes
how these conflicts were stopped by the intervention of the
military in January 1967. It was the military that provided the
leadership for the formation of the provincial revolutionary
committee. In the case of Honan, only after reorganization of
the provincial military district did it become feasible to form
a revolutionary committee. Chang analyzes the leadership in
these two revolutionary committees. In Heilungkiang the rebels
from the Red Guards were given an important position in the
revolutionary committees, while in Honan the former cadres were
given important positions. The appendix listing leaders for 23
revolutionary committees is a useful guide.

215 CHINA NEWS ANALYSIS, The Editor.
"Provincial Party Congresses," No. 746, February 28, 1969,
pp. 1-7.
This article is a three-part report on the events at the provincial level in the spring of 1969, just prior to the convocation
of the Ninth Party Congress. The first part discusses the need
for the central government to reorganize the country, particularly the disintegrated Chinese Communist Party. The second
portion deals with the provincial party congresses' preparation
for reorganizing the party at the provincial level. A province
by province report is given to show how the reorganization was
set in motion. The final part discusses the question of locus
of power during the preparatory stage of party reorganization.
It describes the power of the party committees inside the military. These military party committees, which were undisturbed
by the Cultural Revolution, appeared to be giving orders and
providing direction for the party reorganization in many
provinces.

216 CURRENT SCENE, The Editor.
"Stalemate in Szechwan," Vol. VI, No. 11, July 1, 1968, pp. 1-13.
This article examines the reasons behind the slow and bloody

establishment of the new revolutionary committee structure in the key province of Szechwan. A detailed review of the activities and confrontations is given as background for the analysis. There were at least four sets of problems which seemed to have retarded progress in Szechwan. One was the strength of the regional party apparatus for the southwest, long dominated by the powerful party official, Li Ching-chuan. Then the various mass organizations formed during the "revolution," not only mushroomed in number and size, but competed with each other, using physical violence. Another problem for Szechwan was that the leadership group designated by Peking to speed up the formation of the revolutionary committee was disunited and its members were incompatible. Finally, the military establishment responsible for law and order in the province was divided, and its members backed opposing factions. Thus, it took over a year of bloodshed and compromise before a provincial revolutionary committee was finally formed.

217 CURRENT SCENE, The Editor.
"Mao Fails to Build His Utopia: A Political Assessment of Communist China," Vol. VI, No. 15, September 3, 1968, pp. 1-9. By looking at the events unfolding in China during 1968, an attempt is made to assess the overall situation. The activities in 1968 indicated that the moderate elements had the highest authority in the provinces. The military's political role in the provinces had restored order, but the opposing forces were uneasy with each other. In addition, the rebel mass organizations' resentment over being pushed aside was increasingly evident. Signs of strained relationships between the military and Mao's supporters in Peking were also presented. The events in 1968 pointed toward instability and a fluid situation throughout China. As Mao's personal prestige waned and the loyalty of the masses eroded, the provincial powers showed signs of independent action at the expense of a weakened center in Peking.

218 CURRENT SCENE, The Editor.
"Revolutionary Committee Leadership - China's Current Provincial Authorities," Vol. VI, No. 18, October 18, 1968, pp. 1-28. This issue is devoted in its entirety to biographic sketches of the chairmen and other leading figures in the provincial revolutionary committees. The biographic summaries are introduced by a brief outline of the stages of formation of these provincial revolutionary committees. A detailed analysis is given for the leading cadre of each province, followed by brief notes on other less influential figures. This issue is a ready reference of provincial leadership during the Cultural Revolution period.

219 CURRENT SCENE, The Editor.
"China's Revolutionary Committees," Vol. VI, No. 21, December 6, 1968, pp. 1-18. This article discusses the origin and the circumstances of the formation of the provincial revolutionary committees. These

committees were designed originally to maintain order and stability while carrying on the Cultural Revolution. The article
also presents an aggregate study of the personnel of the provincial revolutionary committees in terms of age, province of
origin, army clique, and degree of stability provided. The
article assesses the success of these provincial revolutionary
committees in fulfilling their major tasks: consolidation of
their power and establishment of their legitimacy.

220 DAVIS, Deborah S.
"The Cultural Revolution in Wuhan," The Cultural Revolution in
the Provinces, East Asian Research Center, Harvard University,
East Asian Monographs No. 42, Harvard University Press,
Cambridge, 1971, pp. 147-170.
The Wuhan incident was the turning point in the Cultural Revolution; it was here that Mao shifted the Cultural Revolution policy
and first allowed the military to use force to suppress unruly
Red Guard factions. In the end this brought order from the
chaos. This article gives a phase by phase survey of the vicissitudes of the upheaval in Wuhan, which ended with a military
confrontation between the local military-party power structure
and the central government. Davis also analyzes the reasons for
and background behind the rectification campaign, which turned
into a campaign against the military's disloyal and "independent
kingdom mentality" in provincial and regional military commands.
She points out that "the army's intervention in politics had
brought the intervention of politics into the army."

221 DOMES, Jurgen.
"The Role of the Military in the Formation of Revolutionary
Committees, 1967-68," The China Quarterly, No. 44, October-
December 1970, pp. 112-145.
The major theme of this article is that the establishment of
the revolutionary committees--Mao's new revolutionary organ
for local and regional leadership of the party, government, and
production--would not have been possible if the PLA had refused
to intervene. Domes analyzes the pattern of military participation in the formation of the different types of revolutionary
committees in the provinces. In a province by province survey,
five criteria of military response to the intervention order
are used to measure the extent of the military's involvement.
The study shows that the military response varied, with most
responses ranging from a supporting but not dominating role to
a dominating role. In a number of areas the military exhibited
a distinct pattern of reluctance to participate in the formation
of these revolutionary committees, and in some areas revolutionary committees were established only after new military commanders had been appointed. At the other extreme, there were some
instances where the regional military leaders simply used the
formation of these revolutionary committees as a cover for
military rule. This study demonstrates that in most cases the
military consented to intervene in the formation of the revolutionary committees only after disciplinary measures had been

taken against the extremists of the left and after there was
acceptance of the military's leadership role. The final result
of the institution of the revolutionary committees was a military
take-over in the provinces.

222 FEURTADO, Gardel.
"The Formation of Provincial Revolutionary Committees, 1966-68:
Heilungkiang and Hopei," Asian Survey, Vol. XII, No. 12, 1972,
pp. 1014-1031.
The article's main purpose is to use the cases of two provinces,
Heilungkiang and Hopei, to discover the specific problems in
the formation of provincial revolutionary committees. It is
a comparative study of the process of creating new provincial
power under tremendous political pressure from the central
authority supported by militant Red Guards. Heilungkiang was
the first province to organize a revolutionary committee. In
the process, the Red Guards initially were given a share of
power in the structural setup. In Hopei, the process took a
long time, and the Red Guards were never allowed to share power
with the military. In both cases the final outcome was the
same: the exclusion of the Red Guards from power in the
provincial revolutionary committees. The final success in the
formation of the committees in these two provinces points out
two key factors: the degree of factionalism among the Red
Guards and the degree of agreement on issues between the
Cultural Revolution Group in Peking and the Red Guards.

223 EAST ASIAN RESEARCH CENTER, Harvard University.
The Cultural Revolution in the Provinces, Harvard East Asian
Monographs No. 42, 1971, 216p.
This monograph is a collection of four separate studies on the
Cultural Revolution in four locations in China: Heilungkiang
in the northeast, Shanghai metropolitan area on the eastern
coast, Szechwan in the remote southwest, and Wuhan industrial
metropolis in central China. The central theme for these
studies is that while Mao's original goal of reliance upon the
masses for revolution was not implemented after order in the
provinces had been restored, the new provincial revolutionary
committees, nevertheless, did begin to experiment with educational reform and economic innovations. Separate annotations
for each of the four studies in the monograph are listed in
this chapter of the bibliography.

224 HYER, Paul, and HESTON, William.
"The Cultural Revolution in Inner Mongolia," The China Quarterly,
No. 36, October-December 1968, pp. 114-128.
The thesis of this study is that "local nationalism" in Inner
Mongolia played an important role in the Cultural Revolution in
that autonomous region. The authors point out that the Mongols
have resented the Chinese communist programs in Inner Mongolia
because these programs were Sinicized at the expense of Mongol
nationalism. Conflicts between the Mongols and Chinese were
evident on matters such as the Chinese incursions into pastoral

areas, the Mongols' role in decision-making, and lack of attention to Mongol economic life prior to the Cultural Revolution.
The political elite in Inner Mongolia, such as Ulanfu, had
identified themselves with local nationalism and had banked on
local nationalism to resist Peking's instructions on the
Cultural Revolution. A detailed description is given on how
the Cultural Revolution arrived in Inner Mongolia in the form
of purges of party officials and the appearance of Red Guards
dispatched from Peking. The Mongols did receive support from
the Chinese party officials and the military in Mongolia in
their resistance efforts. Although the Cultural Revolution
succeeded in Inner Mongolia in terms of changing the power
structure and forming revolutionary committees, the root problem
of treatment of the Mongol minority remains a thorny one for
the Chinese, the authors conclude in the article.

225 MATHEWS, Thomas Jay.
"The Cultural Revolution in Szechwan," The Cultural Revolution
in the Provinces, East Asian Research Center, Harvard University,
East Asian Monographs No. 42, Harvard University Press,
Cambridge, 1971, pp. 94-146.
This is a detailed account of the Cultural Revolution in
Szechwan, the largest and most difficult province to govern in
China. The revolution came to Szechwan slowly, and the new
party authority there took the longest to show results. Mathews
lists factors to account for the painful and tortuously slow
process. First, the purged leaders in Szechwan had been in
power for almost seventeen years. During these years of "independent kingdom," the leaders in Szechwan were more pragmatic
than ideological. Second, since Szechwan was an important
granary center, the revolution in that province was relegated
to a secondary priority by the leaders and cadres. Third,
because of its size and population, there were more factions
contending for power in Szechwan. It was one of the first
areas where centrally controlled forces were used to coerce the
factions into consolidation. The article illustrates vividly
the differences in view which develop between a remote province
like Szechwan and the central government.

226 SARGENT, Margie.
"The Cultural Revolution in Heilungkiang," The Cultural Revolution in the Provinces, East Asian Research Center, Harvard
University, East Asian Monographs No. 42, Harvard University
Press, Cambridge, 1971, pp. 16-65.
In this study Sargent investigates the proposition that
Heilungkiang was pre-selected by the Peking central authorities
as a model for the establishment of a new nationwide political
power structure. A large portion of the study is devoted to
the change of provincial leadership, from the sudden disappearance of the First Party Secretary, Ouyang Chin, to the appoint-
ment of Peng Fu-sheng, who once was purged for allegedly
opposing collectivization in Honan. The manner in which Peng
handled the complex situation by suppressing disorder while

allowing the Cultural Revolution to proceed led Sargent to comment that Peng exhibited "a suspicious aura of self-confidence amounting almost to arrogance." The article illustrates how the central authorities played a very large part in shaping the Cultural Revolution in the province despite local grievance groups.

227 SHUE, Vivienne B.
"Shanghai After the January Storm," The Cultural Revolution in the Provinces, East Asian Research Center, Harvard University, East Asian Monographs No. 42, Harvard University Press, Cambridge, 1971, pp. 66-93.
Shanghai was the base for Maoist radicals during the Cultural Revolution. The Paris Commune, the 1871 popular revolutionary movement, was the model for Red Guards' power seizure in China during the Cultural Revolution. The theme that the central authorities in Peking were largely involved in shaping the Cultural Revolution in provincial and local administrative units occurs again in this case study. Mao's designation of Chang Chun-chiao to direct the revolution in Shanghai is an illustration of this. The treatment of experienced cadres is discussed to show how the Shanghai type of power seizure was not what Mao and Chou had wanted because the Paris Commune model made no allowance for the reformed, experienced cadres to run the government and economy. Despite abandonment of the Paris Commune model and adoption of the Heilungkiang model, the Shanghai leadership was unable to cope with many problems. The military maintained a very low profile in Shanghai during this period.

CHAPTER VI

CHINA'S ECONOMY AND THE CULTURAL REVOLUTION

There is some general consensus among China scholars and experts that the question of strategy--moderate (pragmatic) or radical (revolutionary)--for accelerated development and rapid social change was a key issue in the Cultural Revolution. There is enough solid evidence to indicate that a serious rift developed among the top leaders at the 1959 Lushan party conference when the Great Leap Forward and the commune program were under severe criticism, largely because of the disruptive effect that these radical programs of mass mobilization had on the orthodox economic base. The 1959 Lushan Conference resolution, as revealed in excerpts released by the Cultural Revolution Group in Peking during the Cultural Revolution listed the following charges against the critics within the top leadership at Lushan: (1) they denied the accomplishment of the Great Leap Forward economic programs, (2) they opposed the speedy advancement of the economy, (3) they were against the use of backyard furnaces in steel making by the masses, (4) they were against the commune program for transforming the countryside, and (5) they were opposed to the party's leadership in building socialism by politics-in-command.

Entries in this Chapter include the major interpretations on economic policy differences by the contending leadership

factions during the Cultural Revolution, on the rationality of
Maoist view on economic development, and on the changes and
innovations introduced during and since the Cultural Revolution.

The immediate impact of the upheaval on the economy in
terms of production, management, and worker and peasant unrest
during the Cultural Revolution is discussed in a number of
entries. Several examine the changes brought about by the
Cultural Revolution which have continued into the post-Cultural
Revolution period, such as decentralized administration and
management within a cellular economy with stress on local
self-reliance and innovation from the masses, worker-peasant
participation in decision-making, changes in wage structure and
incentive system, the Taiching industrial model instituted for
both factories and communes, the reorganization of trade unions,
and new social relationships in industrial organizations.
Several entries present analysis and interpretation of the
"rationality" of these changes and Mao's economic policies in
terms of both social and economic objectives. The long range
implications of the purge of the scientific and management
elite and stress on mass participation in China's modernization
process are also discussed in several entires in this chapter
about the effects of the Cultural Revolution on the economy.

228 ANDORS, Stephen.
"Revolution and Modernization: Man and Machine in Industrializing Society, the Chinese Case," America's Asia: Dissenting
Essays on Asian-American Relations, Edward Friedman and Mark
Selden, eds., Vintage Book, A Division of Random House,
New York, 1971, pp. 393-444.
In this essay Andors takes the position that the Chinese revolutionary experience and ideology are not barriers to modernization as many scholars of modern China assume. Andors' study of
factory management in China, the focus of this essay, is
illustrative of "how man can organize complex human interaction
around the technology he uses to control his environment, so
that he becomes the master rather than the slave of his own
creation." The management in Chinese factories in the aftermath
of the Great Leap Forward during 1960-63 and in the prelude to
the Cultural Revolution during 1963-66 are analyzed. The
experiments in factory management from the post-Great Leap
period reveal unresolved fundamental questions on the goals of
the industrial enterprises, on human participation and cooperation in relation to human capacity and fulfillment, and finally
on the cadres or managers attitudes toward workers. It is from
this perspective that the question of models for development
become crucial for China as she develops her industries. The
Cultural Revolution, Andors argues, was "a full-scale struggle
for control over the future of the revolution." The Cultural
Revolution produced a new factory management system which
contains the following characteristics: profit is not the
criterion for management efficiency or incentive, there is
"multi-layer and multi-stage management" at factory level,
management personnel at factory level participate more directly
in production and less in office work. Andors concludes by
stating that "the system of factory management developing in
China is based on certain conceptions about the capacity of
human development and of how individuals and society evolve
through a process of constant struggle."

229 BETTELHEIM, Charles.
Cultural Revolution and Industrial Organization in China:
Changes in Management and the Division of Labor, Monthly Review
Press, New York, 1974, 128p.
The basic purpose of this book is to indicate recent changes
in China's industrial organizations management and division of
labor and to examine the implications of the Cultural Revolution's impact on China's factories. Bettelheim's thesis is that
the Cultural Revolution, as a political and ideological struggle,
has affected the economic base as well as its superstructure in
that a new set of social relationships have emerged in China's
industrial organizations. In Marxian terms, Bettelheim argues,
the Cultural Revolution discovered "an essential form of the
class struggle for the construction of socialism." One chapter
of the book describes the changes which occurred in the management and decision-making process in the General Knitwear Factory
in Peking. These changes are typical of those that occurred

elsewhere in China during and after the Cultural Revolution. The interrelationship and working arrangement of mass organizations, such as the workers' management teams, the revolutionary committee for the factory, and the party committee, are analyzed in detail. Another chapter centers its discussion on the shift from centralized planning to local and provincial initiative and the workers' participation in decision-making. A portion of the book discusses the campaign for the elimination of distinctions between manual and intellectual labor, between urban and rural, and between performance and administrative tasks in production. The concluding portion of the book attempts to relate changes that occurred in China during the Cultural Revolution to the key Marxian concept of the necessity for revolutionization of ideology before the revolutionization of means of production.

230 CHENG, C. K.
"Two Decades of Experiment in Communization," <u>Journal of Asian and African Studies</u>, York University, Toronto, Canada, Vol. IV, No. 2, April 1969, pp. 81-105.
This is a comprehensive survey of two decades of efforts by the Chinese to institute the commune program in China. It discusses the initial decision and debate in 1956 for speedy collectivization of agriculture and the difficulties encountered thereafter in the implementation of the program. A description is given of commune administration and collective living and the commune militia. Cheng briefly analyzes the economic disaster that resulted from the failure of the Great Leap and China's retreat from mass mobilization in the 1960's to counter the effects of the Great Leap. During 1966-67, however, China suffered severe setbacks in all sectors of her economy resulting from over-emphasis on "politics takes command." Cheng goes on to summarize the events of the initial stage of the Cultural Revolution, which he termed a "dismal failure." He argues that the purging of party officials who disagreed with Mao's line of economic development would hinder further China's industrialization. "When these ideological redundancies are done away with, they will be able to utilize available intellectual-scientific knowledge" for rational economic development, Cheng concludes.

231 CHENG, Chu-yuan.
"The Effects of the Cultural Revolution on China's Machine-Building Industry," <u>Current Scene</u>, Vol. VIII, No. 1, January 1970, pp. 1-15.
Based on scattered evidence, this article investigates the effects of the Cultural Revolution on a key sector of modern industry, the machine building industry. The disruptive effects of the Cultural Revolution were felt by the Chinese industry as a whole in three main areas: the disruption of the transportation system, the breakdown of central planning and management of enterprises due to purging of key officials, and the decline in labor discipline due to widespread absenteeism and work stoppage as factional struggle entered into the factories. An industry by industry survey is presented in this article to

determine the extent of disruption in the machine building
industry caused by the revolution. Generally Cheng believes
that a one-to-two year interruption occurred in both the civilian and defense sectors of the machine building industry. The
downgrading and purging of trained engineers in these industries
by the Cultural Revolution, coupled with the new training
programs aimed at turning out only skilled workers rather than
scientists, will have a long-term harmful effect on the industry.

232 CHI, Wen-shun.
"Sun Yeh-fang and His Revisionist Economics," Asian Survey,
Vol. XII, No. 10, October 1972, pp. 887-900.
This is a study of Sun Yeh-fang, the Director of the Institute
of Economics and State Statistical Bureau, at the beginning of
the Cultural Revolution, and the reasons for his downfall as a
"revisionist economist" in conflict with Mao's radical economic
policies. Chi briefly sketches the main areas of controversy
between the rational planners and those who adhered to Mao's
ideas on economics. Conflicts centered around the definitions
and statistical operations for gross output, constant prices,
the law of value, and the principle of profit. In short, Chi's
essay points out the basic area of contention during the
Cultural Revolution: whether the economy should be run in
accordance with the law of economics or politics in command.

233 CURRENT SCENE, The Editor.
"What Price Revolution: China's Economy in 1967," Vol. V,
No. 18, November 1, 1967, pp. 1-10.
This article is a tentative assessment of China's economy in
1967, the year the Cultural Revolution extended into industrial
enterprises. A survey of industry and transportation, agriculture, foreign trade, and economic policies is presented. The
article concludes that severe disruption of China's economy
resulted from the Cultural Revolution in 1967. This disruption
retarded the advances made during the economic recovery period
of the 1960's. Day-to-day decisions on economic policies were
hampered as administrative apparatus broke down under the impact
of the revolution.

234 CURRENT SCENE, The Editor.
"Sources of Labor Discontent in China: The Worker-Peasant
System," Vol. VI, No. 5, March 15, 1968, pp. 1-28.
This article deals with the origin and development of the
worker-peasant system and the labor unrest during the Cultural
Revolution. The worker-peasant system, widely used in China in
1964-65, called for the use of lower paid seasonal labor from
the communes to replace regular workers in industries and the
dispatch of displaced or old workers to rural communes. When
the Cultural Revolution expanded into industries, disruption
occurred in many industrial enterprises, leading to the dismissal of the temporary and contract workers under the worker-
peasant system. When the plight of these workers was brought
to the attention of the Cultural Revolution Group through

Chiang Ching, attacks on the system were orchestrated. The article examines the development of the unrest which grew out of the discriminatory worker-peasant system as well as other clashes between workers, peasants and students. This article makes an attempt to relate these dissatisfactions to the Maoists intent to impose changes in the wage structure and the incentive system of the economy.

235 CURRENT SCENE, The Editor.
"Communist China Economy at Mid-year 1968: Eighteen Months of Disorder," Vol. VI, No. 12, July 17, 1968, pp. 1-16.
This article discusses the economic performance of the Chinese system from 1967 to mid-1968. It describes the efforts of the central government to restore economic order, including the intervention and control by the military of many key industrial plants and sectors, such as railroads, coal and petroleum. Cultural Revolution factionalism had seriously disrupted production in the economy. Data on the performance in agriculture, industry and foreign trade reveals declining economic conditions resulting from the intensification of the Cultural Revolution. The article also discusses the breakdown in long range economic planning in China.

236 CURRENT SCENE, The Editor.
"China's Taching Oilfield: Eclipse of an Industrial Model," Vol. VI, No. 16, September 17, 1968, pp. 1-10.
Taching Oilfield in northeast China has been regarded as China's success story in self-reliance, a model for China's industrial development. This article examines the factors underlying that success, including increased production, high wages, material incentives in the form of bonuses, free social services to the oil field workers and their dependents, and technological breakthroughs. The article analyzes the reasons for the series of disruptions which followed the arrival of the Cultural Revolution in 1967. By 1968 Taching had lost its status as China's industrial model.

237 CURRENT SCENE, The Editor.
"The Conflict between Mao Tse-tung and Liu Shao-chi over Agricultural Mechanization in Communist China," Vol. VI, No. 17, October 1, 1968, pp. 1-20.
This is a reconstruction, based on Chinese official media publications and an agricultural technical journal, of the dispute between Mao and Liu Shao-chi over mechanization of agriculture in China. It summarizes and examines the arguments of these two men on the question of state responsibility for mechanizing agriculture and the problems of political theory associated with the question. It also tries to delineate the areas of uncertainty and to determine facts in the controversy. The controversy began with the 1958 Chengtu Conference when Mao allegedly laid down his strong views: mechanization on the collective must be achieved on a decentralized basis with emphasis on local initiative and self-reliance.

238 CURRENT SCENE, The Editor.
"Industrial Development in China: A Return to Decentralization,"
Vol. VI, No. 22, December 20, 1968, pp. 1-18.
This article discusses the dispute among the leadership over the
crucial question in China's industrial development: whether to
have a vertical, centralized administration and management or a
decentralized management with decision-making at the lowest
possible level. The discussion is based on official media rev-
elations and articles from the pro-Mao periodical Agricultural
Machine Technical in which policies of specialization and
vertical leadership in managing farm machinery were attacked.
The differences in approach to industrial management between Mao
and Liu Shao-chi are illustrated by comparing the Anshan Iron
and Steel's constitution using Mao's model for worker participation with other enterprises using Liu's vertical "trusts"
concept. The article also discusses the worker-peasant propaganda team's role in the simplification of bureaucracy, the wage
system, and innovation introduced via the Cultural Revolution
slogans at Anshan Iron and Steel.

239 CURRENT SCENE, The Editor.
"Peking's Programs to Move Human and Material Resources to the
Countryside," Vol. VII, No. 18, September 15, 1969, pp. 1-17.
The link between Mao's May 7, 1966 directive, issued just prior
to the Cultural Revolution, and China's desire to place emphasis
on increased agricultural production through greater rural collectivization is explored in this article. By analyzing the
follow-up instructions in the provinces, the article establishes
the intent of Mao's famous directive to reduce the differences
between the city and countryside. Another objective of the
May 7 directive was to decentralize administration of industrial
plants and to stress the principle of self-reliance in financing
local plants to support agricultural production. Since the
beginning of the Cultural Revolution, many localized small
plants had been built to produce fertilizer and farm tools and
to generate electricity. Sources for financing the small plants
in rural area came from locally accumulated funds within the
communes. The article also discusses the emphasis on vocational
training, urban dispersal, and the youth to the countryside programs. Questions are raised by the article concerning the new
"rural strategy" which emerged during the Cultural Revolution.

240 DERNBERGER, Robert F.
"Economic Realities and China's Political Economics," Bulletin
of the Atomic Scientists, Vol. XXV, No. 2, February 1969,
pp. 34-42.
This article begins its discussion of the effects of the Cultural Revolution on China's economy with a brief summary of
China's economy from the recovery in the 1960's to the eve of
the upheaval. It then presents an analysis of the economic
policy differences between the contending factions in the
revolution: the Maoists, or radical ideologists, who advocated
mass mobilization of manpower and the "technologists," who relied

on orderly planning and the development of a technical bureaucracy. The Cultural Revolution seriously affected industry and
transportation. 1967 was a very good agricultural year; 1968,
however, showed a decline in agricultural output. Dernberger
sees the Chinese achievement of more equitable distribution of
income and the success in weathering agricultural crises during
the past 20 years as positive achievements. However, he questions the long-term effects of Mao's attempts to achieve
economic goals by political and sociological means.

241 DIAO, Richard K.
"The Impact of the Cultural Revolution on China's Economic
Elite," The China Quarterly, No. 42, April-June 1970, pp. 65-87.
This study on the purge of China's economic elite--those who
directed, planned and managed the economy--is largely a statistical tabulation of the impact of these purges during the
Cultural Revolution. It shows that the higher ranking positions
were more vulnerable to the purge and that party members suffered more than non-party members. A detailed analysis of the
purges is given by groups and ministerial rank, as well as the
specific economic units such as planning, finance and trade, and
national defense industries. Data such as age, social origin,
and education are given to show the background of the victims
and survivors of the purge. According to Diao, over one third
of the members of the economic elite in 1968 were purged during
the Cultural Revolution. The new economic elite, which has
emerged since 1969 after the Ninth Party Congress, is less
dominated by intellectuals and includes a large proportion of
persons with worker and peasant social backgrounds.

242 DONNITHORNE, Audrey.
"China's Cellular Economy: Some Economic Trends Since the
Cultural Revolution," The China Quarterly, No. 52, October-
December 1972, pp. 606-618.
This essay discusses China's stress on local economic self-
reliance and self-sufficiency since the Cultural Revolution.
It also analyzes the extent of China's fragmented, or cellular,
economy. The decentralization in the economy and industry has
brought about the development of local control and protection
in the distribution of goods: "Local administrative boundaries
(are) apt to assume a greater importance in an economy controlled by the political administration than in a market
economy ... When a local authority controls the manufacturing
as well as the distribution of goods in its area, administrative
protection is almost bound to exist through priority being
given to local produce."

243 DONNITHORNE, Audrey.
China's Economic System, Frederick A. Praeger Publishers,
New York and Washington, 1967, 592p.
This is a study of the Chinese economy with ample quantitative
data for an assessment of industrial institutions. The book
covers topics such as collective agriculture, state farms and

machinery stations, electric power, industrial organization,
labor management, mining and transport, foreign trade, fiscal
systems, banking, price policy, and economic planning. It
contains only fragmentary information about the effects of the
Cultural Revolution. However, it is a basic and comprehensive
work on China's economic system. The book addresses itself to
the question of the limits of the Chinese economy subject to
centralized control. Donnithorne finds that the central government controlled no manufacturing of consumer goods by 1958.
But the central ministries did exercise complete control over
producer goods industries as well as the key industries of
transport, water conservation, banking, and foreign trade. The
role of the CCP in the control of industrial institutions is
also analyzed. Donnithorne discusses the importance of the role
of the provinces in China's future development. The cellular
nature of the Chinese economy is stressed. Donnithorne concludes that the movement for modernization will continue: "New
patterns will emerge, but in the long run they will be molded
by economic requirements and not primarily by political desire.
For the superstructure of even a Marxist state is not above
being shaped by the play of productive force."

244 GOODSTADT, Leo.
China's Search for Plenty: The Economics of Mao Tse-tung,
Weatherhill, New York and Tokyo, 1973, 266p.
The book attempts to translate Mao's economic policies and
thinking into western terms to make them understandable from
the western point of view. It presents the thesis that Mao's
views on China's economic development are similar to a number
of western economists' views on economic development. Mao's
views on cooperative farming with emphasis on the application
of scientific farming predated the "Green Revolution" of the
1960's. His concept of reform in land tenure has been widely
accepted as a must for any introduction of change in a predominantly rural economy. Mao, in many ways, was well ahead of
most Asian leaders and western development strategists on rural
development. Similarly, Mao's view of placing priority on the
development of light industry before heavy industry was novel
by Chinese and European communists standards. Mao's belief in
man's ability to conquer hard realities and his conviction that
the masses can contribute to the building of a new society are
shared by other western social scientists. The Cultural Revolution, argues Goodstadt, reflected Mao's serious concern about
the failure of China's intellectuals, technicians, rural cadres,
and economists to understand and appreciate the essence of his
development strategy. Mao felt obliged to make a revolution to
prevent China from following the wrong path to prosperity. The
last section of the book discusses the economic roots of the
Cultural Revolution as the focal point of the upheaval: development goals; industrial management and rural administration;
financial and accounting practices; manual labor in the countryside by the young as well as by the intellectuals and administrators in government and party. Goodstadt concludes: "And if

140

the final result of the Cultural Revolution were to prove the permanent adoption of Mao Tse-tung's economic strategy, lending idealism and hardheaded analysis of the barriers to progress, then Mao's upheaval may be counted by China's future historians a cheap price to have paid for prosperity."

245 GOODSTADT, Leo F.
"Wages in Command," Far Eastern Economic Review, No. 32, August 6, 1970, pp. 52-54.
Goodstadt discusses the rationale for the emphasis on labor-intensive production during both the 1958 Great Leap Forward and the Cultural Revolution. He explains the approach to rural development adopted during the Cultural Revolution as "hard-headed economics." Local plants were built during this period to serve the needs of modern agriculture. The establishment of rural industrial centers and the transfer of people from urban areas to the countryside had political as well as economic implications. The joint impact of these two programs made possible a considerable decline in the national wage level. Goodstadt sees problems inherent in these two policies. He notes that as the wage level declines, the price of capital goods must also decline. Another problem is the persistent effort of rural families to protect their traditional outlooks against ideological campaigns.

246 GRAY, JACK.
"The Economics of Maoism," Bulletin of the Atomic Scientists, Vol. XXV, No. 2, February 1969, pp. 42-51. Also in Richard Baum with Louise B. Bennett, eds., China in Ferment: Perspectives in the Cultural Revolution, Prentice-Hall, Inc., Englewood Cliffs, N. J., 1971, pp. 78-94.
This article attempts to explain Mao's views on economics and economic development policies as they apply to China. A close examination of Mao's writings since 1949 reveals Mao's expressed concern for economic matters, rather than indifference as is commonly assumed in the west. Examples of Mao's views on China's economic development policy are given, including the 1958 Chengtu Conference on agricultural mechanization through the collectives and the strategy of the 1962 10th Plenum of 8th Central Committee of the CCP for achievement of mechanization of Chinese agriculture. The article presents a detailed discussion of Mao's views on economic issues that have confronted the regime for some time: local initiative and control of technology to develop local industries, the degree of "educational fallout" in the use of machines for the peasants, and the appropriateness of the Soviet model for development. Finally, Gray argues that Mao is less concerned about economics than about the final elimination of conflicts between industry and agriculture, town and country, and mental and manual labor--necessary conditions for Marx's classless society.

247 GRAY, Jack.
"Mao's Economic Thoughts," Far Eastern Economic Review,

January 15, 1970, pp. 16-18.
The assumption that Mao is not interested in economics is a
fallacious one, according to Gray. Based on an examination of
Mao's writings, which have been neglected by the west, Gray
outlines the main features of Mao's economic views: the importance of material incentive, production before procurement, and
entrepreneurship within the collective organizations. The
article also summarizes arguments over the question of agricultural mechanization, taken from the Chinese agricultural technical journal. Gray argues that Mao's ideas and policies on
economic issues are not irrational but are close to many ideas
advanced by western economists on development for underdeveloped
countries: the employment of the labor-intensive method, the
relationship between the educated minority and illiterate
masses, "creative inbalanced" growth via crash programs, and a
high level of collectivisation, which is necessary to "provide
the appropriate social framework for the operation of his
economic system."

248 GRAY, Jack.
"Politics in Command: the Maoist Theory of Social Change and
Economic Growth," The Political Quarterly, Vol. 45, No. 1,
January-March 1974, pp. 26-48.
Mao's strategy of "politics in command of the economy" is the
focus of this study. A discussion of the uniqueness and relevance of Mao's economic strategy to the developing world is also
included. The paper begins with the background for the development of such a strategy, the economy of the guerrilla bases.
Then China's experience with the Russian model for heavy industry development is analyzed. Gray points out the validity of
Mao's argument for development in local communities. The
concept of "politics in command" was intended to achieve an
equitable distribution of resources which would yield incentives
for local development and to maintain mass-line politics in
decision-making. The mass-line concept in politics was translated into the Great Leap Program. Its failure in 1959
sharpened the policy differences between Mao and Liu on China's
modernization. The controversy over the mass-line concept in
China's economic development must be considered a key dispute,
which eventually resulted in the Cultural Revolution. Thus the
purpose of politics-in-command is to prevent "the distortion of
the appropriate pattern of income distribution leading to the
reemergence of elitism."

249 GRAY, Jack.
"The Two Roads: Alternative Strategies of Social Change and
Economic Growth in China," Authority, Participation and Cultural
Change in China, Stuart Schram, ed., Cambridge University Press,
Cambridge, 1973, pp. 109-157.
This is a three-part discussion of the controversy over the "two
roads" for China's economic development: the Maoist and the
Liuist. In the first part, Mao's economic strategy is analyzed
in terms of Marxian influence, especially in terms of class

142

consciousness and the avoidance of creeping privileges for the few as wealth increases for a society. In the second section, Gray discusses the emergence of Liuist views. Evidence of differences of opinion within the party appeared in the land reform of 1949-50, in the socialization period of 1951-56, in Mao's response to de-Stalinization which advocated less bureaucracy and more local initiative, and in the debate on the Great Leap Program in 1958-59. In the third portion of the paper, the open debate on policy and strategical differences during the Cultural Revolution, particularly the debate over the problem of agricultural mechanization, is discussed. On this issue there seemed to be two clear-cut alternative strategies, as revealed by documents published during the Cultural Revolution. Gray's conclusion is that Mao has long advocated that "socialism should be based on popular power," not on "paternalistic administration.

250 GURLEY, W.
"Maoist Economic Development: The New Man in the New China,"
The Center Magazine, Center for Study of Democratic Insitutions,
Santa Barbara, California, Vol. III, No. 3, May-June 1970,
pp. 25-33.
Gurley, a western economist, tries to explain the rationality of the Maoist view on economic development in terms of Marxist-Leninist tradition. Mao's emphasis on the development of human beings on an egalitarian basis, on the transformation of ideas, on the breaking down of specialization, and on the dismantling of bureaucracies--all of these have the origin in Marxism. Gurley maintains: "most of the economic researchers have approached China as though it were little more than a series of tables in a yearbook which could be analyzed by western economic methods and judged by capitalist values." Gurley argues that the failure of many economic experts to tell the story of China's economic development fully and accurately is bad enough, but worse still is that they fail to deal with China on her own terms, within the framework of her own goals and methods for attaining these goals. The west, thus, gets a distorted picture of China's economic development. Gurley appeals for the west to take the Maoist model of development seriously. The essay gives a summary of China's economic advances over the past two decades, not only in industrial output and the feeding of an enormously large population, but also in the medical and public-health fields as well.

251 HOWE, Christopher.
"Economic Trends and Policies," The Political Quarterly, Vol. 45,
No. 1, January-March 1974, pp. 12-25.
This paper discusses China's industrial output, agricultural production, income and wages, as well as policy changes affecting China's economy. Summary tables are given on production. Based on the data gathered, Howe analyzes changes in China's industrial policies: the reemphasizing of centralized planning, the de-emphasizing of regional and local initiatives, the

reactivation of technical and disciplinary rules and precedents, and the tightening of wage policy. The paper also briefly covers China's awareness of population pressures on food and other consumer industries.

252 HOWE, Christopher.
"Labour Organization and Incentives in Industry Before and After the Cultural Revolution," Authority, Participation, and Cultural Change in China, Stuart Schram, ed., Cambridge University Press, Cambridge, 1973, pp. 233-256.
This paper on China's labor organizations and system of reward examines the Cultural Revolution's effects on the system in terms of fundamental changes. In the 1960's there were no real wage increases for workers; emulation campaigns which stressed shop innovation and political performance were used to increase production. The work force was controlled through the trade unions, which in turn were controlled by the party. During the Cultural Revolution, the trade unions, Liuist organizations, were attacked for expanding the contract labor system and for defending the privileges of permanent workers. The effects of the Cultural Revolution included: recognition of incentives, reduction of sharp urban-rural differences, and reorganization of the trade unions.

253 HUGHES, T. J.
"China's Economy - Retrospect and Prospect," International Affairs (Catham House), Vol. 46, No. 1, January 1970, pp. 63-73.
This article reviews China's economic development for the two decade period from 1949 to 1969. The development is examined in five separate phases: economic rehabilitation, the transformation of economic institutions, the introduction of large-scale planning, the Great Leap, and the Cultural Revolution. Hughes takes the position that although the Cultural Revolution was a political conflict, it has a considerable impact on China's economy: disruptions in the industrial sector affected the production of iron and steel and disruptions in transport caused shortages of food, fuel and raw materials. Hughes estimates that there was a ten to twenty percent decrease in output during 1966-67; however, some recovery was made during 1968-69. He concludes that there will be an element of uncertainty in China's future economic development as long as the dispute over the priorities of politics and economics remains unresolved.

254 LEE, Rensselaer W., III.
"Ideology and Technical Innovation in Chinese Industry, 1949-1971," Asian Survey, Vol. XII, No. 8, August 1972, pp. 649-661.
This essay deals with the subject of promoting technical innovation by the masses in Chinese industries, a concept derived from Marxist theories and applied in China during the Cultural Revolution. The paper analyzes in detail worker's innovations during the 1950's and the changes that took place during the Great Leap of 1958-59. The separation of politics and technology

144

occurred in 1966, after the Leap period. When the Cultural
Revolution was launched emphasis was placed on workers' innovations for technological improvement. Lee lists the themes
which tended to link technology and politics during the Cultural
Revolution. The author also argues that while the concept of
innovations by the masses is Marxist, it is also an issue of
"Chinese identity in modernization": native technical power
must replace "foreign and expert" technical power. This concept
is both ideological and nationalistic.

255 MAC DOUGALL, Colina.
"The Cultural Revolution in the Communes: Back to 1958?,"
Current Scene, Vol. VII, No. 7, April 11, 1969, pp. 1-11.
According to the author, the widespread effort in 1968-69 to
decentralize control of economic and social life in the communes
was a strong indication that features of the 1958 Great Leap
Forward were being reinstituted in the agricultural sector.
During the Cultural Revolution, communes were made self-reliant
and self-supporting; they provided their own education, health
and agricultural mechanization. MacDougall reviews the manner by
which the Cultural Revolution, in the form of a rural "struggle-
criticism-transformation" campaign aimed at ousting the more
conservative leaders, arrived in the communes toward the end of
1968. The campaign involved the use of the military for propaganda and enforcement purposes. Other changes introduced by
the campaign were adoption of the Tachai work-point system; the
amalgamation of production units into larger teams, brigades,
and communes; localization of rural trade; development of
commune-managed supply and marketing systems; and development
of medical care through commune self-support.

256 MAC DOUGALL, Colina.
"Revolution on China's Railroads," Current Scene, Vol. VI,
No. 14, August 16, 1968, pp. 1-16.
This article describes the difficulties which confronted the
railroads in China during the Cultural Revolution. There were
two basic problems for the railroad, which were administered by
a complex chain of bureaus: Red Guard travels which strained
the capacity of the lines and the factional struggle among the
railroad workers, particularly between skilled and unskilled
workers. Information about these disturbances and difficulties
are analyzed for several provinces. Railway workers also had
grievances because of reductions in their pay and bonuses during
the Cultural Revolution, which led to frequent work stoppages.
These disturbances resulted in a coal shortage for many parts of
China in the winter of 1967. The central government's efforts to
improve the railroad service and the results of these efforts
are analyzed.

257 PERKINS, Dwight.
"Economic Growth in China and the Cultural Revolution (1960 -
April 1967)," The China Quarterly, No. 30, April-June 1967,
pp. 33-48.

This article gives a description of China's economic policies
and growth from 1960 through 1965. During this period there was
some growth in agriculture, a complete recovery with increased
production in heavy industry, but very little gain in light
industries, as compared with 1957, the last year before the
chaotic Great Leap Program. Perkins attributes slow growth in
consumer industries to the slow growth in agriculture. Perkins
states that on the eve of the Cultural Revolution, a large
segment of the party leaders and cadres favored achieving
economic growth through prudent planning and skilled management
of the economy. He notes that it was during 1966 that the
prudent economic policies of Sun Yeh-fang and Liu Shao-chi were
criticized by adherents of Mao's radical views. However,
Perkins saw little disruptive effects on the economy in 1966
when the Cultural Revolution was launched; it was a good year
for agriculture and an even better one for industry.

258 PERKINS, Dwight W.
"Mao Tse-tung's Goals and China's Economic Performance," Current
History, Vol. IX, No. 1, January 7, 1971, pp. 1-13.
This article dismisses the popular argument that mistaken
economic policies, such as the Great Leap Program, have retarded
China's economic growth. The central theme of this article is
that the slow growth rate for China during the 1960's was due
primarily to the fact that priority was given to other non-
economic goals. The evolution of China's economic policies from
the mid-1950's to the eve of the Cultural Revolution and Mao's
role in them are discussed. During this period, Mao insisted
on the continued pursuit of his revolutionary social goals along
with pursuit of the economic goal of increased productive
capacity. Central to Mao's revolutionary social goals was the
elimination of classes and the modes of thought that tend to
promote class structure. Educational reform and other ideological campaigns were the means of attaining these goals. Mao's
political and social experiments did affect the rate of economic
growth in the 1960's. Perkins makes the point that a greater
China is far more important than a rich China in Mao's thinking.
The question for the future is "will China want to pay the
political and social price for rapid growth?"

259 PRYBYLA, Jan.
"The Economic Cost," Problems of Communism, Vol. XVII, No. 2,
March-April 1968, pp. 1-13.
The main purpose of the article is to show how the Cultural
Revolution affected China's economic development. Fragmentary
statistics from a comparative survey of Chinese agriculture,
industry and foreign trade for the years 1957-58, 1961 and
1966-67 showed a decline in output as the activities of the
Cultural Revolution expanded into the economic sectors. Jasny's
hypothesis of politically induced business cycles in Russia
under Stalin was applied to the Chinese case to show that there
was a correlation between the rise in political activities and
the decline in industrial output. The upward swing in Chinese

economy from 1950-58 was followed by a downward swing from
1958-62, during the Great Leap Program. Signs of recovery for
1962-65 were followed by a downward swing in 1966-67, when the
Cultural Revolution occurred. The author concludes that "the
Great Proletarian Cultural Revolution still appears to be the
political agent of another recession in China's socialist
economy, perhaps mild by the standards of the Great Leap debacle,
yet with serious long-range repercussions on China's progress
toward modernization."

260 RICHMAN, Barry.
"Ideology and Management: The Chinese Oscillate," Columbia
Journal of World Business, Vol. VI, No. 1, January-February
1971.
Richman believes that it is the combination of ideology (Mao's
vision of a Chinese communist society) and pragmatism that has
brought about the impressive industrial progress in China. The
"ideological pendulum" has resulted also in severe economic
crises and damage to the industrial system. Richman reviews the
regime's oscillation approach to industrial management from
ideological extremism in the late 1950's to moderation in the
early 1960's. The Cultural Revolution represents Mao's concern
about the shape of the Chinese society and Mao's conclusion
"that he could not rely on the regular party apparatus, including enterprise ideologists, to implement effectively on a
national scale the ideological programs, policies or aims so
cherished by him." Richman believes that Mao "is more concerned
with ideology, human values and relations, than technical or
formal organization." The party, operating on the principle of
a modern bureaucracy, could not possibly revolutionize either
industrial management or society. Thus purge became necessary.
Richman concludes that "the ideological excesses of the Cultural
Revolution--and perhaps especially the cadres versus super-
cadres struggle--significantly hindered managerial efficiency
and industrial progress."

261 RISKIN, Carl.
"The Chinese Economy in 1967," The Cultural Revolution: 1967
in Review, Michigan Papers in Chinese Studies No. 2, Chang
Chun-shu, James Crump and Rhoads Murphey, eds., Center for
Chinese Studies, University of Michigan, Ann Arbor, 1968,
pp. 45-71.
This paper gives an assessment of the Chinese economy for the
year 1967. In agriculture there was general disorganization in
rural areas; the decline in grain procurement by the state and
other disruptions caused a slowdown in production, even though
it was a good crop year. However, there was industrial growth,
despite disruptions in many industrial plants. Riskin takes the
position that the disruptions, which occurred in 1966-67 under
the Cultural Revolution, caused less damage to the economy than
those of the Great Leap in 1958-59. He feels that if conditions
of stability were present, the Chinese economy would continue
to grow.

262   SCHRAM, Stuart, ed.
Authority Participation and Cultural Change in China, Cambridge
University Press, Cambridge, 1973, 350p.
This book contains six essays written by members of a European
Study Group on the Cultural Revolution with particular emphasis
on economic and social aspects of the upheaval. In the introduction to this book, Schram places the Cultural Revolution in
historical perspective: it was the continuation of the Chinese
revolution which involves the process of continued cultural
change. The Cultural Revolution was made up, therefore, of
many strands, a revolution in all of its meanings: political,
cultural, economic and social. Mao's aim in the Cultural Revolution was to change the power structure and to permanently
transform the thought pattern and behavior of the Chinese
people. Separate annotation of the articles contained in this
book may be found in various sections of this bibliography under
author entry.

263   SCHRAN, Peter.
"Economic Management," China: Management of a Revolutionary
Society, John M. Lindbeck, ed., University of Washington Press,
Seattle and London, 1971, pp. 195-220.
This paper deals with the organization and management of economic activities in China in the perspective of Mao's repeated
emphasis on "anti-scientific" and "voluntaristic" approaches.
On the eve of the Cultural Revolution, there was in increase in
the number of persons prepared to become technocrats, who
possessed the managerial skills and expertise to run the economy.
The Great Leap had emphasized decentralization in management and
planning, party control, and mass participation. With the
expansion of Cultural Revolution's activities into the economic
sectors and the attack on the party organization, some damage
was done to management. Less damage occurred in agriculture
where "management was less professional and party control was
more dominant" than in industry. Schran concludes that the
Cultural Revolution not only challenged the pattern of organization but the spirit of it as well. It might be possible to
change the "pattern of organization" but not the "organizers"
because the new managers may be more professionally than politically oriented.

264   SCHRAN, Peter.
"Institutional Continuity and Motivational Change: The Chinese
Industrial Wages System, 1950-1973," Asian Survey, Vol. XIV,
No. 11, November 1974, pp. 1014-1032.
This essay is concerned with the socialist transformation of the
wages system in China. A detailed analysis, with statistics for
1955-56, is presented on monthly basic wage scales and wage
differentiation among various industries. Schran points out
that the Chinese wage system did not rely heavily on material
incentives and that for two decades, from 1950 to 1970, attention was focused on "the form of work and of wage payment." A
table in the article shows the wages scale pattern reported by

148

recent visitors to China. Unfortunately, scanty data on the relationship of current and past wages precluded an analysis of this topic.

265 SNOW, Edgar.
"Success or Failure? China's 70,000 Communes," The New Republic, June 26, 1971, pp. 19-23.
The first part of the article gives a general description of the commune system as a whole and specific information about the income and wage conditions and the governance and management of the communes. The second part deals with a poor commune in the northwest, which Snow first visited in 1937. Snow depicts a sharp contrast between the people in 1937 and in 1971 in terms of their achievements. A description of life in prosperous communes is given to show the diversity of conditions among China's communes. Snow contends in this report that agriculture was less affected by the Cultural Revolution than industry and that the influx of China's urban educated youth into the countryside was valuable for the peasants in terms of new talents and services that were made available. According to Snow, China's countryside will face difficulties as well as "broad vistas" in the future, which should "keep China fully occupied with peaceful work--carried out in a revolutionary way--until the year 2,000."

266 WASHENKO, Steve.
"Agriculture in Mainland China - 1968," Current Scene, Vol. VII, No. 6, March 31, 1969, pp. 1-12.
An assessment of China's agricultural production for 1968 is made by Washenko, an officer of the U. S. Department of Agriculture, stationed in Hong Kong. Washenko paints a picture of agriculture adversely affected by the Cultural Revolution: a decrease in irrigation and drainage work, a decrease in supply of fertilizers and pesticides, and a consequent decrease in China's total grain output as compared to 1967. Washenko argues that the Cultural Revolution was disruptive to agricultural policy and that the intervention of the military in the countryside attested to the worsened situation in rural areas. The upheaval also brought reforms to the rural communes: the reduction in the size of private plots, amalgamation of production units into larger collectives, and the work-point system as a symbol of egalitarian remuneration. Washenko compares data on crop production and food supply in China for 1967-68 with previous years.

267 WENMOHS, John R.
"Agriculture in Mainland China - 1967: Cultural Revolution versus Favorable Weather," Current Scene, Vol. V, No. 21, December 15, 1967, pp. 1-12.
Wenmohs portrays the sizable damage to the countryside, particularly in terms of a decline in grain production, that resulted from the Cultural Revolution. China's reduced agricultural production, rural procurement problems, and the reduced

149

supervisory capacity of rural cadres are analyzed to support the
contention that the upheaval did, indeed, interfere with agricultural production. The problem of peasant resistance to the
Cultural Revolution as long-held beliefs and practices were
attacked by Red Guards is also discussed. Peasant resistance
took the forms of looting grain from warehouses, dividing the
harvests among themselves, and stopping work on irrigation and
drainage maintenance.

268 WHEELWRIGHT, E. L., and MC FARLANE, Bruce.
The Chinese Road to Socialism: Economics of the Cultural
Revolution, Monthly Review Press, New York, 1970, 256p.
This is a study of China's political economy by two Australian
economists. Part one of the book deals with China's search for
a revolutionary strategy for modernization and construction of
an economic base. The slow agricultural development and the
problem of regionalism and decentralization of industry are
analyzed in discussing China's economic strategy prior to 1957.
The authors argue that the tendencies for self-reliance in
locally controlled factories and the strengthening of centrifu-
gal politics were the reasons for promoting provincial revolutionary committees during the Cultural Revolution. The second
portion of the book deals with the impact of the Cultural Revolution on economic policies. It presents all the main policy
approaches attributable to Mao and links Mao's views on "mass
technology" and "socialized incentives" to questions of planning, financing, and operating China's economy. The authors
list the reasons for the Maoists emphasis on moral incentives
and discuss features of these moral incentives. The final
portion of the book centers on the economic aspects of Maoist
strategy in terms of regional autarchy, notable changes in the
planning system brought about by the Cultural Revolution and the
need to achieve the correct ratio between agricultural and
industrial development. In the authors' opinion, the Chinese
road to socialism involves, not merely "the maximizing of economic growth," but a choice between making "socialism a mecha-
nism for forced growth" and considering "socialism as a way of
life." The authors conclude that socialism needs "an ideology
and an ethical framework" just as capitalism does.

269 WHYTE, Martin King.
"The Tachai Brigade and Incentives for the Peasant," Current
Scene, Vol. VII, No. 16, August 15, 1969, pp. 1-13.
In a case study of the model Tachai production brigade's rural
remuneration system, this article examines the work-point system
and the related problems of material incentives in revolutionary
China. Although much of the information for this study comes
from questionable sources, Chinese refugees in Hong Kong, the
analysis does shed light on the rural remuneration practices and
the work-point system. A comparison between the work-point
system in the communes before and after the Cultural Revolution
is given. The present work-point system is based on the model
instituted in the Tachai Brigade in 1966, which not only

simplified the recording procedure but also established a set of
abstract political criteria, such as one's devotion to public
service and one's degree for class and political consciousness,
for determining remuneration. The Tachai system is analyzed in
terms of dislocations in the lives and personal relationships
of the brigade members. Whyte raises questions about the implications of incentives for political activation and their effect
on labor morale.

270 WU, Yuan-li.
"Communist China's Economic Prospects and the Cultural Revolution," Contemporary China, Allan A. Spitz, ed., Washington State
University Press, Seattle and London, 1967, pp. 33-42.
Wu prefaces his analysis of China's economic prospects with the
proposition that the purpose of the Cultural Revolution was to
eliminate the bourgeois and capitalist influence in the cultural
and ideological superstructure. The article discusses the
phases of China's economic development from 1949 to 1965. It
emphasizes that by 1963-64, when the Socialist Education Movement was launched, there was a widespread utilization of methods
of private incentive and individual initiative in production.
The ideological revivalism embodied in the Socialist Education
Movement, a forerunner of the Cultural Revolution, provided the
occasion for a reexamination of these practices. Wu makes
different projections of China's economic prospects in terms of
the final outcome of the Cultural Revolution. A victory for
Mao in the aftermath of the upheaval would mean an economic
setback and instability. A victory for the pragmatic approach
to economic development would mean increases in production,
research and development, and possibly even a flow of foreign
economic assistance from the Soviet Union.

271 WU, Yuan-li.
"Economics, Ideology and the Cultural Revolution," Asian Survey,
Vol. VIII, No. 3, March 1968, pp. 223-245.
This article attempts to define the structure of Maoist economics by analyzing the Maoist attacks against Liu Shao-chi's
revisionism during the Cultural Revolution. Wu cites the following as main features of Maoist economics: the abolition of
private plots and all other forms of private ownership, the
elimination of material incentives and substitution of ideological incentives, low standards of personal consumption, and the
concept of industrialization by mass movement. Wu sees the
orthodox Soviet type of bureaucratically planned and administered system and Liu's pragmatic approach in the economic
recovery program as possible alternatives to Mao's strategy.

272 WU, Yuan-li.
"The Economy After Twenty Years," Communist China, 1949-1969:
A Twenty-year Appraisal, Frank N. Trager and William Henderson,
eds., New York University Press, New York, 1970, pp. 123-151.
Using Western economic tools, Wu makes an attempt to assess
China's economic policy and development strategy over a

151

twenty-year period. He deals with China's economic performance
in terms of goals and their fulfillment through policy and
strategy. The paper concludes that "too much haste in becoming
a great power, unquestioned and frequently misplaced faith in
the ideological appeals of communism, too little understanding
of the deep seated desire of the Chinese peasant and worker to
own some property, overconfidence on the part of the leaders in
their ability to adapt revolutionary military tactics to the
solution of economic problems, and undue reliance upon the
'fraternal goodwill' of the Soviet Union--these were the principal factors underlying China's economic failures." The paper
also lists some of the favorable factors for economic growth,
including the exploration and exploitation of iron ore and
petroleum, large capital stock of industrial plants, transportation facilities, and irrigation installations, and tremendous
expansion of the research and development industry.

CHAPTER VII

EDUCATIONAL REFORM, SCIENCE AND TECHNOLOGY,

ARTS AND SOCIAL LIFE

The entries included in this chapter are divided into three sections covering the relationship of the Cultural Revolution to educational reform, to policies and programs for science and technology, and to arts and social life. The Cultural Revolution, as pointed out in the introduction to the first chapter of this bibliography, was, among other things concerned with the Maoist vision of a good society. Since Max Weber's classic thesis on the Protestant ethic and the rise of capitalism, which described the development of a culture as a process of constantly increasing rationalization, contemporary scholars interested in political development and social change have stressed the importance of attitudes and values in the development process. It is, therefore, significant to note that the Cultural Revolution began with literary criticism and a wholesale revamping of the educational system.

A. EDUCATION

To many China experts, the greatest impact of the Cultural Revolution has been in the area of China's educational system. For education is a key to the Maoist vision of a good society, and basic to this vision is the need for "the world outlook"-- emphasis on social consciousness of a new proletarianism rather

than simply on industrialization. Thus, one of the themes for
the entries in Section A is the criticism of the educational
system prior to the Cultural Revolution in terms of faulty content and orientation as well as deficient facilities for rural
schools. Another theme analyzed is the issue of technical
education (elite) as opposed to proletarian education (mass).
A third theme is the Maoist concept of education which stresses
political ideology and physical labor. Other related topics
deal with economic necessity as a factor in educational reform,
changes in primary and secondary education, the expansion of
work-study programs, decentralization of educational administration in rural schools systems, changes in structure and content
of education, resettlement of urban school graduates, the low
level of training of technicians in rural areas, worker-peasant
colleges, the May 7th Cadre Schools, reform in medical education,
duration of schooling, change in university admission policy, the
question of quality in education, and, finally, the concept and
implementation of education as a tool for building a new socialist and egalitarian society.

B. SCIENCE AND TECHNOLOGY

It is generally recognized that in economic development
the choice of techniques is a critical factor in developing a
country's resources and potentials. The political upheaval and
the disarray on display in China during the Cultural Revolution
were but manifestations of the leadership's dispute over the
most appropriate approach and strategy to promote the regime's
economic and social goals. Many key issues of the Cultural

154

Revolution raised questions closely related to science and technology. To what extent should China follow the Soviet model for economic development? Should China adopt policies which rely on a mixture of modern technology and traditional methods, "walking on two legs"? What are the implications of restricting further growth of functional differentiation and specialization? Can the gap between manual and mental labor be narrowed so that "grass root technology" may be developed? Can the Chinese masses without formal scientific training make scientific and technological innovations in the productive process. Is there a role for advanced and theoretical research in China's technological development? Entries in Section B explore and analyze these questions while examining the evolution of Chinese policies on science and technology prior to and since the Cultural Revolution. Specifically, they discuss topics such as the rate and direction of technological change, the rationale for emphasizing the applied aspect of scientific research, the application of the principle of self-reliance to technological development, the role of modernization under an egalitarian framework and mass participation in technological innovation, the state of scientific education in universities and research institutions, the rise of a new kind of expert in China, the implication of collectivization of knowledge in China since the Cultural Revolution, the interplay of technology and ideology, effects of reform in eliminating elitism from scientific and technological activities, and, lastly, the impact of the Cultural Revolution on China's scientific and technological development in terms of shifts in

155

policy emphasis and organizational changes.

C. <u>ARTS AND SOCIAL LIFE</u>

The last section for this chapter includes annoted items about the politics of reform in Peking opera in terms of transmitting Maoist values and ideology. New development in popular theatre during and since the Cultural Revolution as well as drama techniques are discussed in several entries. Other items deal with topics such as the emancipation of women, the impact of the Cultural Revolution on Buddhism, and life in a commune at the time of the upheaval by a participating cadre and a visitor's impression of daily life in China.

A. EDUCATIONAL REFORMS

273 BASTID, Marrianne.
"Economic Necessity and Political Ideals in Educational Reform During the Cultural Revolution," The China Quarterly, No. 42, April-June 1970, pp. 16-45.
Bastid reviews criticisms of the educational system prior to the Cultural Revolution: inadequate school enrollment and faulty content, method and general orientation of the old system. Reform proposals for education during the Cultural Revolution are analyzed to show that these reforms were related to the economic needs of the country. For instance, China needed versatile people because jobs did not fall exactly within the scope of special training and because the young had to be able to adapt to a variety of situations. Most of the reform proposals in primary and secondary education in rural areas were concerned with control of the schools by the production brigades, based on economic considerations: "The brigade could benefit immediately from the help of the schools in such difficult tasks as accounts; later on, the new type of school graduate would meet local needs better." The author concludes that the Cultural Revolution has opened the way for "a really new education" which is based on the mass line of the Yenan period and of the Great Leap. These reforms in education meet both political ideas and economic necessities for building a new nation.

274 CHEN, Theodore Hsi-en.
"Education in Communist China," Communist China, 1949-1969: A Twenty-year Appraisal, Frank N. Trager and William Henderson, eds., New York University Press, New York, 1970, pp. 175-198.
This essay discusses a variety of topics dealing with China's education: characteristics of the system, form and content of education prior to 1966, types of schools in China, party control over educational development, and significant achievements in education, such as the language reform and worker-peasant education. The paper also points out the shortcomings of China's educational system in terms of the dominance of politics and the distrust of intellectuals. The Cultural Revolution extended political interference in education to such an extent that the upheaval must be considered "disruptive and destructive." The reform programs in education launched during and since the Cultural Revolution involved a shortening of the schooling period and the downgrading of the prestige and authority of the intelligentsia. The concluding portion of the paper raises questions about the impact of the reduced number of students receiving training for the future, the value of increased political and ideological content in the curricula, the long run effects of the neglect in training and the education necessary for nation-building.

275 CHU, Hung-ti.
"Education in Mainland China," Current History, Vol. 59,

No. 349, September 1970, pp. 165-182.
This essay first describes the characteristics of the educational system prior to 1966, when the Cultural Revolution began in earnest. China's education then was characterized by ideological indoctrination, the expansion of the work-study program, the teaching of technical subjects in regular schools, the establishment of research institutes and the rapid enrollment in schools. In higher education, universities and colleges were reorganized into general or composite and polytechnical institutions. Technical colleges specializing in one subject area were created and the comprehensive higher education concept was rejected. The Soviet system of education for China was abandoned in 1958 when the half-work and half-study program was introduced in both rural and urban areas. This paper points out that the issue of technical education requiring the acquisition of hard knowledge versus proletarian education of half-work and half-study was one of the key controversies in the dispute between the Maoists and Liu Shao-chi on the eve of the Cultural Revolution. Chu gives a brief review of the events in the 1966-67 educational crisis, which finally led to a near collapse of the entire Chinese educational system. The restoration of China's education system after 1968 bore the imprint of Mao's ideas on educational reform: emphasis on political education; integration of workers, peasants and soldiers with students in schools and universities; and stress on development of skills in farming and industrial labor, rather than in the academic and intellectual pursuits. Other topics discussed in the article are the decentralization of the educational administration, reform in university admissions policies, and an overall evaluation of China's educational reform and its implication for the future in terms of modernization.

276   CURRENT SCENE, The Editor.
"Educational Reform in Rural China," Vol. VII, No. 3, February 8, 1969, pp. 1-17.
This report about rural secondary schools as models for educational reform in China during the Cultural Revolution is based on Chinese media reports. It deals with the structure and content of the new educational policy for rural areas. Primary education became the basis of rural education, with the commune or production brigade responsible for planning, financing and administering the programs. Under the reform, the control of provincial middle schools has been taken away from the professional educators and placed in the hands of peasants and party representatives. Priority in enrollment for middle schools is given to students from poor and lower-middle peasant families. In terms of curriculum, academic subjects have been eliminated and replaced by ideology, basic practical training, and actual physical labor. Thus, the most important aspect of educational reform for rural China has been the radical change in the content of education which now stresses political ideology and physical labor, not improvement of educational opportunities for rural youth.

277 CURRENT SCENE, The Editor.
"Education Reform and Rural Settlement in Communist China,"
Vol. VIII, No. 17, November 7, 1970, pp. 1-7.
This article summarizes the factors which have influenced the
education system from 1949 to 1966: the large surplus of urban
school graduates, the low level of training of technicians in
rural areas, the traditional attitude toward physical labor, and
the mistrust of intellectuals by some top leaders. Resettlement
of urban school graduates became a major program during the
Cultural Revolution. Reform in primary and middle school education in rural areas was centered on two points: (1) the change
to decentralized administration and funding at the commune
brigade level, and (2) heavy emphasis on the study of political
ideology and on student participation in farm labor. These
reforms, according to this paper, seem to be suited to fulfill
the regime's goals, but the conflict between de-elitism and
technological progress is still unresolved.

278 FRASER, Stewart E., and HAWKINS, John N.
"Chinese Education: Revolution and Development," Phi Delta
Kappan, April 1972, pp. 487-500.
This comprehensive study of the revolution and development in
Chinese education is arranged in four parts. Part one gives a
brief sketch of China's educational policies and the problems
of planning for educational development prior to the Cultural
Revolution, particularly reforms introduced during the Great
Leap period of 1958 to 1960 and the Socialist Education movement
of 1962-65. According to the authors, the Cultural Revolution
was intended to introduce drastic reform into education at all
levels so that the distinction between mental and manual labor
would be eliminated, resulting in the emergence of a "new
homogenized man." Part two of this study deals with the rationale for the new directives which called for the abolition of
the examination system, a reduced curricula, and de-emphasis of
theoretical research. A comprehensive chart which shows clearly
the major changes in China's education system from the 1960's to
the 1970's is presented in the study. Mao's educational goals
underlying the reform measures introduced during the Cultural
Revolution are also analyzed. Part three gives a detailed
description of China's education for the post-Cultural Revolution era from pre-school through higher education. The final
section presents a case study of new models in education: the
worker-peasant colleges, such as the Shanghai Machine Tool Plant
for technical education; a reformed medical education for
"barefoot" doctors; and the May 7th Cadre Schools for the reeducation of party and government bureaucrats.

279 FRASER, Stewart E., and HSU, Kuang-liang.
Chinese Education and Society: A Bibliographic Guide, International Arts and Sciences Press, Inc., White Plains, N. Y.,
1972, 204p.
This is a bibliographic guide on Chinese education in all of its
aspects, primary, secondary, teacher training, higher education,

agricultural education, international relations education, educational development and the Cultural Revolution, and Mao's educational thought. Sources for the items in this bibliographic guide are derived predominantly English and Chinese language publications, with some from Japanese, French, German, and Italian publications. Several sections of the bibliographic guide are worth noting: a list of general reference tools on the People's Republic of China, a general survey of recent works on China, and a list of major works on the Cultural Revolution. The bulk of the entries listed in the guide deal with Chinese education.

280 GARDNER, John, and IDEMA, Wilt.
"China's Educational Revolution," Authority, Participation and Cultural Change in China, Stuart R. Schram, ed., Cambridge University Press, Cambridge, 1973, pp. 257-289.
This essay is concerned with the reorganization of primary and secondary formal education institutions for the young during and since the Cultural Revolution. Problems for rural primary and secondary schools before the Cultural Revolution included: (1) schools were often located only in heavily populated areas or in towns and the largest villages, forcing children from remote or sparsely populated areas to travel long distances, (2) middle, or secondary, schools were the preserve of the able and those willing to be boarders, (3) school time tables disregarded local conditions and agricultural cycles, and (4) state subsidies often went only to big schools in towns and large villages. Examples are given to show the development of a new educational policy designed to ameliorate these problems. Primary schools are now run by the production brigades, while the communes administer middle schools. School courses have been shortened so that primary education can be completed in five years, with two additional years each for junior and senior middle school. The curriculum is designed to impart knowledge of immediate applicability, and young teachers recruited for the schools often have a low cultural level and lack teacher training. The authors believe that Chinese educational reform since the Cultural Revolution constitutes a rational approach for solving some of the cultural problems facing many countries of the world. The article discusses the desirability of imparting practical knowledge to students and the need to enable the peasants to make changes through a rational system of dissemination of knowledge. The authors conclude that the reformed Chinese educational system is designed to give a basic and useful education to all, which should contribute to rapid modernization of an essentially agrarian society.

281 HAWKINS, John N.
Educational Theory in the People's Republic of China: The Report of Chien Chun-jui, Asian Studies at Hawaii No. 6, University of Hawaii Press, Honolulu, 1971, 120p.
This study discusses the theoretical controversy in China over the type of education that the regime should implement: an elite

education or a mass education. Hawkins examines the theoretical
background of China's educational system and the problems that
it has encountered. The Cultural Revolution was one of the many
attempts made to resolve the key issue of elite versus mass
education. The accomplishment of the Cultural Revolution was to
once again emphasize Mao's approach to education: the need to
provide education for the workers and peasants, the need to
combine theory and practice, and the need to develop middle-
level technicians. The study contains a translation of a report
of the former vice minister for education in China, Chien
Chun-jui.

282 MAC DOUGALL, Colina.
"Education in China: Bringing Up Baby," Far Eastern Economic
Review, January 30, 1969, pp. 194-195.
This is a report on the drastic changes made in the educational
system by the Cultural Revolution. It describes the changes in
the rural education system brought about by the state's turning
over management of the schools to the production brigades in the
communes. Urban education reform involved workers in the factories administering the schools. According to the author, the
purpose for decentralization in education was financial rather
than ideological--it reduced the burden on the central government. Decentralization also gave the local party committee
control over education.

283 MACHETZKI, Rudiger.
"China's Education Since the Cultural Revolution," The Political
Quarterly, Vol. 45, No. 1, January-March 1974, pp. 59-74.
Basically this is an evaluation of Chinese education since 1966.
The key controversy in the struggle for education reform on the
eve of the Cultural Revolution was over the retention of the
half-work and half-study program versus emphasis on the acquisition of academic knowledge and academic performance. Machetzki
analyzes criticisms directed at other related educational policy
matters, such as the development of selected primary and secondary schools, the lack of support for rural schools, and the
university admission policy which tended to favor better academ-
ically prepared school students. Models of reformed educational
institutions, introduced during the Cultural Revolution, were
based on the principle of "the unity of theory and practice"
and the work-study concept. Essential elements of educational
reform, such as the abolition of the examination system, a practical curricula, and emphasis on political education, are also
discussed. The results of the reform in education have been to
extend education facilities in the rural villages of poor and
lower-middle class peasants, to provide more local funding for
primary schools in villages, and to integrate labor and learning
in schools. Machetzki concludes that there is at present a
healthier balance between rural and urban educational requirements. But despite the reforms, the educational system still
falls far short of the objectives of the revolutionary cadres
and students.

284 MUNRO, Donald J.
"Egalitarian Ideal and Educational Fact in Communist China,"
China: Management of a Revolutionary Society, John M. Lindbeck,
ed., University of Washington Press, Seattle and London, 1971,
pp. 256-301.
This paper investigates the use of China's educational system as
a tool to implement the egalitarian ideal espoused by Mao. The
paper questions whether it is possible to have egalitarian
education without some dilution in the quality of the education
which is so essential for developing scientific and technological skills in the modernizing process. The paper examines the
educational issues of centralization and decentralization,
egalitarianism and quality education, education and labor,
political indoctrination and man power needs. According to
Munro, the Maoist approach to education is intended to meet
local needs, particularly those of the rural areas, through the
school system and curricula. Mao's educational policies have a
heavy value content aimed at the realization of a revolutionary
and egalitarian society.

285 ONG, Ellen K.
"Education in China Since the Cultural Revolution," Studies in
Comparative Communism, Vol. 3, Nos. 3-4, July-October 1970,
pp. 158-176.
This article discusses the control agencies formed during the
Cultural Revolution which were responsible for the implementation of Mao's October 1968 directive for a new program of
worker-peasant run schools. These agencies were: the Worker
Mao Tse-tung Thought Propaganda Teams; the Poor and Lower Middle
Peasant Mao Thought Propaganda Teams and the Street Mao Thought
Propaganda Teams. A detailed analysis is given in this paper
on the goals of worker-peasant run schools, propaganda teams'
management of schools and support of these teams given by the
military stationed in the schools. The article also discusses
changes brought about in students, teachers, and course content
by the propaganda teams.

286 PEPPER, Susan.
"Education and Political Development in Communist China,"
Studies in Comparative Communism, Vol. 3, Nos. 3-4, July-
October 1970, pp. 132-157.
A large part of this article is devoted to a discussion of
educational changes since 1949 and the reform measures undertaken to meet the demands of the Cultural Revolution. Pepper
argues that most of the educational reforms introduced during
the Cultural Revolution, such as revision of university entrance
requirements, increase in physical labor, and the shortening of
years of schooling, are related to the general problems of
building a socialist society. These problems include the need
for setting up a system of mass education, the expense of building academic institutions in the rural areas, the unemployment
among educated groups, and the "growing divergence, over time,
between the values and goals of the student-age population and

162

those of the older generation responsible for making and implementing education policy." The existence of these problems
reflects both "a blend of ideological predispositions and a
pragmatic concern for scarce resource investment in education."

287 REECE, Bob.
"Education in China: More of the Same," Far Eastern Economic
Review, June 13, 1968, pp. 563-565.
This is a visitor's account of the state of China's primary and
secondary education when schools were ordered to reopen during
the Cultural Revolution. A picture of secondary schooling prior
to the Cultural Revolution is presented in terms of curriculum
content, enrollment, and compensation for teachers. The author
describes conditions at a senior middle school in Peking in
1968. Comparisons are given in education between these two
periods to show some of the changes introduced as a result of
the Cultural Revolution.

B. SCIENCE AND TECHNOLOGY

288 DEAN, Genevieve.
"China's Technological Development," New Scientist, May 18, 1972,
pp. 371-373.
In this article Dean discusses China's technological development
in terms of China's stress on the principle of self-reliance,
which governs China's aid and trade relations with the rest of
the world. Since the principle of self-reliance does appeal to
developing countries, Dean explores the applicability of China's
means for economic development to countries with different
systems and objectives. She presents a summary of findings from
the University of Sussex, Science Policy Research Unit: "The
consensus of participants on both sides was that science and
technology in China cannot be examined apart from the social,
economic, political and ideological setting in which scientific
activities and technological development are pursued." The
origin of China's policy and experience of "walking on two
technological legs" are examined in this article. The Cultural
Revolution strongly stressed the policy of local self-reliance
in that "the initiative and all the material and labor resources for a local enterprise must (ideally) be found by the
county, commune or city neighborhood committee." Dean presents
arguments to show that policies adopted during the Cultural
Revolution which may seem irrational, such as the closing of
universities for three years when China needed qualified
scientists, were quite rational; the skills and knowledge of
the university graduates were more sophisticated than required
by "the relatively simple technological base in all but the
State-owned sector of the economy." Dean concludes that the
Chinese and the rest of the developing countries have the same
development goals, but other countries differ "in the social,
economic, and political means available to Chinese policy-
makers to acquire modern technologies and apply them to the
development objectives."

289 DEAN, Genevieve.
"Science, Technology and Development: China as a Case Study,"
The China Quarterly, No. 51, July-September 1972, pp. 520-534.
This is one participant's summary of discussions by the Sussex
Study Group on Science and Technology in China's development.
According to Dean, Chinese technological policies, which emerged
as a result of changes brought about by the Cultural Revolution,
resemble those of the 1958 Great Leap. That is the policies
call for a strategy of "walking on two legs," or technological
development in both traditional and modern sectors of industry
and the economy. The article provides information on the rate
and direction of technological change and the sources of such
change. Dean concludes that Chinese research programs are
essentially applied and are undertaken in the Academy of
Sciences and in ministry institutes. According to Dean, one
aim of the Cultural Revolution was to make scientific-technical
skill development indistinguishable from production by linking
specialized institutions with production.

290 DEAN, Genevieve.
Science and Technology in the Development of Modern China: An
Annotated Bibliography, Mensell Information/Publishing, Limited,
London, 1974, 265p.
This is a most comprehensive bibliography on the subject of
science, technology and development in relation to the role of
technological advances in economic and social development in
China. The bibliography was originally compiled for a study
group at the University of Sussex in January 1972. It contains
a total of 944 entries, arranged into the following subject
headings: technology and economic growth, technology policy,
science policy, scientific activities and technology in China.
Author indices are arranged according to primary, secondary
and tertiary material.

291 LEE, Rensselaer W., III.
"The Politics of Technology in Communist China," Ideology and
Politics in Contemporary China, Chalmers Johnson, ed.,
University of Washington Press, Seattle and London, 1973,
pp. 301-325.
This paper is concerned with the relationship between technical
democracy, or mass participation in the technological sphere,
and the economic objectives of China's leaders. It gives a
brief description of the evolution of China's technological
policies. According to Lee, Mao's ideology development is
primarily concerned with the role of modernization within an
egalitarian framework "by emphasizing that the masses are intel-
ligent participants in the building of a new China, not passive
objects of manipulation from above." The paper points out that
the Chinese have repudiated the western concept that theoretical
science and modern technology require professionally based
scientific training. The Chinese adhere to the concept of
technological innovation. They view mass participation, without
formal scientific training, in technological innovation as a way

164

in which "native elements" might be incorporated into a modern industrial state: "Distinctively native technical reference works and machines or product designs, reflecting the 'rich experiences' of the masses in production, may become the source of new hierarchies in Chinese economic life."

292 LINDBECK, John M. H.
"An Isolationist Science Policy," China After the Cultural Revolution, A Selection from Bulletin of the Atomic Scientists, Vol. XXV, No. 2, February 1969, Vintage Books, New York, 1970, pp. 181-195.
This paper presents a picture of scientific and technical exchange between China and the rest of the world and the impact of the Cultural Revolution on this exchange. The Cultural Revolution brought the programs of exchange to a standstill. A program for purchasing modern equipment was begun with Japan, Europe, North America and Asia following the withdrawal of the Soviet Union's aid to China. Lindbeck concludes that the re-opening of scientific and intellectual activities between China and the rest of the world will require the lowering of the political temperature in China.

293 LUBKIN, Gloria B.
"Physics in China," Physics Today, December 1972, pp. 23-28.
This is a summary of the impressions on the state of China's physics, gathered by a delegation of United States scientists who visited many scientific research institutions and universities in China during 1971. China has made remarkable progress in applied physics, according to Lubkin. This report provides insights about China's universities and the scientific education offered by them since the Cultural Revolution. Examples of topics covered include: admissions policies to higher education and the remedial work provided for those lacking sufficient academic preparation, the university's role in applied industrial research for neighboring factories, and the use of sophisticated instruments at higher educational institutions.

294 OLDHAM, C. H. G.
"Science Travels the Mao Road," China After The Cultural Revolution, A Selection from Bulletin of the Atomic Scientists, Vol. XXV, No. 2, February 1969, Vintage Books, New York, 1970, pp. 219-228.
This essay gives a brief sketch of the struggle which took place within the Chinese Academy of Sciences during the Cultural Revolution. Criticisms leveled against the academy included: (1) promoting research by worshipping foreign ideas and by engaging in theoretical matters, and (2) creating a special privileged class of scientists in society. Disputes over the policies for science and the way science should serve the national goals are analyzed and illustrated in case studies of atomic energy development and the choice of technology for agriculture. Liu Shao-chi is described here as the one who opposed the development of the atomic bomb as a waste of China's

165

resources when China could have relied on the Soviet Union's protection. Mao is said to advocate a "walking on two legs" policy for agricultural mechanization: use whatever modern technique is available but employ less modern and more labor-intensive techniques. Finally, the essay points out that the sharpest divergence between Mao and Liu has been over educational policies--Mao preferring more political and ideological education and Liu advocating emphasis on scientific and technical education.

295 OLDHAM, C. H. G.
"Technology in China: Science for the Masses?," Far Eastern Economic Review, May 16, 1968, pp. 353-355.
This article discusses the controversy over emphasis on grass root technology for the masses versus more advanced research. The author briefly reviews China's policy on science and technology before the Cultural Revolution. The struggle against scientific leaders who supported Liu Shao-chi during the Cultural Revolution is described in detail to illustrate the violent struggle that took place in China. Oldham concludes that "one result of the Cultural Revolution has been an apparent change in priorities--with more of China's scientists switched to working on projects of immediate relevance to China's development needs. This will be a loss to world science and the freedom of some of China's scientists, but overall it may be a gain for China's development."

296 OLDHAM, C. H. G.
"Science and Technology Policies," China's Developmental Experience, Michel Oksenberg, ed., The Academy of Political Science, Columbia University, Praeger Publishers, New York, Washington, and London, 1973, pp. 80-94.
This paper summarizes China's science policies within the context of science and technology as tools for development. Chinese scientific organizations were originally modeled on the Russian system with the Academies of Science, Agricultural Sciences and Medical Sciences operating their own research institutions and carrying out most of the advanced research in China; few universities carried out advanced research. The 1958 Great Leap program changed these original policies, which were closely tied in with central planning priorities, to policies which emphasized innovations from peasants and workers to solve immediate practical problems. The Cultural Revolution made it necessary to de-emphasize foreign influence in the development of science and technology. A brief survey of the status of scientific and technological development in industry, agriculture, medicine and defense is made to reveal the reforms introduced since the Cultural Revolution. Oldham concludes that if Mao could not make communists out of the experts, then he at least wanted to make "a new kind of expert of the communists." The Cultural Revolution, then, must be seen as Mao's attempt to arrest the widening disparity between manual and mental labor in China. However, Oldham questions whether a country can be

166

modernized in the long run without a technocratic elite.

297 SCIENCE FOR THE PEOPLE.
China: Science Walks on Two Legs, Avon Books, New York, 1974,
316p.
This is a report of a visit to China in February 1973 by a
delegation of American scientists, organized as Science for the
People. The report begins with the delegation's visit to a
commune on the Red Flag Canal in north China and the insights
revealed by the peasants' achievement in building this canal and
overcoming scientific and technological obstacles through the
determination and the will of the people. Their visits and
interviews at agricultural communes, industrial plants, research
institutions, health care and mental health program facilities,
and schools revealed how the Chinese people, the masses, have
participated in the solution to their problems of modernizing
China through the application of science and technology, always
in human terms. The final section of the report deals with the
political theory underlying Chinese application of science:
"Science, for the Chinese people is a methodology, a way of
acting upon and understanding their world, so it must be shared
by all the members of the society if they are all to be free.
Knowledge is power. Those who possess it will control themselves and their world. The collectivization of knowledge is,
therefore, as fundamental to the Chinese as the collectivization
of material production."

298 SHIH, Joseph Anderson.
"Science and Technology in China," Asian Survey, Vol. XII,
No. 8, August 1972, pp. 662-675.
This is a general survey of the development of science and technology in China over the past two decades to provide an "understanding of the interplay of technology and ideology." One
section presents a summary and statistical analysis of the major
achievements of science and technology in China since 1960.
China's success in science and technology after 1960, the year
China ceased relying on Soviet technical aid, was due to a
number of factors: educational reform based on the integration
of theory and practice, utilization of foreign research, special
treatment of scientists, emphasis on both "red and expert," the
sharing of technological knowledge in the countryside through
massive dispersal of technical personnel during and since the
Cultural Revolution. Shih finds that there is a special concern
about the influence of science and technology by the party, as
evidenced by the debate, discussion, and criticism about the
role of science in a modernizing society. With over seventy
percent of China's university students enrolled in scientific
and technological fields, the influence of scientists will
continue to grow in the future.

299 SIGNER, Ethan, and GALSTON, Arthur W.
"Education and Science in China," Science, Vol. 175, No. 4017,
January 7, 1972, pp. 15-23.

The theme of this report by two scientists who visited China in
May 1971 is that the Chinese are searching for new ways to
closely integrate scientific research with the needs of industries and agriculture. A section of the report deals with the
impact of the Cultural Revolution on education and the reasons
for reform. Another section discusses the organization and
reform of China's universities in terms of admissions policy,
decentralized administration, and curriculum changes. The new
role of the intellectuals, not as elites but as individuals who
serve the masses, is revealed in the report through conversations with Chinese scientists and professors. The report points
out that the one change which will have long-term effects on
science in China is the decision to devote time and effort to
applied scientific research rather than to basic research. This
research policy often involves scientists working in factories
or communes. Another important change reported is the shifting
of medical care facilities and personnel from cities to the
countryside as a way of correcting the inequities that existed
prior to the Cultural Revolution. The report concludes that
"potentially the most far-reaching reform is the attempt to
eliminate elitism from scientific, technical, and intellectual
activity. The priorities and attitudes of scientists may
already be affected by the emphasis on workers and peasants, or
practical common sense knowledge, and on 'serving the people.'"

300 SUTTMEIER, Richard P.
"Science Policy Shifts, Organizational Change and China's
Development," The China Quarterly, No. 62, June 1975,
pp. 207-241.
Suttmeier analyzes the evolution of China's science policy and
organization since 1949. He classifies China's "science
system," defined as "an interrelated set of organizations that
pertain to science," into models, each corresponding to the
periodization in China's development process. From 1949 to
1957 was the period of Soviet influence when Chinese science
policy was based on the Soviet Union's model, or in Suttmeier's
classification, "the professional and bureaucratic model."
Next came the period of the Great Leap Forward during 1957-61
when the "mobilization model" of science development emerged.
The policy for this period was that "scientific development is
a function of social and economic factors external to science
itself." The "mobilization model" was followed by a return to
the "professional and bureaucratic model," which corresponded to
the period of consolidation and rationalization of 1961-66.
During this period the party and government adopted the policy
of managing science development by rational organization, not
by mass movement. Finally, the Cultural Revolution returned
China once again to the "mobilization model." Suttmeier takes
the position that key issues of the Cultural Revolution were
related to science and technology: "Questions of national
defense, industrial and agricultural strategies, and the
cultural transformation of the Chinese masses, all impinge upon
science policy." Suttmeier analyzes the impact of the Cultural

Revolution on Chinese scientific and technological development
in terms of organizational changes and policy emphasis and
shifts. These policy emphasis and shifts have been functional
in science development for China, according to Suttmeier, in
that the "competing models for the organization and administration of science have contributed significantly, and in a way no
single model could, to meeting the systemic requisites for the
establishment of an indigenous science system in the service of
production."

301 UNGER, Jonathan.
"Mao's Million Amateur Technicians," Far Eastern Economic
Review, April 3, 1971, pp. 115-118.
This article examines the Chinese efforts to decentralize
industries and to transfer technicians for work in rural areas
and small factories in the communes. By using reports and
stories disseminated in the Chinese media, Unger describes
China's determination to place technical advances under the
control of workers and peasants. A concerted effort has been
made to train blue-collar workers in middle schools, factories,
and universities to become engineers. Local county authorities
sponsor basic training classes for developing technical skills
among the peasants and rural laborers. Mass, low-level,
technical training and education as a preparatory step to
developing a highly specialized corps of experts for China has
been the major emphasis since the Cultural Revolution.

C. ARTS, LITERATURE, AND SOCIAL LIFE

302 AHN, Byung-joon.
"The Politics of Peking Opera, 1962-1965," Asian Survey,
Vol. XII, No. 12, December 1972, pp. 1066-1081.
The focus of this essay is on the debate over Peking opera
reform between the Shanghai radicals and adherents of the Peking
orthodoxy that took place during 1962-65. A background discussion of the attacks by young art and literary critics on the
party's policy toward cultural reform in the early 1960's is
given. The significance of Chiang Ching's campaign in Shanghai
for the revolutionization of Peking opera in 1963-64 is analyzed
to show that the disagreement was not only over artistic expression but also over the substantive content of opera. Chiang
Ching's prominent role in the controversy is detailed. A
sequence of events is reconstructed describing the rectification
campaign and purge launched by the radicals to bring about
reform in culture, a key issue of the revolution.

303 CHEN, Jack.
A Year in Upper Felicity: Life in a Chinese Village during the
Cultural Revolution, Macmillan Company, New York and London,
1973, 383p.
Chen, formerly a cartoonist and an associate editor for the
English edition of The Peking Review, presents his personal
account of daily life in a rural village from his experiences

as a hsia-fang (downward transfer) cadre in a commune for six
months in 1968. He describes the method of selecting cadres to
be sent down to the commune in the midst of the Cultural Revolution, the feelings and reactions of the cadres and their
families who had to endure hardships in the commune, and their
reception by the village and their relations with the villagers.
Detailed information is given about the work and hard physical
labor shared with other members of the commune and how the
cadres coped with the problems of unfamiliar life in the village.
Chen vividly portrays the daily life of the commune members and
their children, who remain subject, to a large extent, to the
influence of their parents, particularly in matters of marriage
through matchmakers. In the final chapters, Chen describes how
the cadres were transformed by the hard physical labor and their
experiences in the commune.

304 FOKKEMA, D. W.
"Maoist Ideology and Its Exemplification in the New Peking
Opera," Current Scene, Vol. X, No. 8, August 1972, pp. 13-20.
This essay deals with the changes that have taken place in
Chinese drama, particularly the Peking opera, since the Cultural
Revolution by focusing on the transformation, from opera to
revolutionary ballet, of the drama entitled The White-Haired
Girl. The 1966 libretto is compared to the 1950 opera text to
illustrate the inclusion of Mao's ideology in modern Peking
opera. Moreover, it is through the medium of modern Peking
opera and ballet that the new ethics of the party, class
struggle and revolutionary fervor, are inculcated in the minds
of the populace. The paper also discusses the influence of
Chiang Ching in the introduction of contemporary themes into
the model theatrical works during and since the Cultural
Revolution. Political themes, personified by operatic heroes,
have become predominant in all the model works being performed
in China today, both on stage and in films. Fokkema concludes
that "Maoism was chosen for a proletarian literature, for the
combination of revolutionary idealism and revolutionary romanticism, and for the description of what is as it ought to be."

305 HUANG, Joe C.
Heroes and Villains in Communist China: The Contemporary Chinese
Novel as a Reflection of Life, C. Hurst, London, 1973, 345p.
This is a study of twenty-five of the most important novels
published in China since 1949. In his study Huang describes
and analyzes the behavior of the heroes and villains depicted
in these Chinese novels. The main purpose of the study is to
examine the literature as a social document of the regime and
fiction as a social-political history. Unfortunately, almost
two-thirds of the novels selected for study deal with pre-1949
communist experience. The book also contains a bibliographical
index for reference.

306 HUANG, Lucy Jen.
"The Role of Religion in Communist Chinese Society," Asian

170

Survey, Vol. XI, No. 7, July 1971, pp. 693-708.
Although this study describes the religious movement in China
before 1949, a large part of the paper deals with the attitude
of the communist regime toward religion and religious elements
during the Cultural Revolution. Huang's analysis points out
that Chinese communist policy toward religion had been, for the
most part, confusing and inconsistent. The author views the
Red Guards in the Cultural Revolution as performing "the role
of missionaries and disciples of the religious movement." The
spirituality of the Long March, the adulation of Mao as a sage,
and pilgrimage to Mao's birthplace are ingredients for a religious experience. Huang argues further that "the participation
in the Red Guard movement resembled for many youth, an adoles-
cent religious conversion experience." The Cultural Revolution
contains many religious dimensions, in the tactics used and
ideology preached, even though the state professes to be opposed
to religion and superstition.

307 LEADER, Shelah Gilbert.
"The Emancipation of Chinese Women," World Politics, Vol. XXVI,
No. 1, October 1973, pp. 55-79.
This is a study of China's policy toward women in terms of the
various theories advanced at various times by the leaders representing competing factions. Specific topics discussed include:
the change from feudal to democratic marriage, the release of
women for productive labor since the Great Leap, and the new
role and image of women. The article presents the thesis that
the issue about the status and role of women was one on which
disagreement existed between Mao and Liu Shao-chi. Mao is
depicted in this article as one concerned about "the continued
oppression of women," while Liu Shao-chi is depicted as one
representing the "reactionary line." A detailed analysis is
given to show the divergent views of Mao and Liu on the emancipation of Chinese women. Leader also explores the question of
whether Chinese women are still considered "inferior to men."
Emancipation of women in China, Leader concludes, "has always
been subordinated to economic and political priorities." Women
can gain equality with men if allowed to engage fully in socialist activities. She sees Mao taking the view that "a meaningful
liberation of women cannot be imposed from above" since "sexist
beliefs and values persist in the face of economic, social and
political change." Thus, "women will be truly equal only in the
period of full communism."

308 MACCIOCCHI, Maria Antonetta.
Daily Life in Revolutionary China, Monthly Review Press, New
York and London, 1972, 506p.
This book is a visitor's account of life in China in 1970. The
topics covered touch upon various aspects of social life in
China affected by the Cultural Revolution. Chapters on the
Cultural Revolution in the universities, the May 7th Cadre
Schools, the Cultural Revolution in Shanghai and Tientsin,
factory life changed by the Cultural Revolution, technical

171

innovation and models for industrialization, peasant conditions
and the Cultural Revolution in the countryside, and the emancipation of women give a vivid picture of life in China. Much of
the book reports direct verbatim conversations with the Chinese
interviewed by the author.

309 MACKERRAS, Colin.
"Chinese Opera After the Cultural Revolution (1970-1972),"
The China Quarterly, No. 55, July-September 1973, pp. 478-510.
This essay discusses the Chinese theory of drama in light of the
Cultural Revolution. Three current Peking operas, as revised to
meet the ideological demands of the Cultural Revolution, are
selected for discussion to show the application of contemporary
ideological and theoretical messages to drama. Difficulties in
"popularizing" the revised model dramas are analyzed. Implications of the new developments during and since the Cultural
Revolution in Chinese opera, such as the regional theatre,
travelling troupes in the countryside, and amateur theatre are
also included. Mackerras sees "signs of similarity with the
pre-1966 period" in the music and the variety of operas. However, the Cultural Revolution has produced changes in the
ideological approach to theatre and has resulted in more dis-
criminating application of historical tradition to drama. In
fact, Mackerras thinks that the Cultural Revolution has channelled the ability of the masses into good, creative theatre:
"Indeed the heavy stress on mass involvement in the theatre
could easily lead, in the long run, to a more universal flower-
ing and the production of a folk theatre finer than anything
China's past can offer."

310 SNOW, Lois Wheeler.
China on Stage: An American Actress in the People's Republic,
Vintage Books, New York, 1973, 328p.
This book on China's drama was written by the wife of Edgar
Snow, an actress on the New York stage. In the introduction,
Lois Snow describes the development of Peking opera through the
ages and devotes considerable time to the evolution of post-
liberation Peking opera. Her main focus is on the transformation of the Peking opera during the Cultural Revolution. Mao's
1942 talks on literature and art at Yenan are analyzed in view
of the 1966 reforms in Peking opera. Five examples of popular,
modern Peking operas are presented in translation with explana-
tory introductions for each. The last chapter of the book
describes staging techniques and theatre construction used in
do-it-yourself versions of Peking opera which are suitable for
any occasion and for any place, village, school, or factory.

311 WELCH, Holmes.
"Buddhism Since the Cultural Revolution," The China Quarterly,
No. 40, October-December 1969, pp. 127-136.
Prior to the Cultural Revolution, the Chinese Buddhist leaders
suffered a number of setbacks in their many efforts to be useful
as an instrument of Chinese foreign policy. Welch gives an

account of the Chinese failure to win leadership in the World
Fellowship of Buddhists, to improve relations with Asian
Buddhist countries, and to pacify Tibet through the use of
Buddhism. When the Cultural Revolution began, in the summer of
1966, Buddhist organizations in China became a prime target for
attack by the Red Guards. Welch describes the situation that
existed during 1966-68 when all Buddhist temples were closed
and monks and nuns were sent back to their villages for productive labor. Patronage to temples had ceased entirely by 1967.
Based on Welch's interviews with visitors to China, however,
some monks from a number of illustrious monasteries appeared to
be living as communities of monks and to be working in the
communes during 1968-69. Welch concludes that religious policy
in China is still in a fluid state.

312 WILKINSON, Endymion.
Translations of The People's Comic Book, Anchor Press, New York,
1973, 272p.
This is a selection of Chinese comics with the Chinese captions
translated into English. Popular Peking opera pieces, both old
favorites and productions since the Cultural Revolution, are
included. This collection is a good illustration of the employment of a popular art form as a vehicle for imparting desired
revolutionary ideals to the masses.

CHAPTER VIII

FOREIGN POLICY AND FOREIGN POLICY-MAKING
DURING THE CULTURAL REVOLUTION

The entries in this chapter present divergent views on the extent of the impact of the internal struggle on China's foreign policy during the Cultural Revolution. Some analysts see little fundamental change in foreign policy during the Cultural Revolution, although some note a directionlessness; while others maintain either that foreign policy actions during the upheaval were essentially influenced by the dissension and rivalry of top leaders at home or that events abroad had triggered the domestic dissension. The Sino-Soviet border dispute, which erupted into armed clashes in 1969, was attributed by several authors to the effects of the Cultural Revolution on China's foreign policy. Some of the entries present the position that Red Guard excesses against foreign nations in 1966-67 were not a part of China's foreign policy. There seems to be some agreement, however, on the negative impact of the Cultural Revolution on China's prestige and influence abroad.

The entries in this chapter cover a wide range of aspects of China's foreign policy. Some items deal with the management of the Ministry of Foreign Affairs, with particular reference to the period when the radicals controlled the ministry during the upheaval. Other analyses and interpretations cover topics such

174

as China's use of revolution as an instrument for foreign policy, changes brought about by the Cultural Revolution on China's support for national liberation, factors contributing to changes in Sino-United States relations, and the cautious and moderate attitude of the Chinese military toward neighboring countries.

313 ACHMINOW, Herman F.
"Crisis in Mao's Realm and Moscow's China Policy," Orbis,
Vol. 41, No. 4, Winter 1968, pp. 1179-1192.
The purpose of this article is to present the Soviet view of
the Cultural Revolution and to examine Moscow's foreign policy
toward China. Based on Soviet press sources, Achminow presents
the Soviet view of the Cultural Revolution. According to
Achminow, the Soviet Union looked upon Mao's attack on the
party as a betrayal of the basic postulate of Leninism that
the party is the vanguard of the proletariat. By placing the
military in a leading position in Chinese domestic politics,
"Mao reverses the historic communist attitude toward military
leaders." According to Achminow, the Soviet interpretation
of the rise of the military and Lin Piao during the Cultural
Revolution was that "Mao expects China to become involved in
a war, and in wartime it could be advantageous for a marshal
to head both state and party." Achminow briefly reviews the
Sino-Soviet rift and concludes that the rift is so deep-rooted
that the "Kremlin is not likely to change its cautious policies toward China while Mao is still alive." He also sees
the possibility of intervention by Moscow in China's domestic
politics on the side of anti-Mao forces. Moscow's attitude
toward China, Achminow feels, is one of increased hostility and
of anticipation of a civil war in China after Mao. Achminow
sees Moscow attempting to encourage the formation of pro-
Soviet forces in China by establishing contacts with Chinese
intellectuals, discredited cadres, and scientists. He also
sees the Cultural Revolution as offering some advantages for
the Soviet Union: "It helps them to consolidate their own
position at home and abroad, for in comparison with Chinese
excesses the Soviet communist regime seems moderate and acceptable."

314 ADIE, W. A. C.
"China Returns to Africa," Current Scene, Vol. X, No. 8,
August 1972, pp. 1-12.
This is a brief summary of the development of Sino-African
relations from early contacts to the eve of the Cultural
Revolution in 1966. China's activities in Africa from 1955
to 1959 are viewed as a reflection of Peking's readiness to
compete with Moscow for influence in the Third World. During
this period China was encouraging and aiding armed struggle
in Algeria and Morocco. From 1959 to 1962 China shifted its
sphere of activities to West and Central Africa; from 1962 to
1965 Chinese activities centered mainly in east and central
Africa. During the Cultural Revolution, essential Chinese
diplomatic relations were maintained in Africa by means of
aid and trade projects, exploitation of local revolutionary
movements, and by using the Congo (Brazzaville) model for
supplying arms and training to para-military and regular
forces. According to Adie, the Chinese attempted to consolidate their Africa activities throughout most of the Cultural
Revolution.

315 BARNETT, Doak A.
"China and U.S. Policy: A Time of Transition," Current Scene,
Vol. VIII, No. 10, May 15, 1970, pp. 1-10.
This essay considers the implications of the Cultural Revolution
in terms of an aging utopian revolutionary, Mao, who lost faith
in, and almost lost control of, his revolutionary regime.
China, in Barnett's view, is in the midst of a transition
period. Barnett discusses China's diplomatic decline in international relations and her dramatic change of attitude toward
Sino-Soviet relations. Changing United States attitudes and
policies toward China, which led to Nixon's decision to revise
United States-China policy in the summer of 1969, are also
analyzed. The essay lists and explains key factors contributing
to the process of change in United States-China policy: the
gradual cooling off of emotions since the early 1950's, revised
views about China as a threat, and Chinese caution and restrained behavior in dealing with explosive situations outside
her border. Barnett offers some suggestions on how the United
States could improve relations with China: explore every
avenue for increased contacts and trade, adjust to China's
claim to a UN seat, remove United States military presence in
Taiwan, and make a pledge with the Soviet Union at the SALT
talks not to build anti-China ABM's.

316 BARNETT, Doak A.
A New U.S. Policy Toward China, The Brookings Institution,
Washington, D.C., 1971, 132p.
This book explores China-United States relations in the 1970's.
In the first part of the book Barnett briefly discusses the
pattern of United States-China relations over the past twenty
years. The changes that took place in the United States'
attitude toward China after the Korean War and the adjustments
contemplated in light of these changes in attitude are analyzed.
Chinese policy modifications toward the United States and their
probable motives for these changes are discussed. In the second
part of the book Barnett outlines proposals for effecting
changes in United States policy toward China and the problems
inherent in such change. He notes that China's acquisition of
nuclear power capability poses problems for the United States
and that the Cultural Revolution and its aftermath created
uncertainty about China's leadership pattern, which is responsible for China's foreign policy.

317 BARNETT, Doak A., and REISCHAUER, Edwin O., eds.
The United States and China: The Next Decade, The National
Committee on U.S.-China Relations, Praeger Publishers, New York
and London, 1970, 249p.
This is a collection of summary comments made by leading
scholars and experts on China at a national conference held in
New York in March 1969 under the sponsorship of the National
Committee on U.S.-China Relations. The volume is arranged by
the topics discussed at the conference: political trends
in China today, China and world security, China's economic

development, and United States-China policy. The bulk of the
volume deals with the basic issues and problems of relations
between China and the United States from the perspectives of a
number of scholars and policy-makers in the United States.

318 COHEN, Jerome H., ed.
The Dynamics of China's Foreign Relations, East Asian Research
Center, East Asian Monographs No. 39, Harvard University, 1970,
129p.
This monograph contains six essays on China's foreign policy in
the 1960's. These essays examine specific problems that China
encountered in major areas of the world at that time. One
essay considers the Sino-Soviet border dispute a trivial issue
which each side finds advantageous to perpetuate. China's
relations with India and Pakistan, in terms of a triangular
diplomacy, and China's relations with Japan and the thorny issue
of Taiwan, which the authors consider to be dominated by
economic factors, are discussed. China's skillful use of small
aid programs to Tanzania in East Africa is contrasted with the
decline of the national liberation movements in the rest of
Africa and in Latin America, where Peking is seen as lacking
sensitivity in forcing its revolutionary model upon foreign
revolutionary leaders. All of the essays in this volume indicate that the Cultural Revolution had little effect on China's
policies in the areas studied.

319 CURRENT SCENE, The Editor.
"Peking and Latin America: Rewriting Scenario," Vol. IX, No. 4,
April 7, 1971, pp. 1-6.
According to this report, the principle concern for Chinese
diplomatic activities in Latin America in the 1960'a was focused
on Soviet ideological influence, rather than on the United
States role in the area. China's strategy in the 1960's was
aimed at splintering pro-Soviet parties and organizations in
Latin America. This essay interprets Chinese efforts in Latin
American to create opposition to established communist parties
as a reflection of the attempts to root out revisionism inside
China during the Cultural Revolution. The paper also discusses
the shift in Peking's policy towards Latin America after the
Cultural Revolution from one of support for "revolutionary
struggles" to one of support for struggles against United States
domination and economic exploitation. Chinese support for
popular Latin American issues, such as the 200 mile territorial
water claim and the return of Panama Canal, is viewed as a
"united front" strategy against the United States in order to
pave the way for China to be more closely identified with the
"Third World."

320 FITZGERALD, C. P.
"A Revolutionary Hiatus," China After the Cultural Revolution,
A selection from Bulletin of the Atomic Scientists, Vol. XXV,
No. 2, February 1969, Vintage Books, New York, 1970, pp. 145-166.
This essay discusses the disruption of China's foreign policy

178

development caused by internal struggle during the Cultural Revolution. According to Fitzgerald, Red Guard excesses against a number of foreign countries in 1967 were not authorized by the policy-makers and were not part of the foreign policy. Anti-British incidents in Hong Kong are interpreted as part of the struggle by local party cadres in Canton to show Peking that they were revolutionary. Fitzgerald concludes that during this period military action by the Chinese was highly improbable because the military leaders in control of the country were employing a cautious and moderate attitude toward frontier nations, particularly the Soviet Union, over border situations. He sees Chinese foreign policy as drifting directionless "in the gorge of the Cultural Revolution."

321 FITZGERALD, Stephen.
"Overseas Chinese Affairs and the Cultural Revolution," The China Quarterly, No. 40, October-December 1969, pp. 103-126. This is a two-part study of overseas Chinese affairs and the impact of the Cultural Revolution on Peking's policies toward the overseas Chinese. In part one Fitzgerald traces the development of these policies prior to and during the Cultural Revolution. By using a few Red Guard tabloids selectively, Fitzgerald tries to piece together the problems within the Overseas Chinese Affairs Commission led by Liao Cheng-chih and the reasons for his purge during the Cultural Revolution. In part two the impact of the Cultural Revolution on the Commission's organizational apparatus and its policy toward Chinese abroad, particularly in Hong Kong, Macao, Burma, Cambodia and Indonesia, are analyzed.

322 GURTOV, Melvin.
"The Foreign Ministry and Foreign Affairs in the Chinese Cultural Revolution," The Cultural Revolution in China, Thomas W. Robinson, ed., University of California Press, Berkeley and Los Angeles, 1971, pp. 313-366. Also see "The Foreign Ministry and Foreign Affairs During the Cultural Revolution," The China Quarterly, No. 40, October-December 1969, pp. 65-102, and China and Southeast Asia--The Politics of Survival: A Study of Foreign Policy Interaction, Chapter 5, "China's Foreign Relations: Foreign Relations in Flux," Heath Lexington Books, D. C. Heath and Co., Lexington, Mass., Toronto and London, 1971, pp. 113-124.
This study based mostly on material from Red Guard publications, is not only about the Chinese foreign ministry but also about the relationship of foreign affairs to China's domestic development during the Cultural Revolution. It begins with a detailed account of the struggle against Foreign Minister Chen Yi and Chen's adamant resistance to the Red Guard's intrusion into the Foreign Ministry. According to Gurtov, the impact of the radicals' take-over of the ministry in the summer of 1967 was to further weaken Foreign Minister Chen's authority and prestige in areas of foreign policy-making. The study shows that foreign affairs for China were "in a state of suspended animation" for

most of the Cultural Revolution. Foreign relations were limited, during the period, to perfunctory receptions and visits by
foreign dignitaries. Chinese officials and all of her ambas-
sadors abroad, except one, were recalled to Peking. Although
the Cultural Revolution paralyzed the foreign ministry and much
of China's foreign policy-making capability; the regime, even
when under the brief control of radical extremists, did not
embark on any military actions abroad. On the contrary, the
study shows that since the fall of 1967, the regime has sought
to stabilize its foreign relations.

323 HINTON, Harold.
China's Turbulent Quest: An Analysis of China's Foreign Relations Since 1949, Indiana University Press, Bloomington, Ind.,
1972, 352p.
This book gives an overview of developments in Chinese foreign
policy since 1949. Part one presents a detailed analysis of
the phases of China's foreign policy evolution, which Hinton
divides into five periods: (1) Stalinism and armed struggle in
the early 1950's, (2) the Bandung peaceful co-existence period,
(3) the challenge to Mao from the Soviet's 20th Party Congress
in 1956 to the shelling of offshore islands, (4) the breakaway
from the Soviet orbit, and (5) the Cultural Revolution in the
late 1960's. According to Hinton the immediate impact of the
Cultural Revolution was to reduce China's prestige and influence
abroad. He believes that China's foreign policy is motivated
by national interest rather than revolutionary ideology. Part
two deals with China's specific policies toward specific regions
and groups. Part three describes the normalization of China's
foreign relations after the Cultural Revolution and examines
the prospects for future development.

324 HINTON, Harold C.
"Sino-Soviet Relations in the Brezhnev Era," Current History,
Vol. 61, No. 361, September 1971, pp. 135-141 and 181.
In Hinton's opinion, the Cultural Revolution represented the
greatest shock the Chinese ever gave to the Soviet Union. This
paper presents an analysis of the Sino-Soviet border dispute
and the maneuvers by Peking on the border issue. Hinton describes the aspects of the Cultural Revolution which most
irritated Moscow: the repeated demonstrations staged on the
border by the Chinese against Soviet "revisionism"; and the
attacks against the very concept and organizational principles
of Lenin, the sanctity of the party. Hinton makes the point
that it was mainly on the issue of party apparatus that Moscow
contemplated, but never dared to carry out, military intervention against China.

325 HINTON, Harold.
"Vietnam Policy, Domestic Factionalism, Regionalism, and Plot-
ting a Coup," Cases in Comparative Politics: Asia, Lucian W.
Pye, ed., Little, Brown and Company, Boston, 1970, pp. 119-156.
In this essay Hinton attempts to show that domestic Chinese

180

developments complicated the plan for a Soviet-Chinese solution to United States escalation in Vietnam. First Hinton points out the close parallel in the differences among Chinese leaders over domestic policies and foreign policies, particularly with respect to Sino-Soviet relations. Then he analyzes the inter-relationship between Chinese intra-party differences and the rejection of the Soviet request for air base rights in southwest China in 1965, when the United States was escalating war in Vietnam. The rejection was illustrative of Peking's concern over the increased regional power of border provinces, such as Szechwan and Kwangsi. Hinton concludes: "There can be no doubt that the Cultural Revolution, and in particular such develop-ments as domestic disorder (notably the disruption of service on the railway leading through Kwangsi to North Vietnam), the heavy involvement of the army in political activity, and the slowing of the nuclear weapons program, harmed both China's image and its actual influence in foreign affairs."

326 KIM, Samuel S.
"The Peoples Republic of China in the United Nations: A Preliminary Analysis," World Politics, Vol. XXVI, No. 3, April 1974, pp. 299-330.
Kim presents his thesis that with the termination of the Cultural Revolution in the spring of 1969, a "new and revolu-tionary" Chinese foreign policy began. This new Chinese foreign policy was more than a policy of moderation and pragmatism; "it demonstrated an extraordinary--almost unprecedented--degree of flexibility and moderation by extending the permissible limits of normalization toward former enemies such as the United States, Japan, and Yugoslavia." With the inauguration of this new foreign policy, China's attitude towards the United Nations also changed from the "polemic indictments against the United Nations" to a conciliatory posture. Kim analyzes Peking's strategy in winning the campaign for the United Nation's seat launched in 1970. The strategy called for visiting China "banquet diplo-macy," people-to-people exchanges, a drive for state-to-state relations, China's agitation on the eve of the 26th session of the General Assembly, and the step-up on Chinese aid activities in the Third World. A detailed analysis is given on the voting record in the General Assembly and on China's intentions and strategies in the United Nations after the expulsion of the Taiwan government and the seating of the Peking representatives. Finally Kim makes a few broad assessments of China's role in the United Nations: pursuance of national interests concealed under the mantel of a "cautious and diligent apprentice" rather than "an operational wrecker"; defender of Third World causes. Kim also feels that China has the appearance of "the status of a superpower" despite her frequent disclaimers.

327 KLEIN, Donald.
"The Management of Foreign Affairs in Communist China," China: Management of a Revolutionary Society, John M. Lindbeck, ed., University of Washington Press, Seattle and London, 1971,

pp. 305-342.
This study of the management of Chinese foreign affairs focuses
on "the institutionalization of the foreign affairs apparatus."
The study traces the development of the foreign affairs apparatus from the Kiangsi period to the Yenan days. Tables and
charts show the make-up of the Ministry of Foreign Affairs
personnel and its functional development from 1949 to 1969.
This study provides information and analysis on the unofficial
foreign affairs apparatus such as the complex network of "mass,"
or "people-to-people," organizations. The organizational and
hierarchical structure of the foreign affairs apparatus is also
discussed. The impact of the Cultural Revolution on the foreign
affairs personnel is examined in the concluding segment of the
study. According to Klein, the disappearance of a number of
foreign relations specialists during and after the Cultural
Revolution and the rise of a new corps of experienced diplomats
abroad since 1969 indicates a certain degree of continuity and
stability in the institutional apparatus in foreign relations
for the future.

328 KLEIN, Sidney.
"The Cultural Revolution and China's Foreign Trade: A First
Approximation," Current Scene, Vol. V, No. 19, November 17,
1967, pp. 1-11.
This study examines the impact of the Cultural Revolution on
the size, direction and composition of China's foreign trade.
Statistics on the volume of trade with individual countries for
the years 1965-67 are given to estimate the extent of the
Cultural Revolution's effect. Klein's tentative evaluation of
the data in the study indicates no change in the total volume
of trade. Thus, it appears that the Cultural Revolution in
1966-67 neither helped nor harmed China's trade and her general
economic development.

329 OJHA, Ishwer C.
Chinese Foreign Policy in an Age of Transition: The Diplomacy
of Cultural Despair, Beacon Press, Boston, 1969, 234p.
This book is predominantly concerned with the trauma a nation
suffers when it becomes modernized and at the same time tries
to save its own cultural values and traditions. Sections of
this book deal specifically with China's experience in domestic
and international politics and the effect on China's culture in
psychological and sociological terms. The last chapter of the
book discusses the impact of the Cultural Revolution on China's
foreign policy. Ojha presents the view that the upheaval had
a limited and transitory effect on China's foreign policy.
"Chinese foreign policy is concerned with China's vital interests," a policy that calls for "self-strengthening at home"
and "self-reliance abroad" which can only be interpreted as
cautious and prudent. Ojha views the Cultural Revolution as a
failure in terms of social revolution and argues that major
foreign policy actions during the upheaval were external in
origin.

330 PAN, Stephen C. Y.
"China and Southeast Asia," Current History, Vol. 57, No. 337,
September 1969, pp. 164-167 and 180.
This article presents evidence to show that the Cultural Revo-
lution had impact, not only on domestic life in China, but on
the rest of Asia as well. Pan believes that disturbances in
Hong Kong, Macao and Burma during the Cultural Revolution were
reflections of events in China. The increased Chinese aid to
North Vietnam and the fear of Chinese activities overseas by
Thailand, Malaysia and Singapore are offered as additional evi-
dence of the impact of the upheaval. Responses to the Cultural
Revolution by southeast Asian nations, the United States,
Australia and New Zealand, as well as collective security for
southeast Asia, are analyzed.

331 RAVENAL, Earl C., ed.
Peace with China? U.S. Decisions for Asia, Liverwright, New
York, 1971, 248p.
This book is a collection of essays and comments made by a group
of experts at a conference held at the Institute for Policy
Studies in Washington, D.C., in 1970. The collection begins
with a discussion of the Nixon Doctrine on disengagement in
Asia and its implication for China. The second part is concerned with the policy consequences of defense management procedures. A portion of the book deals directly with the question
of Nixon's China policy of accommodation versus the policy of
containment. Alternatives to the basic U.S. policy in Asia,
such as anti-communist roadblocks, containment and coexistence,
are suggested by several experts. One expert suggests that to
end the permanent confrontation with China a change in rhetoric
or a trivial concession is not sufficient; the abandonment of
Saigon, Phnom Penh, and Vietiane as bastions of United States
power is required: "getting out of Indochina is the key to a
new relationship with China."

332 ROBINSON, Thomas W.
"The Sino-Soviet Border Dispute," The American Political Science
Review, Vol. LXVI, No. 4, December 1972, pp. 1175-1202.
Robinson's article gives a full account of Sino-Soviet relations
from 1956 to 1969, when clashes occurred along the frontier.
One of the author's purposes in this article is to establish the
linkage between domestic politics and foreign policies of China
and the Soviet Union. By using the method of qualitative
content analysis as an approach, Robinson was able to conclude:
"Apparently border relations became much worse in 1967. There
were reports of a clash along the Ussuri River in January 1967,
and the Soviets accused the Chinese of wildly provocative
behavior in connection with the excesses of the Cultural Revolution." Robinson then illustrates the connection between
domestic politics and external policies for both China and the
Soviet Union in the border dispute. He finds that "border
problems did not occupy a major place in either state's attitude
toward the other until relations began to deteriorate for other

reasons." He blames both sides for creating the seriousness of the border situation during the Cultural Revolution: "The Chinese apparently allowed extremist partisans of the Cultural Revolution to cross at will over the border, causing the Russians to worry about allegedly irrational Chinese behavior and conjuring up old fears about large numbers of Chinese sweeping in from the East to settle like locusts upon Soviet soil. The Russians, for their part, overreacted to Cultural Revolution incursions by fortifying their border forces much beyond the level necessary to cope with propaganda demonstrations by unruly Chinese crowds and by policing the border with an iron hand."

333 SCALAPINO, Robert.
"The Cultural Revolution and Chinese Foreign Policy," The Cultural Revolution: 1967 in Review, Michigan Papers in Chinese Studies No. 2, Chang Chun-shu, James Crump and Rhoads Murphey, eds., Center for Chinese Studies, University of Michigan, Ann Arbor, 1968, pp. 72-96. Also see, Current Scene, Vol. VI, No. 13, August 1, 1968, pp. 1-15.
This essay discusses two aspects of Chinese foreign policy and the Cultural Revolution: the effects of the upheaval on China's security policy and the relationship between the upheaval and China's external influence. Scalapino argues here that it was the escalation of the Vietnam War by the United States in 1965-66 that again triggered the issues that were involved in the dismissal of Marshal Peng Teh-huai: the priority of the nuclear development and the erroneous economic policies of the Great Leap. If China were attacked by the might of the United States, what posture could China take--reliance on the Soviet Union for nuclear protection or a revival of Mao's guerrilla strategy? The purging of party leaders by Mao during the Cultural Revolution resulted in the readoption of Mao's military doctrine of a purely defensive posture. In terms of China's external relations, the Cultural Revolution was seen as an important factor which contributed to the decline of China's prestige abroad and to the low morale of China's professional diplomats.

334 SHAW, Brian.
"China and North Vietnam: Two Revolutionary Paths, Part I and Part II," Current Scene, Vol. IX, Nos. 11 and 12, November 7 and December 7, 1971, pp. 1-12 and 1-11.
This study develops the theme that events in Vietnam since the 1954 Geneva Conference have changed China's perception of possible United States and Soviet military threat as well as China's judgment in the use of ideology in foreign policy-making. Shaw believes that Hanoi has developed a posture independent from both the Chinese and the Soviets. Part I traces the development of China's aid to Hanoi since 1954 and Hanoi's reasons for cautious acceptance of such aid. Sino-Soviet disputes also affected Hanoi as the North Vietnamese became more dependent on Soviet economic and technical assistance. Part II

focuses on the Chinese response to United States military escalation in the Indochina conflict. According to Shaw, Chinese
commitment intensified in both North and South Vietnam (the
Vietcong) in terms of military aid prior to the Cultural Revolution, but the leaders in Hanoi maintained some distance from
the internal upheaval in China. Shaw concludes that "ideological and national security considerations rather than Hanoi's
interests have played a major role in Peking's position on the
Vietnamese conflict."

335 TRETIAK, Daniel.
"The Chinese Cultural Revolution and Foreign Policy," Current
Scene, Vol. VIII, No. 7, April 1, 1970, pp. 1-26.
This study points out the areas in which the Cultural Revolution
affected Chinese foreign policy: the removal of Liu Shao-chi
from foreign policy decision-making; the reduction of influence
of regular foreign service personnel in policy-making; the rise
of second echelon diplomats in the management of foreign
affairs; and loss of direction for Chinese foreign policy for
a brief period during the upheaval. Sources of conflict and
stages of development in attacks within the Foreign Affairs
Ministry during the Cultural Revolution are analyzed and summa-
rized in a convenient chart. The specific attacks levelled
against Liu Shao-chi and other senior diplomats are also
categorized. As the radical tide of the Cultural Revolution
began to ebb in 1967-68, foreign affairs management was placed
in the hands of a more moderate group of diplomats, and Foreign
Minister Chen Yi's power and influence was gradually restored.
Tretiak concludes that Chinese foreign policy alternates between
moderation and radicalism which reflects domestic political
currents.

336 TRETIAK, Daniel.
"Is China Preparing to 'Turnout'? Changes in Chinese Levels of
Attention to the International Environment," Asian Survey,
Vol. XI, No. 3, March 1971, pp. 219-237.
This study shows that Chinese attention to the international
environment was on the increase, or "turnout" during 1966-69.
By quantifying the international news coverage in the Peking
Review for that four year period, Tretiak reaches the conclusion
that, with the exception of the period from July 1966 to June
1967, at least half of the news coverage in the Peking Review
was on international events occurring outside of China. A
comparative quantitative picture is given for 1968-69 to show
the degree of China's attention with respect to various nations
of the world. Tretiak's conclusion is that in the aftermath of
the Cultural Revolution, there was an increase in China's
attention to the world outside and less hostility toward neighboring countries.

337 VAN NESS, Peter.
Revolution and Chinese Foreign Policy: Peking's Support for
Wars of National Liberation, University of California Press,

185

Berkeley, Los Angeles and London, 1970, 266p.
The main concern of this book is China's use of revolution as an
instrument of its foreign policy. Van Ness attempts to answer
the often raised question of whether China's foreign policy is
dictated by ideology or national interests. Part one of the
book presents a discussion of Mao's theory of wars of national
liberation as a basis for an analytical framework. A Chinese
revolutionary model, based on Mao's writings and official statements before 1965, is built for analysis. Part two analyzes
China's actual support of wars of national liberation prior to
the Cultural Revolution. From a theoretical point of view,
China is committed to the support of all revolutions against
imperialism and oppression. In practice China does not support
all armed struggles in the Third World. The cases of Kenya,
Kashmir, Burma, and Indonesia are used in support of this contention. The last portion of the book focuses on the changes
brought about by the Cultural Revolution on China's support for
the national liberation movement. The Cultural Revolution is
seen as a major shift, in theoretical terms, from China's concern for revolutionary strategy abroad to her attention to
post-revolutionary development and the maintenance of the
"dictatorship of the proletariat." This change consequently
affected China's support of wars of national liberation abroad.
After the Cultural Revolution, the Chinese "seemed to become
largely preoccupied with the replication of the Chinese revolutionary model, and they appeared to be extremely eager to see
Maoist revolutionary strategy prove to be successful abroad."

338 WARREN, Susan.
China's Voice in the United Nations, World Winds Press, New
York, 1974, 146p.
This booklet deals with the role of the Chinese delegation to
the 28th Session and the 6th Special Session of the United
Nations General Assembly in the fall of 1973 and the spring of
1974. It contains speeches and statements made by the Chinese
at these world gatherings which present the Chinese view of
world problems. The book also includes the major items discussed by the General Assembly upon which the Chinese outlined
their positions: Cambodia, Korea, the Middle East, world
disarmament, law of the seas, and economic development. There
are extensive direct quotes from the speeches of Chinese representatives on each of the topics mentioned above. The concluding portion of the book deals with the question of whether
China is a superpower. The author feels that the answer to
that question is found in Teng Hsiao-ping's statement to the
6th Special Session of the General Assembly.

339 WU, Yuan-li.
As Peking Sees Us, Hoover Institution Press, Stanford University,
Stanford, 1969, 98p.
The objective of this book is to interpret Peking's views on the
turmoil within the United States in the 1960's and to analyze
Peking's perception and policy toward the United States. Wu

first presents a documentary analysis of the evolution of China's perception of the United States by focusing on a few selected public pronouncements made in 1968. The views of the black militants in the United States and their relation to Mao's perception on revolution are analyzed. For instance, Mao viewed the Negro's struggle as an independent movement of a colony. One of the book's conclusions is that a parallel exists between Peking's view of the unrest in the United States and the goals and methods advocated by the black militants. This parallel might lead Peking to exert influence on the development of an armed rebellion in the United States.

340 YAHUDA, Michael B.
"China's Nuclear Option," China After the Cultural Revolution, A Selection from Bulletin of Atomic Scientists, Vol. XXV, No. 2, February 1969, Vintage Books, New York, 1970, pp. 198-212. This essay discusses China's nuclear deployment in relation to her foreign policy goals. China's nuclear doctrine is essentially a defensive one, predicated on survival after a nuclear attack and the employment of a "people's war" against invaders on the ground. According to Yahuda, factors which influenced China's decision to develop nuclear weapons were: the quest for power, the symbol of self-reliance, and the need to fill the defense gap. Yahuda discusses China's delivery options, targets for her missiles, and the possibility of China's long-range missile development.

341 YAHUDA, Michael B.
"Chinese Foreign Policy after 1963: The Maoist Phase," The China Quarterly, No. 36, October-December 1968, pp. 93-113. Yahuda describes Chinese foreign policy from the end of 1963 to 1968 in two distinct phases of development. In the first phase, from 1963 to the summer of 1965, there was an international united front strategy against the United States and against Soviet revisionism. The second stage, from the autumn of 1965 to 1968, was characterized by verbal militancy, which called for a war of national liberation of the rural areas of the world (the Third World) to encircle the cities of the world. Yahuda sees a loss of direction and coherence in Chinese foreign policy after 1965. In Yahuda's opinion, the impact of the Cultural Revolution on foreign policy came in the form of attacks on the Foreign Affairs Ministry and on the foreign policies of Chen Yi and Liu Shao-chi. According to Yahuda, the only coherent and consistent factor in Chinese foreign policy from 1965 to 1968 was China's desire to secure her borders and to avoid a clash with the United States in southeast Asia. Otherwise the Chinese foreign policy for the period was paradoxical: "the more global the aspirations, the more introverted and regional the operationalizations."

342 YU, George T.
"Working on the Railroad: China and the Tanzania-Zambia Railway," Asian Survey, Vol. XI, No. 11, November 1971, pp. 1101-1117.

This study covers the impact of the Cultural Revolution on
Chinese foreign policy-making in the case of the African railway. Yu gives a brief history of events that led to the Chinese
aid commitment for the Zambian railway construction in 1965.
The stages of negotiation from 1966 to July 1970 and the financial terms involved in the final agreement are analyzed. Yu
explores the Chinese motives, in terms of Chinese foreign policy,
for extending her scarce resources to faraway East Africa. He
suggests the following motivating factors: enhancement of
China's international status, the demonstration of China's
capabilities and power, and China's reputation for international
activism. Yu notes that the successful negotiations for the
railway aid coincided with the Cultural Revolution, a period of
domestic chaos and disruption in China. The rational decision-
making process in this case, Yu argues, disproves the popular
hypothesis that there was a complete breakdown in state authority and power in China during the Cultural Revolution.

343 ZAGORIA, Donald S.
Vietnam Triangle: Moscow, Peking, Hanoi, Pegasus, New York,
1967, 286p.
While this book is mainly concerned with the triangular diplomacy of China, the Soviet Union, and North Vietnam on the United
States military action in Indochina, interspersed throughout the
book are implications of the Cultural Revolution's impact on
China's foreign policy. Zagoria takes the position that there
were fundamental foreign policy questions in the Cultural
Revolution struggle: the United States involvement in Vietnam
served as a "catalyst" which "triggered" the policy disagreements among China's top leaders. Furthermore, Zagoria's analysis points out the parallel between ideological disputes among
leaders during the Cultural Revolution and ideological disputes
in China's quarrel with the Soviet Union. Zagoria explores the
divergent views of the Chinese leaders on foreign policy, with
specific reference to Vietnam, as those of "hawks," "doves,"
and "dawks." The Cultural Revolution represented "a deep-seated
and long-standing division of opinion among the Chinese leaders
on basic questions of domestic and foreign policy." The key
foreign policy documents on Vietnam from China located in the
appendixes are useful references on China's attitudes toward the
conflict.

CHAPTER IX

THE CULTURAL REVOLUTION AND ITS AFTERMATH

Included in this chapter are major analyses and interpretations about the results, or consequences, of the upheaval on all
aspects of Chinese society, as well as evaluations of the success
of the Cultural Revolution in terms of goals and objectives
achieved. In the area of politics, attention is focused on the
ascendency of the provincial military-party power structure and
the extent of erosion of power at the center in Peking. The
evolving relationship between the rebuilt party structure and
the revolutionary committees is also analyzed. Finally, the
question of whether the Cultural Revolution has resulted in the
establishment of a "Sino-Marxist Communist Party" dedicated to
the institutionalization of mass line communications between the
ruler and the people is examined.

Analysis in the area of economics is concentrated on the
effects of changes, such as decentralization in decision-making
and management, de-emphasis on elitism in science and technology,
and changes in the remuneration system, on production and future
prospects for modernization. The extent of structural and
ideological changes resulting from the Cultural Revolution and
their implications are explored.

The impact of the Cultural Revolution on society is discussed, directly or indirectly, in most entries since all changes

189

affect the social system. Some scholars in this and other
chapters have indicated that the upheaval, indeed, was meant to
be a revolution of the Chinese culture in all of its ramifica-
tions. Particular attention is paid in these entries to the
goals of the Cultural Revolution for a truly egalitarian Chinese
communist society to be reflected in all institutions. The
question of the viability of such a society for China and of
whether China after the Cultural Revolution is an integrated
society are raised in a number of works. Students of contemporary China will find the analyses and interpretations on the
above questions in the entries included in this chapter.

344 ASIAN SURVEY.
"The Cultural Revolution and Its Aftermath," Vol. XII, No. 12,
December 1972, pp. 999-1100.
This is a collection of six articles dealing with various
aspects of the Cultural Revolution and its aftermath. Parris
Chang's article on the regional military power shows that the
leaders in the Chinese central government have expressed concern
over the erosion of power at the center and over the fragmenta-
tion of regional power in the provinces in the aftermath of the
Cultural Revolution. Gardel Feurtado describes the formation
of the provincial revolutionary committees in Hopei and
Heilungkiang to illustrate the problems of increased localism
and anti-center bias. Juliana Heaslet's article on the Red
Guard movement points out the possibility of a larger role for
a new generation of youths schooled in political infighting.
Robert Dernberger sees China doing well in continued economic
growth since the Cultural Revolution. Byung-joon Ahn's article
on the politics of the Peking opera points out the underlying
issues of the Cultural Revolution. The last article by Ralph
Powell and Chong-kun Yoon discusses the reorganization of China's
public security system after the Cultural Revolution and describes the continued influence of the military in public security
affairs, which is linked to the political power of the military
in the provinces. Entries for these articles are annotated
separately in this bibliography.

345 BASTID, Marianne.
"Levels of Economic Decision-making," Authority, Participation
and Cultural Change in China, Stuart R. Schram, ed., Cambridge
University Press, Cambridge, 1973, pp. 159-197.
This study analyzes the distribution and functioning of economic
decision-making power during the post-Cultural Revolution
period. The article begins by describing the controversy over
the merits of strong centralization in key industries and local
decision-making in a limited sector of economic life in 1965.
A detailed survey of the central decision-making process since
the Cultural Revolution is given. Through the introduction of
a number of new administrative practices following the Cultural
Revolution, decision-making powers were vested in the unit which
had the power in the field. Bastid concludes that "the real
efficiency of the present system, however, relies on the potential of energy and enthusiasm which was liberated when the
Cultural Revolution overthrew barriers and taboos, on the willingness of local people and leaders to voice their opinion and
contribute a selfless effort."

346 BRUGGER, William.
"The Ninth National Congress of the Chinese Communist Party,
The World Today, Vol. 25, No. 7, July 1969, pp. 297-305.
This article evaluates the programs and issues brought about by
the Cultural Revolution. It focuses on the Ninth Party Congress
of the CCP, held in April 1969, and measures the congress in
terms of the goals achieved by the Cultural Revolution. A

summary is given at the beginning of the article on the progress of the Cultural Revolution in terms of decentralized party structure and mass participation in the decision-making process, overall commitment of individuals to goals of transforming society, the permanence of the Cultural Revolution spirit, training of revolutionary youth, reform in literature and art, and the enshrining of Mao's thought. Brugger then examines the party documents of the Ninth Party Congress for indications of success in solving problems such as democratic centralism, status differences within the party, the red versus expert polemic, the problem of succession, the permanence of revolutionary spirit, the role of China's youth in light of the Cultural Revolution, and the stress on Mao's thought as a Maoist model. Brugger concludes by stating: "Lin Piao's political report sums up the experiences of the Cultural Revolution during the past few years but gives little indication as to the future course of events."

347   BRYAN, Derek.
"Changing Social Ethics in Contemporary China," The Political Quarterly, Vol. 45, No. 1, January-March 1974, pp. 49-57.
This short essay takes the position that Mao felt that the Cultural Revolution was necessary to inculcate the proletarian ethic into the masses in China's vast countryside. Bryan links Mao's concept of a new socialist man with Mao's "aim of developing the creative powers of the individual on an egalitarian basis." This new type of human being was projected into the minds of the Chinese through the mass media as "able and creative, but open and unsophisticated, very much an individual but also a member of a strong and wise community." Bryan describes China after the Cultural Revolution as "an integrated society" and a nation that can live by the Maoist maxim, "serve the people."

348   CHANG, Parris H.
"Regional Military Power: The Aftermath of the Cultural Revolution," Asian Survey, Vol. XII, No. 12, December 1972, pp. 999-1013.
This essay is about the changes brought about by the Cultural Revolution, particularly the changes in the distribution of power between the central and local authorities. Chang reviews the rising political influence of the military in the early 1960's and its involvement in the Cultural Revolution. When the 9th Party Congress met in April 1969, the political prominence of the military had become apparent both at the central and local levels. According to Chang one consequence of this change is the conflict between the more conservative party bureaucrats and military-regional forces and the radicals of the Cultural Revolution. Chang analyzes the nature of the central-provincial relationship and the problems involved in exercising control over the provincial authorities. However, he also points out the leverage the central authority has in eliciting compliance from the provincial authorities. Chang

192

concludes with remarks on the possible future role of the military in Chinese politics by projecting an increase in the military's political influence as the leaders face the inevitable crisis of succession.

349 CURRENT SCENE, The Editor.
"The Revolutionary Committee and the Party in the Aftermath of the Cultural Revolution," Vol. VIII, No. 8, April 15, 1970, pp. 1-10.
In exploring the relationship between the party committees and the revolutionary committees in the aftermath of the Cultural Revolution, the author finds that the complicating factor was the role of the military, which had assumed the leadership of many party organs as well as dominance over the revolutionary committees. As background, the article gives a brief overview of the provincial level revolutionary committees and the basic level revolutionary committees in cities, towns and communes during 1969. According to the author, it was in the basic level revolutionary committees that party members reemerged in leadership positions. He finds that a crucial point in China's political development was the "evolving relationship between the rebuilt party apparatus and the revolutionary committee." This study points out the emerging trend in China of relying less on the military for leadership. However, the study concludes, the military could remain a potent force in provincial and municipal politics.

350 CURRENT SCENE, The Editor.
"The Food and Population Balance: China's Modernization Dilemma," Vol. IX, No. 6, July 7, 1971, pp. 1-7.
This article briefly summarizes various estimates of China's population and food production for the period 1952-70. It points out that the increase in food production for the period under study just kept pace with the rate of population growth. A section of the article, devoted to China's birth control campaigns, quotes Edgar Snow's conversation with Chou En-lai, which revealed that the population increase during the Cultural Revolution was due to early marriages among the young. Since the Cultural Revolution an intensive birth control campaign has been carried out in the rural areas. United States government studies indicating that China will have problems producing enough food to meet the increasing demand of an increasing future population are included in this article. The study concludes that it is imperative that China reduce its birthrate as rapidly as possible.

351 CURRENT SCENE, The Editor.
"Recent Developments in Chinese Education," Vol. X, No. 7, July 1972, pp. 1-6.
Phases of China's educational restoration and reform from 1968 to 1971 are discussed as examples of post-Cultural Revolution development. According to this article, a new educational campaign in the aftermath of the upheaval was directed at three

major areas of educational reform. One reform objective, a goal
of the Cultural Revolution, was the extension of educational
opportunities to the rural areas by providing a universal five
year primary education, using urban middle school graduates as
teachers. Another area of reform was the rapid nationwide
recruitment of worker-peasant-soldier students for university
work under fixed quotas for designated national universities for
each province. The third area of reform was a return to traditional academic content. In addition, there were signs of
revival of the examination system for admission to university
work. The Cultural Revolution, this article contends, not only
disrupted higher education but also failed to solve the problem
of providing a steady supply of trained specialists and skilled
workers for China's development.

352 DERNBERGER, Robert.
"Radical Ideology and Economic Development in China: The
Cultural Revolution and Its Impact on the Economy," Asian Survey,
Vol. XII, No. 12, December 1972, pp. 1048-1065.
A major premise of this study is that the Cultural Revolution
represented the culmination of a series of economic policy
debates. The key economic arguments which resulted in the
Cultural Revolution are analyzed to show the irreconcilable
differences of opposing leadership groups on the prime question
of the appropriate model for China's economic development.
Dernberger feels that the short run effects of the Cultural
Revolution on China's economic policy were insignificant: the
disrupted economy was restored and radical institutional change
occurred in the economy. But the Cultural Revolution resulted
in significant long run changes in China's economic structure in
terms of reorientation of the values of economic activities, the
de-emphasis of elitism, the fostering of mass participation in
economic development programs, reforms in higher education,
revised wage differentials, abolition of bonuses, recognition of
the need for self-reliance and a planned allocation of resources.
Dernberger concludes that if China could achieve long-run
economic growth and, at the same time, acquire qualitative
improvement, then she would have developed a successful new
model of economic development.

353 GOLDMAN, Merle.
"The Aftermath of China's Cultural Revolution," Current History,
Vol. 61, No. 361, September 1971, pp. 165-170 and 182.
Goldman argues that the Cultural Revolution did not yield tangi-
ble progress toward the realization of Mao's vision. She
believes that the restructuring of the political institutions
reflects little of Mao's revolutionary values and that reforms
in economic institutions only partially reflect these values.
The political aftermath led to military dominance in the rebuilding of the party and in local provincial power structures.
Goldman argues that there was no infusion of new blood or youth
into the provincial administration after the breakdown of the
bureaucratic party hierarchy. The only new blood in the central

administration was that of military officers, not the revolutionary representatives of the mass organizations which emerged during the Cultural Revolution. Economic systems were affected mainly by the creation of more decentralized, self-reliant economic operations with emphasis on narrowing the gap between urban and rural life and between experts and workers. Goldman feels that the Cultural Revolution's greatest impact was on education. Curriculum and teaching methods were reorganized and educational opportunities opened for those of non-elite background. Educational content has become more practical and less theoretical. According to the author, a true Cultural Revolution has taken place in the area of production of literary works by amateur writing groups of workers, peasants, and soldiers. Goldman questions however, the reality of reform in the political system. She implies that the dominance of the new bureaucratic-military elite and the uncertain loyalty of the millions of young who were sent to the countryside to be silenced for their political activism could cause future trouble. She concludes: "It is possible that Mao's Cultural Revolution may produce a greater threat to his vision than the threat he set out to eliminate."

354 GOLDMAN, Merle.
"In the Wake of the Cultural Revolution," Current History, Vol. 65, No. 385, September 1973, pp. 129-131 and 136. Goldman believes that the Cultural Revolution created political chaos at all levels of government, and, therefore, the regime's post-Cultural Revolution tasks were to rebuild the party and to curb the military's involvement in politics. She describes the regime's attempt to resurrect the party and army under Lin Piao's leadership, a move which culminated in the military coup attributed to Lin Piao and his military lieutenants in 1971. According to Goldman, after the death of Lin, old party leaders reappeared and the pre-Cultural Revolution status quo was reestablished. She sees less certainty in the central leadership and greater control by the government-bureaucracy than by the party in the post-Revolution period. In Goldman's opinion, the major impact of the Cultural Revolution on the economy was ideological rather than economic, creating a change in attitude rather than in the system of economics. She concludes by saying that Mao's "vision of building a truly revolutionary society still remains and contradicts the current adjustment now under way."

355 LIU, Alan P.
"Mass Campaign and Political Development in China," Current Scene, Vol. XI, No. 8, August 1973, pp. 1-9. This study of mass campaigns in China categorizes mass campaigns from 1949 to 1966 in terms of functionally diffuse or specific and in terms of presence or absence of target groups. The Cultural Revolution is classified under this scheme as functionally diffuse with a target group. In discussing the styles of mass campaigns, Liu describes the Cultural Revolution as one

with heavy accent on ideology and radicalism. The techniques
used were the same ones used for the pre-1953 campaigns, involving "the designation of specific target groups for the public
to struggle against, the dispatch of special cadres to the
provinces to conduct the campaign, and an ad hoc command structure." Liu also discusses the unique features of the Cultural
Revolution: the Red Guards, the public humiliation of officials,
and the use of the military.

356 MALONEY, Joan M.
"Chinese Women and Party Leadership: Impact of the Cultural
Revolution," Current Scene, Vol. X, No. 4, April 10, 1972,
pp. 10-15.
This essay discusses the improved status of women in China
during and since the Cultural Revolution. Statistics are given
to show representation of women on the Central Committee of the
party in 1969 and the increased number of women placed in high
positions in the party apparatus at the local and provincial
level since the Cultural Revolution. The article also reports
increased recruitment of women into low-level party positions.
Propaganda campaigns have also been launched on the glorification of careers for women party activists. However, this report
indicates that there are some unresolved problems related to the
status of women: the avoidance of equal pay for women in the
communes and the denial of party membership to women in some
areas. The article concludes that the status of women in China
has improved greatly since the Cultural Revolution.

357 MICHAEL, Franz.
"China after the Cultural Revolution: The Unresolved Succession
Crisis," Orbis, Vol. XVII, No. 2, Summer 1973, pp. 315-333.
Professor Michael views the Cultural Revolution as but a continuation of a series of party purges for the specific objective
of enabling Mao "to assert his power and policy over the Chinese
communists." He reviews the factors which, during the Cultural
Revolution, led Mao "to tamper with the chief ingredients" of
Lenin's recipe for communist revolution and power control" by
challenging the role of the party. Mao's attempts to deviate
from orthodox communist thinking and behavior are traced back
to the 1956 Soviet Twentieth Party Congress. Subsequent programs that Mao engineered, such as the Great Leap Forward, are
analyzed. The result of the "party-army structure" in 1959, in
Michael's view, was to place in Mao's hand "a reliable means to
secure his power." Thus on the eve of the Cultural Revolution,
Mao had secured a power base in the PLA and placed himself in a
position above the established party apparatus. Michael analyzes the modification of Mao's original plan to substitute his
own mass-based organization for the party organization as events
got out of control in the later stages of the Cultural Revolution. The structure of the revolutionary committees was adopted
as a compromise to unite contending factions. Lin Piao's over-
extension of his power eventually led to his rejection as Mao's
successor. Michael concludes: "The post-Cultural Revolution

scene in China is considerably changed. The military leadership
has been decimated, and though the PLA still predominates in the
revolutionary committees and the new party positions, there is
no commanding military personality who could challenge the
Maoist supremacy." Although Chou En-lai's policy has prevailed
since Lin Piao's demise, Michael sees uncertainty and doubt for
leadership stability in the future.

358 OKSENBERG, Michel.
"Political Changes and Their Causes in China, 1949 to 1972,"
The Political Quarterly, Vol. 45, No. 1, January-March 1974,
pp. 95-114.
This essay describes the changes which took place in the Chinese
political system over the past two decades. Oksenberg sketches
some of the principal trends and developments: the emergence of
strong institutions suited to Chinese conditions, the increasing
strength of government and party bureaucrats, the gradual loss
in effectiveness of the mass campaign techniques developed
during the guerrilla days, the increased differentiation and
specialization of the bureaucracy, the improved communications
system, and the changing focus of decision-making. Oksenberg
postulates that some changes resulted from economic, political
and international developments. For instance, he argues, the
Cultural Revolution was Mao's response to United States escalation of the war in Vietnam and that economic changes were a
result of the availability of resources and the changing relationships of key leaders. Oksenberg concludes that "the changes
since 1949 reflect the continued search for a Chinese political
order suited to the rapidly changing world and domestic environments."

359 ORLEANS, Leo A.
"China: The Population Record," Current Scene, Vol. X, No. 5,
May 10, 1972, pp. 10-19.
Orleans is mainly concerned with the problem of making estimates
of China's population growth rate. He gives a brief survey of
China's population policies and programs since 1949, with some
reference to the discontinuance, beginning with the Cultural
Revolution, of any public information with respect to family
planning or planned parenthood programs. Orleans considers that
the down-transfer of medical personnel from the cities to the
countryside during and after the Cultural Revolution indicates
that they have responsibility for implementing effective birth
control programs in rural areas. Orleans presents a table of
population estimates and projections for China from 1960 to 1980.

360 PFEFFER, Richard M.
"Serving the People and Continuing the Revolution," The China
Quarterly, No. 52, October-December 1972, pp. 620-653.
This article explains the Cultural Revolution in terms of the
Chinese revolutionary movement's need for "a continuing vanguard
to direct the revolutionary change that China's conditions
demand" and its need to institutionalize "the appropriate degree

of accountability and responsiveness to the masses of people."
The article stresses Mao's theory of mass participation and
community control as a key to understanding the Cultural Revolution. The author discusses four examples of this "vanguard
system" to illustrate his thesis: the open door rectification
process, educational reform, the May 7th Cadre Schools, and
direct class representation in the decision-making processes at
all levels. Pfeffer concludes by saying: "The Cultural Revolution and its aftermath represents the return to the integrated
Maoist model of rule and development, incorporating the revival
and institutionalization of mass influence as an integral part
of China's political system."

361   THE POLITICAL QUARTERLY
China in Transition, Vol. 45, No. 1, January-March 1974,
pp. 1-114.
The effects of the Cultural Revolution are analyzed in this
issue in separate essays dealing with the interrelationship
between bureaucrats and technocrats, and the process of industrialization: China's ability to recover from the disruption
caused by the Cultural Revolution in the economic and industrial
sectors; the acceptance of gradual institutional and social
change; educational reform to provide equality; the Chinese
leaders' adaptation of their roles in a changing world; and,
finally, causes for political change in China during the past two
decades. Entries on these articles are annotated separately in
this bibliography.

362   PRYBYLA, Jan S.
"China's Economy: Experiments in Maoism," Current History,
Vol. 59, No. 349, September 1970, pp. 159-180.
The theme of this article is that the wounds inflicted on
China's political and economic systems by the Cultural Revolution had gradually healed between 1969 and 1970 and that a
general outline of Mao's new society had emerged by 1970. Mao's
concept of China's future communist society is described using
two policy documents emphasized by the leaders after the 9th
Party Congress, which concluded the Cultural Revolution: the
Anshan Constitution and the October 14, 1969, Red Flag editorial
on China's road to socialist industrialization. The five basic
principles of the Anshan Constitution revised the orthodox
Soviet-type socialism. These principles were: (1) correct
politics in command of economics; (2) strengthened party
leadership in economics; (3) mass line in economics; (4) cadre
participation in productive labor; and (5) worker's technical
innovation and revolution. The rural variant of the Anshan
principles was the Tachai work-point system. The Red-Flag
editorial stated that the principal guide lines for China's
road to socialist industrialization consisted of (1) recognition of agriculture as the foundation for China's economic
development, (2) self-reliance, (3) mutual technical aid from
friendly nations, and (4) rational planning in the use of
resources.

363 SNOW, Edgar.
"Mao and the New Mandate," The World Today, Vol. 25, No. 7,
July 1969, pp. 289-297.
The main purpose of Snow's article is to ascertain China's
domestic and foreign policies following the convening of the
Ninth Party Congress in April 1969, which proclaimed the success
of the Cultural Revolution. One of Snow's conclusions is that
by the Ninth Party Congress "Mao had largely replaced the
Central Committee majority with a new coalition of forces
pledged to maintain his absolute authority." Snow states that
"there was indeed a revolutionary seizure of power" as evidenced
by the massive purge within the top levels of the party. The
Cultural Revolution had, in essence, established "a Sino-Marxist
Communist Party or a Maoist Revolutionary Communist Party."
Among the many results of the Cultural Revolution were, according to Snow, the institutionalization of the mass-line direction
communication between the leaders and the people, the prevention
of "the formation of a corruptible (revisionist) elite," and the
loyalty of the military to secure internal unity. Snow also
believed that the new structure of party and government would
uphold "the Cult of Mao as a unifying faith." Maoist solutions
would be used to resolve inherent contradictions between revolutionary society and modernization. In foreign affairs, Snow
sees "a more flexible diplomacy" toward the world as a whole;
even though "to Mao, China is the world, and it's for the others
to beat a footpath there."

364 WALLER, Derek J.
"Revolutionary Intellectuals or Managerial Modernizers," The
Political Quarterly, Vol. 45, No. 1, January-March 1974,
pp. 5-12.
This essay discusses a perennial problem in Chinese politics--
the conflict between the revolutionary intellectual and the
"managerial modernizers." Based on the developmental experiences of both the Soviet Union and China, Waller argues that
the communist party as a ruling elite must inevitably incorporate the "managerial modernizers" into its membership. He
illustrates the nature and depth of the "red versus expert"
question in China by describing the rectification campaigns of
1954 and 1959 and the Cultural Revolution of 1966. The Cultural
Revolution is explained as a result of Mao's concern over the
development of complex and specialized bureaucratic institutions
which wielded too much power and influence and were dominated by
careerists. Educational reforms introduced during and after the
Cultural Revolution were aimed at curbing the growth of these
bureaucratic tendencies. Waller sees some relaxation in attacks
against the bureaucrats during the post-Cultural Revolution
period but warns that "the difficulties in finding an effective
balance between the conflicting demands of political purity and
technical expertise will remain with China for the foreseeable
future."

AUTHOR INDEX

The reference numbers used in this index are the numbers for the annotated bibliographic entries. Under the alphabetized authors' names are the citations for the works annotated in this bibliography, followed by the appropriate entry numbers.

ACHMINOW, Herman F.
"Crisis in Mao's Realm and Moscow's China Policy," Orbis, Vol. 41, No. 4, Winter 1968, pp. 1179-1192.   313

ADIE, W. A. C.
"China Returns to Africa," Current Scene, Vol. X, No. 8, August 1972, pp. 1-12.   314

ADIE, W. A. C.
"China's 'Second Liberation' in Perspective," China After the Cultural Revolution, Vintage Books, New York, 1970, pp. 27-56.   1

AHN, Byung-joon.
"The Cultural Revolution and China's Search for Political Order," The China Quarterly, No. 58, April-June 1974, pp. 249-285.   2

AHN, Byung-joon.
"The Politics of Peking Opera, 1962-1965," Asian Survey, Vol. XII, No. 12, December 1972, pp. 1066-1081.   302

AN, Tai Sung.
Mao Tse-tung's Cultural Revolution, Pegasus, A Division of the Bobs-Merrill Company, Inc., Indianapolis, Ind., 1972, 211p.   3

ANDORS, Stephen.
"Revolution and Modernization: Man and Machine In Industrializing Society, the Chinese Case," America's Asia: Dissenting Essays on Asian-American Relations, Edward Friedman and Mark Selden, eds., Vintage Books, A Division of Random House, New York, 1971, pp. 393-444.   228

ARMBRUSTER, Frank E., LEWIS, John W., MOZINGO, David, and TANG TSOU.
China Briefing, University of Chicago, Center for Policy Study, the University of Chicago Press, Chicago, 1968, 72p.   4

ASIAN RESEARCH CENTRE.
The Great Cultural Revolution in China, Charles E. Tuttle Company, Rutland, Vt., and Tokyo, 1968, 507p.   5

ASIAN RESEARCH CENTRE.
The Great Power Struggle in China, Hong Kong, 1969, 303p.   6

ASIAN SURVEY.
"The Cultural Revolution and Its Aftermath," Vol. XII,
No. 12, December 1972, pp. 999-1100.   344

BARNETT, Doak A.
China After Mao, Princeton University Press, Princeton,
N.J., 1967, 287p.   7

BARNETT, Doak A.
"China and U.S. Policy: A Time of Transition," Current
Scene, Vol. VIII, No. 10, May 15, 1970, pp. 1-10.   315

BARNETT, Doak A.
A New U.S. Policy Toward China, The Brookings Institution,
Washington, D.C., 1971, 132p.   316

BARNETT, Doak A., and REISCHAUER, Edwin O., eds.
The United States and China: The Next Decade, The
National Committee on U.S.-China Relations, Praeger
Publishers, New York and London, 1970, 249p.   317

BASTID, Marianne.
"Economic Necessity and Political Ideals in Educational
Reform During the Cultural Revolution," The China
Quarterly, No. 42, April-June 1970, pp. 16-45.   273

BASTID, Marianne.
"Levels of Economic Decision-making," Authority,
Participation and Cultural Change in China, Stuart R.
Schram, ed., Cambridge University Press, Cambridge,
1973, pp. 159-197.   345

BAUM, Richard.
"China: Year of the Mangoes," Asian Survey, Vol. IX,
No. 1, January 1969, pp. 1-17.   212

BAUM, Richard.
"Elite Behavior under Conditions of Stress: The Lesson
of 'Tang-chuan Pai' in the Cultural Revolution," Elites
in the People's Republic of China, Robert A. Scalapino,
ed., University of Washington Press, Seattle and London,
1972, pp. 540-574.   102

BAUM, Richard.
"Ideology and Redivivus," Problem of Communism," May-June
1967, Vol. XVI, No. 3, pp. 1-11.   8

201

BAUM, Richard.
"'Red and Expert': The Politico-Ideological Foundations
of China's Great Leap Forward," Asian Survey, Vol. IV,
No. 9, September 1964, pp. 1048-1057.   9

BAUM, Richard, with BENNETT, Louise B., eds.
China in Ferment: Perspectives on the Cultural Revolution,
Prentice-Hall, Inc., Englewood Cliffs, N.J., 1971, 246p.   10

BAUM, Richard, and TEIWES, Frederick C.
"Liu Shao-chi and the Cadres Question," Asian Survey,
Vol. VIII, No. 4, April 1968, pp. 323-345.   103

BENNETT, Gordon.
"China's Continuing Revolution: Will It Be Permanent?"
Asian Survey, Vol. X, No. 1, January 1970, pp. 2-17.   213

BENNETT, Gordon.
"Military Regions and Provincial Party Secretaries:
One Outcome of China's Cultural Revolution," The China
Quarterly, No. 54, April-June 1973, pp. 294-307.   159

BENNETT, Gordon, and MONTAPERTO, Ronald N.
Red Guard: The Political Biography of Dai Hsiao-ai,
Anchor Books, Doubleday and Co., Inc., Garden City,
N.Y., 1972, 258p.   144

BETTELHEIM, Charles.
Cultural Revolution and Industrial Organization in
China: Changes in Management and the Division of Labor,
Monthly Review Press, New York, 1974, 128p.   229

BRIDGHAM, Philip.
"Factionalism in the Central Committee," Party Leadership
and Revolutionary Power in China, John W. Lewis, ed.,
Cambridge University Press, Cambridge, 1970, pp. 203-233.   104

BRIDGHAM, Philip.
"Mao's Cultural Revolution in 1967: The Struggle to
Seize Power," The China Quarterly, No. 34, April-June
1968, pp. 6-36.   160

BRIDGHAM, Philip.
"Mao's 'Cultural Revolution': Origin and Development,"
The China Quarterly, No. 29, January-March 1967, pp. 1-35.   11

BRIDGHAM, Philip.
"Mao's Cultural Revolution: The Struggle to Consolidate
Power," The China Quarterly, No. 41, January-March 1970,
pp. 1-34.   161

BRUGGER, William.
"The Ninth National Congress of the Chinese Communist
Party," The World Today, Vol. 25, No. 7, July 1969,
pp. 297-305.   346

BRYAN, Derek.
"Changing Social Ethics in Contemporary China,"
The Political Quarterly, Vol. 45, No. 1, January-
March 1974, pp. 49-57.   347

BULLETIN OF THE ATOMIC SCIENTISTS.
China After the Cultural Revolution, A Selection from
Bulletin of the Atomic Scientists, Vol. XXV, No. 2,
February 1969, Vintage Books, New York, 1970, 247p.   12

BURTON, Barry.
"The Cultural Revolution's Ultra-left Conspiracy:
The 'May 16 Group,'" Asian Survey, Vol. XI, No. 11,
November 1971, pp. 1029-1053.   162

CHAI, Winberg.
"The Reorganization of the Chinese Communist Party,
1966-1968," Asian Survey, Vol. VIII, No. 11, November
1968, pp. 901-910.   105

CHANG, Chen-pang.
"The Present and Future Situation of the Chinese
Communist Party and Administration," Chinese Communist
Affairs, Vol. 5, No. 5, October 1968, pp. 15-28.   106

CHANG, Chun-shu, CRUMP, James, and MURPHEY, Rhoads, eds.
The Cultural Revolution: 1967 in Review, Michigan Papers
in Chinese Studies No. 2, University of Michigan,
Ann Arbor, 1968, 125p.   13

CHANG, Parris.
"Changing Patterns of Military Roles in Chinese Politics,"
The Military and Political Power in China in the 1970's,
William W. Whitson, ed., Praeger Publishers, New York,
1972, pp. 47-70.   163

CHANG, Parris.
"Mao's Great Purge: A Political Balance Sheet,"
Problems of Communism, Vol. XVIII, No. 2, March-April
1969, pp. 1-10.   14, 107

CHANG, Parris.
"Provincial Party Leaders Strategies for Survival during
the Cultural Revolution," Elites in the People's Republic
of China, Robert A. Scalapino, ed., University of
Washington Press, Seattle and London, 1972, pp. 501-539.   108

CHANG, Parris.
Radicals and Radical Ideology in China's Cultural Revolution,
Research Institute on Communist Affairs, Columbia University,
New York, 1973, 103p.   109

CHANG, Parris.
"Regional Military Power: The Aftermath of the Cultural
Revolution," Asian Survey, Vol. XII, No. 12, December 1972,
pp. 999-1013.   348

CHANG, Parris.
"The Revolutionary Committee in China - Two Case Studies:
Heilungkiang and Honan," Current Scene, Vol. VI, No. 9,
June 1, 1968, pp. 1-37.   214

CHEN, Jack.
A Year in Upper Felicity: Life in a Chinese Village
during the Cultural Revolution, Macmillan Company,
New York and London, 1973, 383p.   303

CHEN, Theodore Hsi-en.
"Education in Communist China," Communist China, 1949-1969:
A Twenty-year Appraisal, Frank N. Trager and William
Henderson, eds., New York University Press, New York,
1970, pp. 175-198.   274

CHEN, Theodore Hsi-en.
"A Nation in Agony," Problems of Communism, Vol. XV,
No. 6, November-December 1966, pp. 14-20.   15

CHENG, C. K.
"Two Decades of Experiment in Communization," Journal
of Asian and African Studies, York University,
Toronto, Canada, Vol. IV, No. 2, April 1969, pp. 81-105   230

CHENG, Chu-yuan.
"The Effects of the Cultural Revolution on China's
Machine Building Industry," Current Scene, Vol. VIII,
No. 1, January 1970, pp. 1-15.   231

CHENG, Chu-yuan.
"The Power Struggle in Red China," Asian Survey, Vol. VI,
No. 9, September 1966, pp. 469-483.   16

CHENG, Peter.
"Liu Shao-chi and the Cultural Revolution,"
Asian Survey, Vol. XI, No. 10, October 1971,
pp. 943-957.   17, 110

CHENG, Peter.
"The Root of China's Cultural Revolution: The Feud
between Mao Tse-tung and Liu Shao-chi," <u>Orbis</u>, Vol. XI
No. 4, Winter 1968, pp. 1160-1178.   18

CHI, Wen-shun, compiler and ed.
<u>Readings in the Chinese Communist Cultural Revolution</u>,
<u>A Manual for Students of the Chinese Language</u>, University
of California Press, Berkeley, Los Angeles and London,
1971, 530p.   19

CHI, Wen-shun.
"Sun Yeh-fang and His Revisionist Economics," <u>Asian</u>
<u>Survey</u>, Vol. XII, No. 10, October 1972, pp. 897-900.   232

CHIEN, Yu-shen.
<u>China's Fading Revolution: Army Dissent and Military</u>
<u>Divisions, 1967-68</u>, Centre of Contemporary Chinese
Studies, Hong Kong, 1969, 405p.   164

CHINA NEWS ANALYSIS, The Editor.
"Army Rule: Part I - Inner Party Relations," No. 707,
May 10, 1968, pp. 1-7.   168

CHINA NEWS ANALYSIS, The Editor.
"Army Rule: Part II - Personnel Changes," No. 708,
May 17, 1968, pp. 1-7.   169

CHINA NEWS ANALYSIS, The Editor.
"Army Rule: Part III - Soldiers in the Maze," No. 710,
May 31, 1968, pp. 1-7.   170

CHINA NEWS ANALYSIS, The Editor.
"Army Rules: Part IV - In Factories," No. 711, June 7,
1968, pp. 1-7.   171

CHINA NEWS ANALYSIS, The Editor.
"Army Rule: Part V - In the Villages," No. 712, June 14,
1968, pp. 1-7.   172

CHINA NEWS ANALYSIS, The Editor.
"Army Rule: Part VI - In Schools," No. 715, July 5, 1968,
pp. 1-7.   173

CHINA NEWS ANALYSIS, The Editor.
"Decline in the Prestige of the PLA," No. 664, June 16,
1967, pp. 1-7.   166

CHINA NEWS ANALYSIS, The Editor.
"Military Rule," No. 655, April 14, 1967, pp. 1-7.   165

CHINA NEWS ANALYSIS, The Editor.
"PLA Soldiers in Politics," No. 751, April 4, 1969, pp. 1-7. 167

CHINA NEWS ANALYSIS, The Editor.
"Provincial Party Congresses," No. 746, February 28, 1969,
pp. 1-7.   215

CHINA NEWS ANALYSIS, The Editor.
"Reconstruction of the Communist Party," No. 790,
February 6, 1970, pp. 1-7.   111

CHIU, S. M.
"China's Military Posture," Current History, Vol. 53,
No. 313, September 1967, pp. 155-160.   174

CHU, Hung-ti.
"Education in Mainland China," Current History, Vol. 59,
No. 349, September 1970, pp. 165-182.   275

COHEN, Jerome H., ed.
The Dynamics of China's Foreign Relations, East Asian
Research Center, East Asian Monographs No. 39, Harvard
University, 1970, 129p.   318

COMMITTEE OF CONCERNED ASIAN SCHOLARS.
China! Inside the People's Republic, Bantam Books, Inc.,
New York, 1972, 433p.   20

CURRENT SCENE, The Editor.
"China's Revolutionary Committees," Vol. VI, No. 21,
December 6, 1968, pp. 1-18.   219

CURRENT SCENE, The Editor.
"China's Taching Oilfield: Eclipse of an Industrial
Model," Vol. VI, No. 16, September 17, 1968, pp. 1-10.   236

CURRENT SCENE, The Editor.
"Communist China Economy at Mid-year 1968: Eighteen
Months of Disorder," Vol. VI, No. 12, July 17, 1968,
pp. 1-16.   235

CURRENT SCENE, The Editor.
"The Conflict between Mao Tse-tung and Liu Shao-chi
over Agricultural Mechanization in Communist China,"
Vol. VI, No. 17, October 1, 1968, pp. 1-20.   237

CURRENT SCENE, The Editor.
"The Cultural Revolution: Act III - The Maoists against
Liu Shao-chi," Vol. V, No. 6, April 5, 1967, pp. 1-10.   114

CURRENT SCENE, The Editor.
"Education Reform and Rural Settlement in Communist
China," Vol. VIII, No. 17, November 7, 1970, pp. 1-7.   277

CURRENT SCENE, The Editor.
"Educational Reform in Rural China," Vol. VII, No. 3,
February 8, 1969, pp. 1-17.   276

CURRENT SCENE, The Editor.
"The Food and Population Balance: China's Modernization
Dilemma," Vol. IX, No. 6, July 7, 1971, pp. 1-7.   350

CURRENT SCENE, The Editor.
"Industrial Development in China: A Return to Decentralization," Vol. VI, No. 22, December 20, 1968, pp. 1-18.   238

CURRENT SCENE, The Editor.
"Lin Piao and the Cultural Revolution," Vol. VIII, No. 14,
August 1, 1970, pp. 1-14.   113

CURRENT SCENE, The Editor.
"Lin Piao: A Political Profile," Vol. VII, No. 5,
March 10, 1969, pp. 1-16.   112

CURRENT SCENE, The Editor.
"Mao Fails to Build His Utopia: A Political Assessment
of Communist China," Vol. VI, No. 15, September 3, 1968,
pp. 1-9.   217

CURRENT SCENE, The Editor.
"Mao's Revolutionary Successors: Part II - Youth to the
Countryside and Back Again," Vol. V., No. 16, October 2,
1967, pp. 1-8.   145

CURRENT SCENE, The Editor.
"Peking and Latin America: Rewriting Scenario," Vol. IX,
No. 4, April 7, 1971, pp. 1-6.   319

CURRENT SCENE, The Editor.
"Peking's Programs to Move Human and Material Resources
to the Countryside," Vol. VII, No. 18, September 15,
1969, pp. 1-17.   239

CURRENT SCENE, The Editor.
"Recent Developments in Chinese Education," Vol. X,
No. 7, July 1972, pp. 1-6.   351

CURRENT SCENE, The Editor.
"The Revival of the Communist Youth League," Vol. VIII,
No. 5, March 1, 1970, pp. 1-7.   146

CURRENT SCENE, The Editor.
"The Revolution Committee and the Party in the Aftermath
of the Cultural Revolution," Vol. VIII, No. 8, April 15,
1970, pp. 1-10.   349

CURRENT SCENE, The Editor.
"Revolutionary Committee Leadership - China's Current
Provincial Authorities," Vol. VI, No. 18, October 18,
1968, pp. 1-28.   218

CURRENT SCENE, The Editor.
"Sources of Labor Discontent in China: The Worker-
Peasant System," Vol. VI, No. 5, March 15, 1968,
pp. 1-28.   234

CURRENT SCENE, The Editor.
"Stalemate in Szechwan," Vol. VI, No. 11, July 1, 1968,
pp. 1-13.   216

CURRENT SCENE, The Editor.
"What Price Revolution: China's Economy in 1967,"
Vol. V, No. 18, November 1, 1967, pp. 1-10.   233

DAUBIER, Jean.
A History of the Cultural Revolution, Vintage Books,
A Division of Random House, New York, 1974, 336p.   21

DAVIS, Deborah S.
"The Cultural Revolution in Wuhan," The Cultural
Revolution in the Provinces, East Asian Monographs
No. 42, Harvard University Press, Cambridge, 1971,
pp. 147-170.   220

DEAN, Genevieve
"China's Technological Development," New Scientist,
May 18, 1972, pp. 371-373.   288

DEAN, Genevieve.
Science and Technology in the Development of Modern
China: An Annotated Bibliography, Mansell Information/
Publishing, Limited, London, 1974, 265p.   290

DEAN, Genevieve.
"Science, Technology and Development: China as a Case
Study," The China Quarterly, No. 51, July-September
1972, pp. 520-534.   289

DERNBERGER, Robert.
"Economic Realities and China's Political Economics,"
Bulletin of the Atomic Scientists, Vol. XXV, No. 2,
February 1969, pp. 34-42.   240

DERNBERGER, Robert.
"Radical Ideology and Economic Development in China:
The Cultural Revolution and Its Impact on the Economy,"
Asian Survey, Vol. XII, No. 12, December 1972,
pp. 1048-1065.   352

DESHINGKAR, G. D.
"The Causes of the Cultural Revolution," China Report,
Vol. 3, No. 1, December 1966-January 1967, pp. 9-12
and 17.   22

DESPHANDE, G. P.
"The PLA and the Cultural Revolution," China Report,
Vol. 3, No. 3, April-May 1967, pp. 12-16.   175

DIAO, Richard K.
"The Impact of the Cultural Revolution on China's
Economic Elite," The China Quarterly, No. 42, April-
June 1970, pp. 65-87.   241

DITTMER, Lowell.
"The Cultural Revolution and the Fall of Liu Shao-chi,"
Current Scene, Vol. XI, No. 1, January 1973, pp. 1-13.   116

DITTMER, Lowell.
"Mass Line and Mass Criticism in China: An Analysis of
the Fall of Liu Shao-chi," Asian Survey, Vol. XIII,
No. 8, August 1973, pp. 772-792.   115

DOMES, Jurgen.
"The Cultural Revolution and the Army," Asian Survey,
Vol. VIII, No. 5, May 1968, pp. 349-363.   176

DOMES, Jurgen.
"Party Politics and the Cultural Revolution," Communist
China, 1949-1969: A Twenty-year Appraisal, Frank N.
Trager and William Henderson, eds., New York University
Press, New York, 1970, pp. 63-93.   117

DOMES, Jurgen.
"The Role of the Military in the Formation of Revolutionary
Committees, 1967-68," The China Quarterly, No. 44,
October-December 1970, pp. 112-145.   221

DONNITHORNE, Audrey.
"China's Cellular Economy: Some Economic Trends Since
the Cultural Revolution," The China Quarterly, No. 52,
October-December 1972, pp. 606-618.   242

DONNITHORNE, Audrey.
China's Economic System, Frederick A. Praeger Publishers,
New York and Washington, 1967, 592p.   243

DORRILL, William F.
"Leadership and Succession in Communist China," Current
History, Vol. 49, No. 289, September 1965, pp. 129 - 135
and 179-180.   23

DUTT, Gardi, and DUTT, Vidya P.
<u>China's Cultural Revolution</u>, Asia Publishing House, Bombay
and Calcutta, 1970, 260p.   24

ELEGANT, Robert S.
<u>Mao's Great Revolution</u>, The World Publishing Company,
New York and Cleveland, 1971, 478p.   25

ELMQUIST, Paul.
"The Internal Role of the Military," <u>The Military and
Political Power in China in the 1970's</u>, William W. Whitson,
ed., Praeger Publishers, New York, 1972, pp. 269-289.   177

ESMEIN, Jean.
<u>The Chinese Cultural Revolution</u>, Anchor Books, New York,
1973, 346p.   26

FAN, Kuang-huan.
<u>The Chinese Cultural Revolution: Selected Documents</u>,
Grove Press, Inc., New York, 1968, 320p.   27

FETOV, V.
"The Army: A Reliable Supporter of Mao," <u>Reprint from
the Soviet Press</u>, Vol. IX, No. 4, August 22, 1969,
pp. 15-25.   178

FEURTADO, Gardel.
"The Formation of Provincial Revolutionary Committees,
1966-68: Heilungkiang and Hopei," <u>Asian Survey</u>, Vol. XII,
No. 12, 1972, pp. 1014-1031.   222

FITZGERALD, C. P.
"A Revolutionary Hiatus," <u>China After the Cultural
Revolution</u>, Vintage Books, New York, 1970, pp. 145-166.   320

FITZGERALD, Stephen.
"China Visited: A View of the Cultural Revolution,"
<u>China and Ourselves: Explorations and Revisions by a
New Generation</u>, Bruce Douglass and Ross Terrill, eds.,
Beacon Press, Boston, 1970, pp. 1-29.   28

FITZGERALD, Stephen.
"Overseas Chinese Affairs and the Cultural Revolution,"
<u>The China Quarterly</u>, No. 40, October-December 1969,
pp. 103-126.   321

FOKKEMA, D. W.
"Maoist Ideology and Its Exemplification in the New
Peking Opera," <u>Current Scene</u>, Vol. X, No. 8, August 1972,
pp. 13-20.   304

FRASER, Stewart E., and HAWKINS, John N.
"Chinese Education: Revolution and Development," <u>Phi
Delta Kappan</u>, April 1972, pp. 487-500.   278

FRASER, Stewart E., and HSU, Kuang-liang.
<u>Chinese Education and Society: A Bibliographic Guide</u>,
International Arts and Sciences Press, Inc., White
Plains, N. Y., 1972, 204p.   279

FRIEDMAN, Edward.
"Cultural Limits of the Cultural Revolution," <u>Asian
Survey</u>, Vol. IX, No. 3, March 1969, pp. 188-201.   29

FUNNELL, Victor.
"Bureaucracy and the Chinese Communist Party," <u>Current
Scene</u>, Vol. IX, No. 5, May 7, 1971, pp. 1-14.   118

FUNNELL, Victor.
"The Chinese Communist Youth Movement 1949-1966,"
<u>The China Quarterly</u>, No. 42, April-June 1970, pp. 105-130.   147

FUNNELL, Victor.
"Social Stratification," <u>Problems of Communism</u>, Vol. XVII,
No. 2, March-April 1968, pp. 14-20.   30

GARDNER, John, and IDEMA, Wilt.
"China's Educational Revolution," <u>Authority, Participation,
and Cultural Change in China</u>, Stuart R. Schram, ed.,
Cambridge University Press, Cambridge, 1973, pp. 257-289.   280

GELMAN, Harry.
"Mao and the Permanent Purge," <u>Problems of Communism</u>,
Vol. XV, No. 6, November-December 1966, pp. 2-14.   31

GITTINGS, John.
"Army-Party Relations in the Light of the Cultural
Revolution," <u>Party Leadership and Revolutionary Power
in China</u>, John Wilson Lewis, ed., Cambridge University
Press, Cambridge, 1970, pp. 373-403.   182

GITTINGS, John.
"The Chinese Army's Role in the Cultural Revolution,"
<u>Pacific Affairs</u>, Vol. XXXIX, Nos. 3 and 4, Fall and
Winter 1966-67, pp. 269-289.   180

GITTINGS, John.
"The Cultural Revolution and the Chinese Army: A Study
in Escalation," <u>The World Today</u>, Vol. 23, No. 4,
April 1967, pp. 166-176.   179

GITTINGS, John.
"The Prospects of the Cultural Revolution," China After
the Cultural Revolution, Vintage Books, New York, 1970,
pp. 57-72.   32

GITTINGS, John.
"A Red Guard Repents," Far Eastern Economic Review,
July 10, 1969, pp. 123-126.   148

GITTINGS, John.
"Reversing the PLA Verdicts," Far Eastern Economic
Review, July 25, 1968, pp. 191-193.   181

GITTINGS, John.
"What Was It All About," Far Eastern Economic Review,
October 20, 1969, pp. 36-37.   33

GOLDMAN, Merle.
"The Aftermath of China's Cultural Revolution," Current
History, Vol. 61, No. 361, September 1971, pp. 165-170
and 182.   353

GOLDMAN, Merle.
"In the Wake of the Cultural Revolution," Current
History, Vol. 65, No. 385, September 1973, pp. 129-
131 and 136.   354

GOLDMAN, Merle.
Literary Dissent in Communist China, Harvard University
Press, Cambridge, Mass., 1967, 343p.   34

GOODSTADT, Leo.
China's Search for Plenty: The Economics of Mao Tse-tung,
Weatherhill, New York and Tokyo, 1973, 266p.   244

GOODSTADT, Leo.
"Wages in Command," Far Eastern Economic Review,
August 6, 1970, pp. 52-54.   245

GRAY, Jack.
"The Economics of Maoism," Bulletin of the Atomic
Scientists, Vol. XXV, No. 2, February 1969, pp. 42-51.   246

GRAY, Jack.
"Mao's Economic Thoughts," Far Eastern Economic Review,
January 15, 1970, pp. 16-18.   247

GRAY, Jack.
"Politics in Command: The Maoist Theory of Social Change
and Economic Growth," The Political Quarterly, Vol. 45,
No. 1, January-March 1974, pp. 26-48.   248

212

GRAY, Jack.
"The Two Roads: Alternative Strategies of Social Change
and Economic Growth in China," Authority, Participation
and Cultural Change in China, Stuart Schram, ed., Cambridge
University Press, Cambridge, 1973, pp. 109-157.   249

GRAY, Jack, and CAVENDISH, Patrick.
Chinese Communism in Crisis: Maoism and the Cultural
Revolution, Frederick A. Praeger, New York, 1968, 279p.   35

GURLEY, W.
"Maoist Economic Development: The New Man in the New
China," The Center Magazine, Center for Study of
Democratic Institutions, Santa Barbara, California,
Vol. III, No. 3, May-June 1970, pp. 25-33.   250

GURTOV, Melvin.
"The Foreign Ministry and Foreign Affairs in the Chinese
Cultural Revolution," The Cultural Revolution in China,
Thomas W. Robinson, ed., University of California Press,
Berkeley and Los Angeles, 1971, pp. 313-366.   322

HARDING, Harry, Jr.
"China: Toward Revolutionary Pragmatism," Asian Survey,
Vol. XI, No. 1, January 1971, pp. 51-67.   36

HARDING, Harry, Jr.
"Maoist Theories of Policy-making and Organization,"
The Cultural Revolution in China, Thomas Robinson, ed.,
University of California Press, Berkeley and Los Angeles,
1971, pp. 113-164.   119

EAST ASIAN RESEARCH CENTER, Harvard University.
The Cultural Revolution in the Provinces, East Asian
Monographs No. 42, Harvard University, 1971, 216p.   223

HAWKINS, John N.
Educational Theory in the People's Republic of China:
The Report of Chien Chun-jui, Asian Studies at Hawaii
No. 6, University of Hawaii Press, Honolulu, 1971, 120p.   281

HEASLET, Juliana Pennington.
"The Red Guards: Instruments of Destruction in the
Cultural Revolution," Asian Survey, Vol. XII, No. 12,
December 1972, pp. 1032-1047.   149

HINTON, Harold.
China's Turbulent Quest: An Analysis of China's Foreign
Relations Since 1949, Indiana University Press, Bloomington,
Ind., 1972, 352p.   323

HINTON, Harold.
An Introduction to Chinese Politics, Praeger Publishers,
New York, 1973, 323p.   37

HINTON, Harold.
"Sino-Soviet Relations in the Brezhnev Era,"
Current History, Vol. 61, No. 361, September 1971,
pp. 135-141 and 181.   324

HINTON, Harold.
"Vietnam Policy, Domestic Factionalism, Regionalism,
and Plotting a Coup," Cases in Comparative Politics:
Asia, Lucian W. Pye, ed., Little, Brown and Company,
Boston, 1970, pp. 119-156.   325

HINTON, William.
Hundred Day War: The Cultural Revolution at Tsinghua
University, Monthly Review Press, New York and London,
1972, 288p.   38

HINTON, William.
Turning Point in China: An Essay on The Cultural
Revolution, Monthly Review Press, New York, 1972, 112p.   39

HO, Ping-ti and TANG TSOU, eds.
China's Heritage and the Communist Political System,
China in Crisis, Vol. 1, Book 2, The University of
Chicago Press, Chicago, 1968, 803p.   40

HOOK, Brian.
"China's Cultural Revolution: The Preconditions in
Historical Perspective," The World Today, Vol. 23,
No. 11, November 1967, pp. 454-464.   41

HOOK, Brian.
"The Post-Plenum Development of China's Proletarian
Cultural Revolution," The World Today, Vol. 22, No. 11,
November 1966, pp. 467-475.   42

HOWE, Christopher.
"Economic Trends and Policies," The Political Quarterly,
Vol. 45, No. 1, January-March 1974, pp. 12-25.   251

HOWE, Christopher.
"Labour Organization and Incentives in Industry Before
and After the Cultural Revolution," Authority,
Participation, and Cultural Change in China, Stuart
Shcram, ed., Cambridge University Press, Cambridge,
1973, pp. 233-256.   252

214

HSIAO, Gene T.
"The Background and Development of 'The Proletarian
Cultural Revolution,'" Asian Survey, Vol. VII, No. 6,
June 1967, pp. 389-404.   43

HSIUNG, James Chieh.
Ideology and Practice: The Evolution of Chinese
Communism, Praeger Publishers, New York, 1970, 359p.   44

HSU, Kai-yu.
"The Chinese Communist Leadership," Current History,
Vol. 57, No. 337, September 1969, pp. 129-136.   120

HUANG, Joe C.
Heroes and Villains in Communist China: The Contemporary
Chinese Novel as a Reflection of Life, C. Hurst, London,
1973, 345p.   305

HUANG, Lucy Jen.
"The Role of Religion in Communist Chinese Society,"
Asian Survey, Vol. XI, No. 7, July 1971, pp. 693-708.   306

HUBERMAN, Leo, and SWEEZY, Paul.
"The Cultural Revolution in China," Monthly Review,
Vol. 18, No. 8, January 1967, pp. 1-17.   45

HUGHES, T. J.
"China's Economy - Retrospect and Prospect,"
International Affairs (Catham House), Vol. 46, No. 1,
January 1970, pp. 63-73.   253

HUNTER, Neale.
Shanghai Journal: An Eyewitness Account of the Cultural
Revolution, Frederick A. Praeger, New York, 1969, 311p.   46

HYER, Paul, and HESTON, William.
"The Cultural Revolution in Inner Mongolia," The China
Quarterly, No. 36, October-December 1968, pp. 114-128.   224

ISRAEL, John.
"The Red Guards in Historical Perspective: Continuity
and Change in the Chinese Youth Movement," The China
Quarterly, No. 30, April-June 1967, pp. 1-32.   150

ITO, Kikazo, and SHIBATA, Minoru.
"The Dilemma of Mao Tse-tung," The China Quarterly,
No. 38, July-September 1968, pp. 58-77.   47

JOFFE, Ellis.
"China in Mid-1966: 'Cultural Revolution' or Struggle
for Power?," The China Quarterly, No. 26, July-September
1966, pp. 123-131.   48

JOFFE, Ellis.
"The Chinese Army After the Cultural Revolution: The
Effects of Intervention," The China Quarterly, No. 55,
July-September 1973, pp. 450-477.   185

JOFFE, Ellis.
"The Chinese Army in the Cultural Revolution: The
Politics of Intervention," The Current Scene, Vol. VIII,
No. 18, December 7, 1970, pp. 1-25.   183

JOFFE, Ellis.
"The Chinese Army Under Lin Piao: Prelude to Political
Intervention," China: Management of a Revolutionary
Society, John M. Lindbeck, ed., University of Washington
Press, Seattle and London, 1971, pp. 343-374.   184

JOHNSON, Chalmers.
"China: The Cultural Revolution in Structural Perspective,
Asian Survey, Vol. VIII, No. 1, January 1968, pp. 1-15.   49

JOHNSON, Chalmers, ed.
Ideology and Politics in Contemporary China, University
of Washington Press, Seattle and London, 1973, 390p.   50

JOHNSON, Chalmers.
"Lin Piao's Army and Its Role in Chinese Society:
Part I and II," Current Scene, Vol. IV, Nos. 13-14,
July 1 and 14, 1966, pp. 1-10 and pp. 1-11.   186

JOHNSON, Chalmers.
"The Two Chinese Revolutions," The China Quarterly,
No. 39, July-September 1969, pp. 12-29.   51

JORDAN, James D.
"Political Orientation of the PLA," Current Scene,
Vol. XI, No. 1, November 1973, pp. 1-14.   187

KARNOW, Stanley.
Mao and China: From Revolution to Revolution, The
Viking Press, New York, 1972, 592p.   52

KAROL, K. S.
The Second Chinese Revolution, translated from the
French by Mervyn Jones, Hill and Wang, New York,
1974, 472p.   54

KAROL, K. S.
"Why the Cultural Revolution?," Monthly Review, Vol. 19,
No. 4, September 1967, pp. 22-34.   53

KEN LING.
The Revenge of Heaven: Journal of a Young Chinese,
Ballantine Books, New York, 1972, 438p.   151

216

KIM, Samuel S.
"The Peoples Republic of China in the United Nations:
A Preliminary Analysis," World Politics, Vol. XXVI,
No. 3, April 1974, pp. 299-330.   326

KIRBY, E. Stuart.
"The Framework of the Crisis in Communist China,"
Current Scene, Vol. VI, No. 2, February 1, 1968,
pp. 1-10.   55

KLEIN, Donald.
"The Management of Foreign Affairs in Communist China,"
China: Management of a Revolutionary Society, John M.
Lindbeck, ed., University of Washington Press, Seattle
and London, 1971, pp. 305-342.   327

KLEIN, Donald.
"A Question of Leadership: Problems of Mobility Control
and Policy-making in China," Current Scene, Vol. V,
No. 7, April 30, 1967, pp. 1-8.   121

KLEIN, Donald.
"The State Council and the Cultural Revolution," The
China Quarterly, No. 35, July-September 1968, pp. 78-95.   122

KLEIN, Donald, and HAGER, Lois B.
"The Ninth Central Committee," The China Quarterly,
No. 45, January-March 1971, pp. 37-56.   123

KLEIN, Sidney.
"The Cultural Revolution and China's Foreign Trade:
A First Approximation," Current Scene, Vol. V, No. 19,
November 17, 1967, pp. 1-11.   328

LA DANY, L.
"Mao's China: The Decline of a Dynasty," Foreign Affairs,
Vol. XIV, No. 4, July 1967, pp. 610-623.   56

LEADER, Shelah Gilbert.
"The Communist Youth League and the Cultural Revolution,"
Asian Survey, Vol. XIV, No. 8, August 1974, pp. 700-715.   152

LEADER, Shelah Gilbert.
"The Emancipation of Chinese Women," World Politics,
Vol. XXVI, No. 1, October 1973, pp. 55-79.   307

LEE, Rensselaer W., III.
"Ideology and Technical Innovation in Chinese Industry,
1949-1971," Asian Survey, Vol. XII, No. 8, August 1972,
pp. 649-661.   254

LEE, Rensselaer W., III.
"The Politics of Technology in Communist China,"
Ideology and Politics in Contemporary China, Chalmers
Johnson, ed., University of Washington Press, Seattle
and London, 1973, pp. 301-325.   291

LEVENSON, Joseph.
"Communist China in Time and Space: Roots and Rootlessness," The China Quarterly, No. 39, July-September
1969, pp. 1-11.   57

LEWIS, John W.
"The Cultural Revolution," China Briefing, University
of Chicago Press, Chicago, 1968, pp. 17-22.   58

LEWIS, John W.
"Leader, Commissar, and Bureaucrats: The Chinese
Political System in the Last Days of the Revolution,"
China's Heritage and the Communist Political System,
Ping-ti Ho and Tang Tsou, eds., China in Crisis,
Vol. 1, Book Two, University of Chicago Press, Chicago,
1968, pp. 449-481.   124

LEWIS, John W., ed.
Party Leadership and Revolutionary Power in China,
Cambridge University Press, Cambridge, 1970, 422p.   125

LIFTON, Robert Jay.
Revolutionary Immortality: Mao Tse-tung and the
Chinese Cultural Revolution, Vintage Books, New York,
1968, 178p.   59

LINDBECK, John M. H., ed.
China: Management of a Revolutionary Society,
University of Washington, Seattle and London, 1971, 391p.   126

LINDBECK, John M. H.
"An Isolationist Science Policy," China After the
Cultural Revolution, Vintage Books, New York, 1970,
pp. 181-195.   292

LIU, Alan P.
"Mass Campaign and Political Development in China,"
Current Scene, Vol. XI, No. 8, August 1973, pp. 1-9.   355

LONDON, Marian, and LONDON, Ivan D.
"China's Lost Generation: The Fate of the Red Guards
Since 1968," Saturday Review World, No. 30, 1974,
pp. 12-15 and 18-19.   153

LUBKIN, Gloria B.
"Physics in China," Physics Today, December 1972, pp. 23-28. 293

MACCIOCCHI, Maria Antonetta.
Daily Life in Revolutionary China, Monthly Review Press,
New York and London, 1972, 506p.   308

MAC DOUGALL, Colina. "The Cultural Revolution in the
Communes: Back to 1958?," Current Scene, Vol. VII,
No. 7, April 11, 1969, pp. 1-11.   255

MAC DOUGALL, Colina.
"Education in China: Bringing Up Baby," Far Eastern
Economic Review, January 30, 1969, pp. 194-195.   282

MAC DOUGALL, Colina. "Revolution on China's Railroads,"
Current Scene, Vol. VI, No. 14, August 16, 1968, pp. 1-16.   256

MAC FARQUHAR, Emily.
"China: Mao's Last Leap," The Economist Brief Booklets,
No. 6, The Economist Newspapers, Ltd., London, 1968,
pp. 1-24.   60

MAC FARQUHAR, Roderick.
The Origins of the Cultural Revolution, Volume I:
Contradictions among the People, 1956-1957, Columbia
University Press, New York and London, 1974, 439p.   61

MACHETZKI, Rudiger.
"China's Education Since the Cultural Revolution," The
Political Quarterly, Vol. 45, No. 1, January-March 1974,
pp. 59-74.   283

MACKERRAS, Colin.
"Chinese Opera After the Cultural Revolution (1970-1972),"
The China Quarterly, No. 55, July-September 1973,
pp. 478-510.   309

MACKERRAS, Colin, and HUNTER, Neale.
China Observed: 1964-1967, Pall Mall Press, London,
1968, 194p.   62

MALONEY, Joan M.
"Chinese Women and Party Leadership: Impact of the
Cultural Revolution," Current Scene, Vol. X, No. 4,
April 10, 1972, pp. 10-15.   356

MATHEWS, Thomas Jay.
"The Cultural Revolution in Szechwan," The Cultural
Revolution in the Provinces, East Asian Monographs
No. 42, Harvard University Press, Cambridge, 1971,
pp. 94-146.   225

MEHNERT, Klaus.
Peking and the New Left: At Home and Abroad, China
Research Monographs No. 4, Center for Chinese Studies,
University of California, Berkeley, 1969, 156p.   127

MICHAEL, Franz.
"China After the Cultural Revolution: The Unresolved
Succession Crisis," Orbis, Vol. XVII, No. 2, Summer
1973, pp. 315-333.   357

MICHAEL, Franz.
"The Struggle for Power," Problems of Communism,
Vol. XVI, No. 3, May-June 1967, pp. 12-21.   63

MILTON, David, MILTON, Nancy, and SCHURMANN, Franz, eds.
People's China: Social Experimentation, Politics, Entry
onto the World Scene, 1966 through 1972, Vintage Books,
A Division of Random House, New York, 1974, 673p.   64

MITS, F.T.
"Mao's Revolutionary Successors: Part I - The Wanderers,"
Current Scene, Vol. V, No. 13, August 15, 1967, pp. 1-7.   154

MONTAPERTO, Ronald N.
"From Revolutionary Successors to Revolutionaries:
Chinese Students in the Early Stages of the Cultural
Revolution," Elites in the People's Republic of China,
Robert Scalapino, ed., University of Washington Press,
Seattle and London, 1972, pp. 575-605.   155

MONTAPERTO, Ronald N.
"The Origins of 'Generational Politics': Canton 1966,"
Current Scene, Vol. VIII, No. 11, June 1, 1969, pp. 1-16.   156

MUNRO, Donald J.
"Egalitarian Ideal and Educational Fact in Communist
China," China: Management of a Revolutionary Society,
John M. Lindbeck, ed., University of Washington Press,
Seattle and London, 1971, pp. 256-301.   284

MUNTHE-KAAS, Harald.
"Problems for the PLA," The Far Eastern Economic Review,
Ocotber 5, 1967, pp. 39-43.   188

MYERS, James T.
"The Fall of Chairman Mao," Current Scene, Vol. VI,
No. 10, June 15, 1968, pp. 1-18.   65, 128

NATHAN, Andrew J.
"A Factionalism Model for CCP Politics," The China
Quarterly, No. 53, January-March 1973, pp. 34-66.   129

NEE, Victor.
The Cultural Revolution at Peking University, Monthly
Review Press, New York, 1969, 91p.   66

NELSEN, Harvey W.
"Military Bureaucracy in the Cultural Revolution,"
Asian Survey, Vol. XIV, No. 4, April 1974, pp. 327-395.   190

NELSEN, Harvey W.
"Military Forces in the Cultural Revolution," The China
Quarterly, No. 51, July-September 1972, pp. 444-474.   189

NEUHAUSER, Charles.
"The Chinese Communist Party in the 1960's: Prelude to
the Cultural Revolution," The China Quarterly, No. 32,
October-December 1967, pp. 3-36.   130

NEUHAUSER, Charles.
"The Impact of the Cultural Revolution on the Chinese
Communist Party Machine," Asian Survey, Vol. VIII, No. 6,
June 1968, pp. 465-488.   131

NOUMOFF, S. J.
"China's Cultural Revolution as a Rectification Movement,"
Pacific Affairs, Vol. XL, Nos. 3-4, Fall and Winter 1967-
1968, pp. 221-234.   67

OJHA, Ishwer C.
Chinese Foreign Policy in an Age of Transition: The
Diplomacy of Cultural Despair, Beacon Press, Boston,
1969, 234p.   329

OKSENBERG, Michel.
"China: Forcing the Revolution to a New Stage," Asian
Survey, Vol. VII, No. 1, January 1967, pp. 1-15.   68

OKSENBERG, Michel, ed.
China's Developmental Experience, The Academy of Political
Science, Columbia University, Praeger Publishers, New York,
Washington, and London, 1973, 227p.   69

OKSENBERG, Michel.
"Communist China: A Quiet Crisis in Revolution,: Asian
Survey, Vol. VI, No. 1, January 1966, pp. 1-12.   70

OKSENBERG, Michel.
"The Institutionalization of the Chinese Communist
Revolution: The Ladder of Success on the Eve of the
Cultural Revolution," The China Quarterly, No. 36,
October-December 1968, pp. 61-92.   132

OKSENBERG, Michel.
"Occupational Groups in Chinese Society and the Cultural
Revolution," The Cultural Revolution: 1967 in Review,
Michigan Papers in Chinese Studies No. 2, Center for
Chinese Studies, University of Michigan, Ann Arbor,
1968, pp. 1-44.   71, 191

OKSENBERG, Michel.
"Political Changes and Their Causes in China, 1949-
1972," The Political Quarterly, Vol. 45, No. 1,
January-March 1974, pp. 95-114.   72, 358

OLDHAM, C. H. G.
"Science and Technology Policies," China's Developmental
Experience, Michel Oksenberg, ed., Praeger Publishers,
New York, Washington, and London, 1973, pp. 80-94.   296

OLDHAM, C. H. G.
"Science Travels the Mao Road," China After the Cultural
Revolution, Vintage Books, New York, 1970, pp. 219-228.   294

OLDHAM, C. H. G.
"Technology in China: Science for the Masses?" Far
Eastern Economic Review, May 16, 1968, pp. 353-355.   295

ONG, Ellen K.
"Education in China Since the Cultural Revolution,"
Studies in Comparative Communism, Vol. 3, Nos. 3-4,
July-October 1970, pp. 158-176.   285

ORLEANS, Leo A.
"China: The Population Record," Current Scene, Vol. X,
No. 5, May 10, 1972, pp. 10-19.   359

PAN, Stephen C. Y.
"China and Southeast Asia," Current History, Vol. 57,
No. 337, September 1969, pp. 164-167 and 180.   330

PARISH, William L., Jr.
"Factions in Chinese Military Politics," The China
Quarterly, No. 56, October-December 1973, pp. 667-699.   192

PEPPER, Susan.
"Educational and Political Development in Communist
China," Studies in Comparative Communism, Vol. 3,
Nos. 3-4, July-Ocotber 1970, pp. 132-157.   286

PERKINS, Dwight.
"Economic Growth in China and the Cultural Revolution
(1960 - April 1967)," The China Quarterly, No. 30,
April-June 1967, pp. 33-48.   257

PERKINS, Dwight.
"Mao Tse-tung's Goals and China's Economic Performance,"
Current History, Vol. IX, No. 1, January 7, 1971,
pp. 1-13.   258

PFEFFER, Richard M.
"The Pursuit of Purity: Mao's Cultural Revolution,"
Problems of Communism, Vol. XVIII, No. 6, November-
December 1969, pp. 12-25.   73

PFEFFER, Richard M.
"Serving the People and Continuing the Revolution,"
The China Quarterly, No. 52, October-December 1972,
pp. 620-653.   360

THE POLITICAL QUARTERLY.
China in Transition, Vol. 45, No. 1, January-March 1974,
pp. 1-114.   361

POSSONY, Stephan T.
"The Chinese Communist Cauldron," Orbis, Vol. XIII,
No. 3, Fall, 1969, pp. 783-821.   74

POWELL, David E.
"Mao in Stalin's Mantle," Problems of Communism, Vol. XVII,
No. 2, March-April, 1968, pp. 21-30.   75

POWELL, Ralph L.
"The Increasing Power of Lin Piao and the Party-Soldiers
in 1959-1966," The China Quarterly, No. 34, April-June
1968, pp. 38-65.   193

POWELL, Ralph L.
"The Party, the Government and the Gun," Asian Survey,
Vol. X, No. 6, June 1970, pp. 441-471.   194

POWELL, Ralph L.
"The Power of the Chinese Military," Current History,
Vol. 59, No. 349, pp. 129-133 and pp. 175-178.   195

POWELL, Ralph L.
"Soldiers in the Chinese Economy," Asian Survey, Vol. XI,
No. 8, August 1971, pp. 742-760.   196

POWELL Ralph L., and YOON, Chong-kun.
"Public Security and the PLA," Asian Survey, Vol. XII,
No. 12, December 1972, pp. 1082-1100.   197

PRAHYE, Prabhakar.
"Why Red Guards?," China Report, Vol. 3, No. 1, December
1966 - January 1967, pp. 4-8.   157

PRYBYLA, Jan.
"China's Economy: Experiments in Maoism," Current History,
Vol. 59, No. 349, September 1970, pp. 159-180.   362

PRYBYLA, Jan.
"The Economic Cost," Problems of Communism, Vol. XVII,
No. 2, March-April 1968, pp. 1-13.   259

PUSEY, James R.
Wu Han: Attacking the Present through the Past, East
Asian Research Center, Harvard University Press,
Cambridge, 1969, 84p.   76

PYE, Lucian W.
The Authority Crisis in Chinese Politics, Center for
Public Policy, University of Chicago Press, Chicago,
March 1967.   78

PYE, LUCIAN W.
"Coming Dilemmas for China's Leaders," Foreign Affairs,
Vol. XLIV, No. 3, April 1966, pp. 387-402.   77

RAVENAL, Earl C., ed.
Peace with China? U.S. Decisions for Asia, Liverwright,
New York, 1971, 248p.   331

REECE, Bob.
"Education in China: More of the Same," Far Eastern
Economic Review, June 13, 1968, pp. 563-565.   287

RICHMAN, Barry.
"Ideology and Management: The Chinese Oscillate,"
Columbia Journal of World Business, Vol. VI, No. 1,
January-February 1971.   260

RISKIN, Carl.
"The Chinese Economy in 1967," The Cultural Revolution:
1967 in Review, Michigan Papers in Chinese Studies No. 2,
University of Michigan, Ann Arbor, 1968, pp. 45-71.   261

ROBINSON, Joan.
"The Cultural Revolution in China," International Affairs:
A Quarterly Review, Vol. 44, No. 2, April 1968,
pp. 214-227.   79

ROBINSON, Joan.
The Cultural Revolution in China, Penguin Books, Ltd.,
Harmondsworth, Middlesex, England, and Baltimore, Md.,
1969 and reprinted with revised postscript, 1970, 154p.   80

ROBINSON, Thomas W.
"Chou En-lai and the Cultural Revolution in China," The
Cultural Revolution in China, Thomas W. Robinson, ed.,
University of California Press, Berkeley and Los Angeles,
1971, pp. 165-312.   134

ROBINSON, Thomas W.
"Chou En-lai's Political Style: Comparisons with Mao
Tse-tung and Lin Piao," Asian Survey, Vol. X, No. 12,
December 1970, pp. 1101-1116.   133

ROBINSON, Thomas W., ed.
The Cultural Revolution in China, University of California
Press, Berkeley and Los Angeles, 1971, 509p.   81

ROBINSON, Thomas W.
"Lin Piao as an Elite Type," Elites in the People's
Republic of China, Robert A. Scalapino, ed., University
of Washington Press, Seattle and London, 1972,
pp. 149-195.   135

ROBINSON, Thomas W.
"The Sino-Soviet Border Dispute," The American Political
Science Review, Vol. LXVI, No. 4, December 1972,
pp. 1175-1202.   332

ROBINSON, Thomas W.
"The Wuhan Incident: Local Strife and Provincial Rebellion
during the Cultural Revolution," The China Quarterly,
No. 47, July-September 1971, pp. 413-438.   198

S. S.
"Army's Role in the Cultural Revolution," China Report,
Vol. IV, No. 2, 1968, pp. 27-32.   199

SARGENT, Margie.
"The Cultural Revolution in Heilungkiang," The Cultural
Revolution in the Provinces, East Asian Monographs No. 42,
Harvard University Press, Cambridge, 1971, pp. 16-65.   226

SCALAPINO, Robert.
"The Cultural Revolution and Chinese Foreign Policy," The
Cultural Revolution: 1967 in Review, Michigan Papers in
Chinese Studies No. 2, Center for Chinese Studies,
University of Michigan, Ann Arbor, 1968, pp. 72-96.   333

SCALAPINO, Robert, ed.
Elites in the People's Republic of China, University of
Washington Press, Seattle and London, 1972, 671p.   136

225

SCALAPINO, Robert.
"The Transition in Chinese Party Leadership: A Comparison
of the Eighth and Ninth Central Commitees," Elites in the
People's Republic of China, Robert A. Scalapino, ed.,
University of Washington Press, Seattle and London,
1972, pp. 67-148.   137

SCHRAM, Stuart, ed.
Authority, Participation and Cultural Change in China,
Cambridge University Press, Cambridge, 1973, 350p.   262

SCHRAM, Stuart, ed.
Chairman Mao Talks to the People: Talks and Letters,
1956-1971, translated by John Chinnery and Tieyun,
Pantheon Books, New York, 1974, 352p.   82

SCHRAM, Stuart R.
"Mao Tse-tung and Liu Shao-chi, 1939-1969," Asian Survey
Vol. XII, No. 4, April 1972, pp. 275-293.   138

SCHRAM, Stuart R.
"The Party in Chinese Communist Ideology," Party Leader-
ship and Revolutionary Power in China, John W. Lewis, ed.,
Cambridge University Press, Cambridge, 1970, pp. 170-202. 139

SCHRAN, Peter.
"Economic Management," China: Management of a Revolutionary
Society, John M.Lindbeck, ed., University of Washington
Press, Seattle and London, 1971, pp. 195-220.   263

SCHRAN, Peter.
"Institutional Continuity and Motivational Change: The
Chinese Industrial Wages System, 1950-1973," Asian Survey,
Vol. XIV, No. 11, November 1974, pp. 1014-1032.   264

SCHURMANN, Franz.
"The Attack of the Cultural Revolution on Ideology and
Organization," China's Heritage and the Communist
Political System, Ping-ti Ho and Tang Tsou, eds., China
in Crisis, Vol. 1, Book 2, The University of Chicago
Press, Chicago, 1968, pp. 525-564.   83

SCHWARTZ, Benjamin I.
"The Reign of Virtue: Some Broad Perspectives on Leaders
and Party in the Cultural Revolution," Party Leadership
and Revolutionary Power in China, John W. Lewis, ed.,
Cambridge University Press, Cambridge, 1970, pp. 149-169. 140

SCIENCE FOR THE PEOPLE.
China: Science Walks on Two Legs, Avon Books, New York,
1974, 316p.   297

226

SHAW, Brian.
"China and North Vietnam: Two Revolutionary Paths,"
Part I and Part II, Current Scene, Vol. IX, Nos. 11
and 12, November 7 and December 7, 1971, pp. 1-12 and
1-11.   334

SHERIDAN, Mary.
"The Emulation of Heroes," The China Quarterly, No. 33,
January-March 1968, pp. 47-72.   200

SHIH, Joseph Anderson.
"Science and Technology in China," Asian Survey, Vol. XII,
No. 8, August 1972, pp. 662-675.   298

SHUE, Vivienne B.
"Shanghai After the January Storm," The Cultural Revolution
in the Provinces, East Asian Monographs No. 42, Harvard
University Press, Cambridge, 1971, pp. 66-93.   227

SIMMONDS, John D.
"The New Gun-Barrel Elite," The Military and Political
Power in China in the 1970's, William W. Whitson, ed.,
Praeger Publishers, New York, 1972, pp. 93-113.   201

SIMS, Stephen A.
"The New Role of the Military," Problems of Communism,
Vol. XVIII, No. 6, November-December 1969, pp. 26-32.   202

SINGER, Ethan, and GALSTON, Arthur W.
"Education and Science in China," Science, Vol. 175,
No. 4017, January 7, 1972, pp. 15-23.   299

SNOW, Edgar.
The Long Revolution, Vintage Books, New York, 1973, 267p. 86

SNOW, Edgar.
"Mao and the New Mandate," The World Today, Vol. 25, No. 7,
July 1969, pp. 289-297.   363

SNOW, Edgar
"Success or Failure? China's 70,000 Communes," The New
Republic, June 26, 1971, pp. 19-23.   265

SNOW, Lois Wheeler.
China on Stage: An American Actress in the People's
Republic, Vintage Books, New York, 1973, 328p.   310

SOLOMON, Richard H.
Mao's Revolution and the Chinese Political Culture,
University of California Press, Berkeley,
1971, 604p.   84

SOLOMON, Richard H.
"On Activism and Activists: Maoist Conception of
Motivation and Political Role Linking State to
Society," The China Quarterly, No. 39, July-September
1969, pp. 76-114.   85

STARR, John Bryan.
"Conceptual Foundations of Mao Tse-tung's Theory of
Continuous Revolution," Asian Survey, Vol. XL, No. 6,
June 1961, pp. 610-628.   87

STARR, John Bryan.
Ideology and Culture: An Introduction to the Dialetic
of Contemporary Chinese Politics, Harper and Row,
New York, 1973, 300p.   88

STARR, John Bryan.
"Revolution in Retrospect: The Paris Commune through
Chinese Eyes," The China Quarterly, No. 49, January-
March 1972, pp. 106-125.   89

SUTTMEIER, Richard P.
"Science Policy Shifts, Organizational Change and China's
Development," The China Quarterly, No. 62, June 1975,
pp. 207-241.   300

TANG TSOU.
"The Cultural Revolution and the Chinese Political System,"
The China Quarterly, No. 38, April-June 1969, pp. 63-91.   90

TANG TSOU.
"The Cultrual Revolution - I," China Briefing, The
University of Chicago, Center for Policy Study, University
of Chicago Press, Chicago, 1968, pp. 9-15.   91

TANNENBAUM, Gerald.
"China's Cultural Revolution: Why It Had to Happen,"
China in Ferment: Perspectives on the Cultural Revolution,
Richard Baum with Louise B. Bennett, eds., Prentice-Hall,
Inc., Englewood Cliffs, N.J., 1971, pp. 60-66.   92

TEIWES, Frederick.
Provincial Leadership in China: The Cultural Revolution
and Its Aftermath, China-Japan Program, Cornell University,
Ithica, N. Y., 1974, 165p.   203

TEIWES, Frederick.
"A Review Article: The Evolution of Leadership Purges in
Communist China," The China Quarterly, No. 41, October-
December, 1970, pp. 123-135.   93

TERRILL, Ross.
"The Siege Mentality," Problems of Communism, Vol. XV,
No. 2, March-April 1967, pp. 1-10.   94

TING WANG.
"The Emergent Military Class," The Military and Political
Power in China in the 1970's, William W. Whitson, ed.,
Praeger Publishers, New York, 1972, pp. 115-132.   204

TRAGER, Frank N., and HENDERSON, William, eds.
Communist China, 1949-1969: A Twenty-year Appraisal,
New York University Press, New York, 1970, 356p.   95

TRETIAK, Daniel.
"The Chinese Cultural Revolution and Foreign Policy,"
Current Scene, Vol. VIII, No. 7, April 1, 1970, pp. 1-26.   335

TRETIAK, Daniel.
"Is China Preparing to 'Turnout'? Changes in Chinese
Levels of Attention to the International Environment,"
Asian Survey, Vol. XI, No. 3, March 1971, pp. 219-237.   336

UNGER, Johathan.
"Mao's Million Amateur Technicians," Far Eastern Economic
Review, April 3, 1971, pp. 115-118.   301

UNION RESEARCH INSTITUTE.
CCP Documents of the Great Proletarian Cultural Revolution,
1966-1967, Hong Kong, 1968, 692p.   96

VAN GINNEKAN, Jaap.
"The 1967 'Plot of the May 16 Movement,'" Journal of
Contemporary China, Vol. 2, No. 3, 1972, pp. 237-254.   141

VAN NESS, Peter.
Revolution and Chinese Foreign Policy: Peking's Support
for Wars of National Liberation, University of California
Press, Berkeley, Los Angeles and London, 1970, 266p.   337

VOGEL, Ezra F.
"From Revolutionary to Semi-Bureaucrat: The 'Regularization'
of Cadres," The China Quarterly, No. 29, January-March
1967, pp. 36-60.   142

VOGEL, Ezra F.
"The Structure-of Conflict: China in 1967," The Cultural
Revolution: 1967 in Review, Michigan Papers in Chinese
Studies No. 2, University of Michigan, Ann Arbor, 1968,
pp. 97-125.   97

WALLER, Derek J.
"China: Red or Expert?," The Political Quarterly,
April-June 1967, pp. 122-131.   98

WALLER, Derek J.
"Revolutionary Intellectuals or Managerial Modernizers,"
The Political Quarterly, Vol. 45, No.1, January-March
1974, pp. 5-12.   364

WANG, James C. F.
"The Political Role of the People's Liberation Army as
Perceived by the Chinese Communist Press in the Cultural
Revolution," Issues and Studies, Vol. X, No. 8, May 1974,
pp. 57-71.   205

WARREN, Susan.
China's Voice in the United Nations, World Winds Press,
New York, 1974, 146p.   338

WASHENKO, Steve.
"Agriculture in Mainland China - 1968," Current Scene,
Vol. VII, No. 6, March 31, 1969, pp. 1-12.   266

WELCH, Holmes.
"Buddhism Since the Cultural Revolution," The China
Quarterly, No. 40, October-December 1969, pp. 127-136.   311

WENMOHS, John R.
"Agriculture in Mainland China - 1967: Cultural Revolution
versus Favorable Weather," Current Scene, Vol. V.,
No. 21, December 15, 1967, pp. 1-12.   267

WHEELWRIGHT, E. L., and MCFARLANE, Bruce
The Chinese Road to Socialism: Economics of the Cultural
Revolution, Monthly Review Press, New York, 1970, 256p.   268

WHITSON, William W.
The Chinese Communist High Command: A History of
Military Politics, 1927-69, Frederick A. Praeger,
New York and London, 1971, 638p.   209

WHITSON, William W.
"The Concept of Military Generation: The Chinese Communist
Case," Asian Survey, Vol. VIII, No. 11, November 1968,
pp. 921-947.   206

WHITSON, William W.
"The Field Army in Chinese Communist Military Politics,"
The China Quarterly, No. 37, January-March 1969, pp. 1-30.   207

WHITSON, William W., ed.
The Military and Political Power in China in the 1970's,
Praeger Publishers, New York, 1972, 390p.   210

WHITSON, William W.
"The Military: Their Role in the Policy Process,"
Communist China, 1949-1969: A Twenty-year appraisal,
Frank Trager and William Henderson, eds., New York
University Press, New York, 1970, pp. 95-122.   208

WHYTE, Martin King.
"Bureaucracy and Modernization in China: The Maoist
Critique," American Sociological Review, Vol. 38, No. 2,
April 1973, pp. 149-163.   143

WHYTE, Martin King.
"The Tachai Brigade and Incentives for the Peasant,"
Current Scene, Vol. VII, No. 16, August 15, 1969, pp. 1-13. 269

WILKINSON, Ednymion.
Translations of The People's Comic Book, Anchor Press,
New York, 1973, 272p.   312

WILSON, Richard W., and WILSON, Amy A.
"The Red Guards and the World Student Movement,"
The China Quarterly, No. 42, April-June 1970, pp. 88-104.   158

WU, Yuan-li.
As Peking Sees Us, Hoover Institution Press, Stanford
University, Stanford, 1969, 98p.   339

WU, Yuan-li.
"Communist China's Economic Prospects and the Cultural
Revolution," Contemporary China, Allan A. Spits, ed.,
Washington State University Press, Seattle and London,
1967, pp. 33-42.   270

WU, Yuan-li.
"Economics, Ideology and the Cultural Revolution,"
Asian Survey, Vol. VIII, No. 3, March 1968, pp. 223-245.   271

WU, Yuan-li.
"The Economy After Twenty Years," Communist China, 1949-
1969: A Twenty-year Appraisal, Frank N. Trager and
William Henderson, eds., New York University Press,
New York, 1970, pp. 123-151.   272

WYLIE, Ray.
"The Meaning of the Cultural Revolution," China and
Ourselves: Explorations and Revisions by a New Generation,
Bruce Douglass and Ross Terrill, eds., Beacon Press,
Boston, 1970, pp. 30-48.   100

WYLIE, Ray.
"Revolution within a Revolution?," China After the
Cultural Revolution, Vintage Books, New York, 1970, pp.29-32.   99

YAHUDA, Michael B.
"China's Military Capabilities," Current History, Vol. 57,
No. 337, September 1969, pp. 142-149 and 182.   211

YAHUDA, Michael B.
"China's Nuclear Option," China After the Cultural
Revolution, Vintage Books, New York, 1970, pp. 198-212.   340

YAHUDA, Michael B.
"Chinese Foreign Policy after 1963: The Maoist Phase,"
The China Quarterly, No. 36, October-December, 1968,
pp. 93-113.   341

YANG, C. K.
"Cultural Revolution and Revisionism," China's Heritage
and the Communist Political System, Ping-ti Ho and Tang
Tsou, eds., China in Crisis, Vol. 1, Book 2, The University
of Chicago Press, Chicago, 1968, pp. 501-524.   101

YU, George T.
"Working on the Railroad: China and the Tanzania-Zambia
Railway," Asian Survey, Vol. XI, No. 11, November 1971,
pp. 1101-1117.   342

ZAGORIA, Donald S.
Vietnam Triangle: Moscow, Peking, Hanoi, Pegasus, New York,
1967, p. 286.   343

SUBJECT INDEX

The reference numbers used in this index are the numbers for the
annotated bibliographic entries. The entries are numbered con-
secutively from the first chapter to the end of the bibliography.

Accounting practices, 244
Agriculture
    collectives and collectivization, 17, 18, 43, 97, 242
        see also communes; commune system
    disorganization, 261, 266
    enterpreneurship, 247
    mechanization, 237, 249
        Chengtu conference, 237, 246
        Mao-Liu dispute, 110, 237
    military supervision of, 196
    production, 266, 267
        see also economy; rural development
    scientific, 244
        see also science and technology
    state farms, 243
Alienation of state, 88
Anarch, 10
Anshan Iron and Steel, 238
Arts, debate and reform, 302, 304
Authority and participation, 78, 262
        see also mass authority and mass line

Bourgeois tendencies, 3, 33, 39, 44, 60, 80, 86, 92, 270
Bureaucracy, 8, 53, 142
    contradictions, 22
    Communist Youth League, 147
    inertia, 131
    military loyalty system, 192
    modernization, 118
    ossification, 70
    party, 34, 67, 85, 91, 130
        see also party; cadre
    prevention of, 352, 353, 358, 363, 364
    routinization, 8, 36, 49, 64, 68, 72, 142, 208
    state, 190
Bureaucratic elite, 46, 55, 64, 99
    see also elite

Interest and occupational groups, 13, 29, 32, 55, 71, 72, 120

Kao-Jao affair, 16, 93, 104
Khrushchev revisionism, 8, 15, 43, 61
Kuang Feng, 109
Kwangtung, 164
Kweichow, 164

Labor
    absenteeism in factories, 231
    discipline enforced by PLA, 171
    labor-intensive, 245
    manual and intellectual, 229
    organizations, 171, 252
    unrest, 231, 234, 267
Leadership
    cleaveage and conflict, 61, 83, 971, 121, 129
        see also factionalism
    control, mobility, and style, 17, 120, 121, 140, 177
    decline of charismatic leader, 91, 101
    development experience, 69
    provincial, 169, 214, 220
    State Council, 122, 156
Leftist upsurge, 14, 32, 79, 127, 148
Line-staff conflict, 98
Lin Piao
    affair and fall, 54, 82, 141
    behavior in Cultural Revolution, 113, 184
    biographic sketch, 112, 135
    relations with Mao and others, 16, 65, 112, 113, 128, 135,
        141
    relations with PLA, 113, 175, 187, 192, 193
Literature, dissent, reform and change, 34, 44, 76, 302, 304
        305, 353
Li Tso-peng, 112
Liu Shao-chi
    attacks on, 3, 9, 16, 17, 19, 39, 55, 65, 76, 93, 106, 110,
        115, 321
    crimes and reasons for dismissal, 103, 110, 116, 184
    disputes with Mao, 18, 52, 97, 114, 116, 124, 138
    pragmatic programs, 101, 238
Localism, 107, 203, 214, 224, 242, 246, 269
Long March veterans, 98
Lushan Conference (1959), 16, 25, 31, 56, 65, 98, 128

Mao Tse-tung
    alliance with Lin Piao, 65, 113, 128
    cult of, 18, 24, 43, 78, 128, 363
    decentralized administration, 239
    departure from Leninist orthodoxy, 139, 351
    directives and speeches, 6, 82

professional commanders, 77, 163, 179, 187, 193, 208, 210
propaganda teams, 196, 212, 238, 258
regional commanders, 162, 179, 183, 190, 196, 199, 201,
    207, 208, 220
relation withLin Piao, 113, 175, 187, 192, 193
relations with masses, 167, 172
revolutionary committees, 194, 205, 221, 344, 349, 357
revolutionary elan, 183, 345, 346, 363
role as mediator, 183, 205
role as police, 197
role as seen by Indian scholar, 199
role as seen by Soviet expert, 178
role in Cultural Revolution, 36, 126, 131, 137, 160, 163,
    174, 180, 186, 205
role in law and order, 183
role in schools, 173
roving units in villages, 172
seizure and supervision of public security forces, 197, 344
self-criticism, 167, 188
stablizing influence, 183, 212
study sessions, 205
support to production, 166
Ultra-left, 162, 163, 187
Personality cult, 18, 24, 43, 78, 128, 363
Political activism, 78, 85
Politics in command, 53, 98, 230, 248, 253
Policy-making theories, 81, 119, 126
Political change, cultural and system, 35, 40, 62, 72, 80, 84,
    92, 117, 163, 262, 361
Population trends, 350, 359
Power struggle, 2, 5, 6, 16, 24, 39, 43, 45, 48, 53, 58, 63,
    72, 99, 104, 120, 138, 182, 224, 262, 357
Pragmatism, 2, 3, 36, 39, 63, 77, 119, 131, 232
Proletarianism, 39, 80
Provinces
    activities, 215, 216
    elites, 108, 136, 212
    future developments, 243
    leadership, 108, 136, 169, 203, 214, 215, 218
    localism, 25, 83, 107, 159, 203, 248
    moderate elements, 217
    power, 90, 217, 222, 246
    revolutionary committees, 203, 215, 218, 219
    role of central authorities, 226
Psychological aspects of revolution, 59, 78, 84
Public Security System, 197, 344
Purges, 6, 11, 14, 28, 44, 105, 106, 107, 122, 124, 131, 159,
    162, 226, 230, 231, 241, 321, 363

Radicalism, 3, 14, 32, 57, 60, 63, 70, 79, 99, 109, 127, 148
    See also ultra-left
Rectification campaign, Cultural Revolution as, 41, 42, 45, 48,

243

52, 67, 86, 104, 119, 120, 130, 132, 194, 360
Red Guards
    alienation theory, 158
    and religion, 5, 306, 311
    at Peita and Tsinghua, 38, 66
    effects of Cultural Revolution on, 102, 144, 145, 149, 153,
        155, 199, 222, 344
    exchange and link up, 102, 127, 151, 256
    factionalism among, 28, 144, 150, 151, 155, 160, 170, 222
    organization of, 5, 6, 10, 35, 38, 149, 150, 158, 183, 212
    origin of, 25, 35, 37, 62, 127, 149, 157, 158, 222
    personal accounts of, 151, 155, 156
    power seizure by, 144, 151, 156, 222
    sheng-wu-lien, 127, 151, 256
    suppression by military, 49, 144, 150, 153, 164, 195, 212,
        214
    wanderers, 154
Red vs. expert, 9, 57, 98, 101, 121, 346
Regionalism, 159, 176, 189, 190, 193, 207, 268
Religion and Cultural Revolution
    Buddhism and monks, 311
    policy, 306, 311
Revolutionary Committees, 3, 20, 85, 106, 161, 194, 205, 212,
    214, 216, 218, 221, 222, 225, 344
Revolutionary elan, immortality, and romanticism, 7, 9, 20, 22,
    32, 45, 59, 78, 90, 104, 130
Revolutionary successors, 7, 22, 42, 67, 75, 80, 86, 92, 147,
    150, 154, 158, 214
Revisionism, 7, 8, 11, 15, 22, 24, 36, 41, 42, 43, 45, 53, 60,
    61, 83, 86, 101, 164, 257, 271
Rightists, 32, 38, 79, 108, 127, 164
Routinization, 8, 36, 49, 64, 68, 72, 142, 208
Rural development, 81, 100, 145, 237, 239, 244, 245, 255, 298,
    299, 301

Sciences and technology
    Academy of Sciences, problems and roles, 289, 294, 300
    achievement and success, 297, 298
    advanced research, 289, 293, 295, 296
    applied scientific and industrial research emphasis, 289,
        293, 295, 296, 299, 300
    Cultural Revolution impact on, 288, 292, 295, 296, 298, 300,
        301
    decentralized industries, 301
    for the masses, 254, 295, 299, 301
    for rural areas, 298, 299, 301
    implication for the future, 296, 298
    models for scientific development, 300
    Red Flag Canal, 297
    remedial classes for students in, 293
    science policy and system
        background, 290, 300
        dispute over policies, 275, 288, 291, 293, 294, 297, 299

For Product Safety Concerns and Information please contact our EU
representative GPSR@taylorandfrancis.com
Taylor & Francis Verlag GmbH, Kaufingerstraße 24, 80331 München, Germany

www.ingramcontent.com/pod-product-compliance
Lightning Source LLC
Chambersburg PA
CBHW070732270326
41926CB00064B/2658

9 7 8 1 1 3 8 3 4 7 8 0 9